4.50

JOSEF
OF
18

G000163187

JOSEPH ASHBY
OF TYSOE
1859-1919

A Study of English Village Life

BY

M. K. ASHBY

With an Introduction by
E. P. Thompson

THE MERLIN PRESS LTD.
London

First published in this edition by
The Merlin Press Ltd.,
3, Manchester Road, London
1974

First published 1961 by The Cambridge University Press
©Cambridge University Press 1961
©The Merlin Press 1974

ISBN 085036 180 X

Reprinted 1979

Printed in Great Britain by
Whitstable Litho Ltd., Whitstable, Kent

INTRODUCTION

One does not often see in one's lifetime the publication by a contemporary of a book which one is certain will become a minor "classic": that is, such a book as Gilbert White's *Selborne*, Mark Rutherford's *Deliverance*, or George Sturt's *The Wheelwright's Shop*. *Joseph Ashby of Tysoe* will certainly join this company. It shares their economy and precision of observation or (as with Rutherford) compels with a similar indisputable authenticity of feeling.

But this book is no throwback to some earlier literary mode. It is the expression of a complex contemporary consciousness, both in its sense of historical process and in its reconstruction of a community's culture. A mind wholly immersed in that culture could not have stood sufficiently apart to take in its shape and structure; a mind wholly detached from it, and returning to it only through historical evidences, could not have unlocked its gestures, its human exchanges, its unarticulated meanings. That is why only this author could have written this book. And that is why its form—part biography, part auto-biography, part historical reconstruction (from many deftly-concealed sources), part imaginative recreation and inference—is exactly right.

It is a carefully-considered, consciously-wrought form. This is certainly not a book which flowed from its author's memory unbidden. Examine chapter 4 and the disclosure of the matter of Tysoe's Town Lands. The artistry is superb and the reader is scarcely conscious of it: he reads and enjoys the story. But what is the artist doing? We start with young Joseph's initiation into working life. But this is also an initiation into a new dimension of the community's culture and into its history as it endures in the minds of the shepherd, the carter, family and neighbours. We are not given the Town Lands story all at once. First we are made curious, as Joseph was made curious; we have a feeling about the problem and we sense its submerged societal energy even before the problem itself is disclosed. It was more shocking and intriguing to the boy that his mother should (in "the old Quaker way") have a brusque encounter with the Vicar's wife than that he should have been given a historical homily. This history is still alive and is sensed in the tension of existing village relationships.

Joseph's mother starts to tell the story and then stops; to recall it opens up old wounds; the boy must not "waaste 'is thoughts on what dooan't matter". But neighbours fill bits of the story in. At length it all comes out, alternately from his mother and from Jasper the carter. But what comes out is not the facts of the story only. (The facts are certainly there, and they are established with precision.) But what comes through is *how these events were experienced* by the labourers and other losers in the conflict—and how these experiences were transmitted to the next generation. Nor is this transmission only in the telling of the story: it is also the transmission of attitudes and of values which this experience (and other similar ones) had helped to form. Nor is there one uniform set of responses to these experiences: this is why the story is put into two mouths—Jasper ("the poor were beaten and kicked too") and Elizabeth, the mother (" 'Tis in their blood to expect fairness. I don't know why, but it is so.") And so to the author's conclusion: it was in such ways as these that there came to young Joseph a sense "that under the wide acreage of grass and corn and woods which he saw daily there was a ghostly, ancient tessellated pavement made of the events and thoughts and associations of other times".

How far, then, can a story told with the selection and control of imaginative fiction be taken as "true"?

I will note two things. First, this is the work of a patient and exact historian. When I first read it I had the curiosity to check one or two parts against more normal historical "evidence"—for example, the dry proceedings of the Reports of the Charity Commissioners. And I was left in no doubt that the author had done this checking, far more thoroughly, for herself. But, second, it is also the work of a moralist. What the author wishes to communicate is the trajectory of her father's life and, as part of this, the experiences and the culture of his community. To do this there must be an imaginative, shaping hand. Were there really, in the initiation of the youth, two opposed mentors, as in an old morality play? John Makepeace, the shepherd, who stands for the old pagan but cruel village culture, and Jasper, the carter, who stands for the culture of the Gospels and the Friendly Society, both of whom wrestle for the boy's soul? Perhaps there were: but, perhaps again, not *exactly* like this.

John Makepeace loses out, and with him one edge of the village culture is less often brought to view. The author's sympathies, which extend in a quizzically critical way to Vicars and to the gentry, show less extension towards the "rough" end of the Lower Town, the customers at "The Peacock", and the more distant sound of rioters in other villages. Some readers, with preconceptions like my own and with urban habits of mind, may feel, now and then, that the morality is structured in ways which give the godly villagers too great an advantage: that the villagers expected "fairness" too patiently and for too long.

The trajectory of Joseph's life can be seen from two aspects. Seen from one aspect it is the rediscovery of village community, in that brief decade or two of rural Liberalism at the turn of the century. From another aspect it is the trajectory of personal self-realisation, of the extension of intellectual and social boundaries, a movement which takes the cottager to a fine old farmhouse, the villager to the magistrate's bench—a trajectory which moves outwards from the village to the more complex national political and intellectual community.

If there is any conflict between these two kinds of movement, we are left to consider and to draw our own conclusions. For this is a recurring truth of human aspiration, both as observed history and as morality. And what we are shown is not only important as an authentic and beautifully-recreated moment of history. It is important also as living political morality. For the essential structure of the book turns upon the exploration of what community is about. The conflict between Vicar and parishioners, between the Trustees of the Town Lands and the labourers, arises, in the end, from "the different patterns of community at the back of minds, the needs, the passions, the fantasies . . ." The climax of Joseph's struggle to translate old community into new context comes (in chapter 18) with his efforts to work out new forms of communal land-holding relevant to the English countryside as, for a life-time, he has known it. The point about chapter 19 is the historical rediscovery by the whole family (the farm kitchen and study littered with documents) of "the ordinary man's vision of a sound co-operative village of free men, free to get a living, free to say yea and nay in their own affairs . . ." How to recreate that now, how to "project it clearly" in new times?

Participatory democracy is what we all talk about now. A test of our maturity might well be found in the response to *Joseph Ashby of Tysoe*. For this shows us, not in a utopian future but in an actual and recent past, all the difficulties and awkwardnesses of a vestigial communal democracy and, beyond that, a "pattern of community" at the back of men's minds. This pattern is yet strong enough to have its occasional moments of triumph, when neighbours suddenly assume the dignity of representatives; when Charlie Reason ("a little shrunken, down-looking man") stands up to challenge the Trustees; or when Ratnitt Hayward, the reluctantly-impressed Waywarden, astonishes the village by mastering, for the first time, the annual floods. In recalling this to us the author has reminded us of an "ancient tessellated pavement" which lies also beneath our urban streets.

If among those who instantly acclaimed *Joseph Ashby of Tysoe* when it was first published there were some readers whom the author had done nothing to court—atheists, Marxists, descendants of those "young doctrinaires of Ruskin College" who are dismissed rather peremptorily in the last chapters of this book—she has shown neither anxiety nor surprise. This is due not only to her tact but also to a kind of historical wisdom. She knows from her own study of history that old aspirations can reappear in new and unexpected forms. The problem—to envisage community and to "project it clearly"—remains her central pre-occupation. She asks of her readers only that they should share her concern.

The author—the Kathleen of the book—is exactly as one would expect the author to be. She has one or two vices. One of them is an assumed diffidence. She amuses herself, when historians call upon her, by pretending to be an "amateur", to be out-of-touch with true professional history. Then, when she has got you off your guard, she knocks you to the floor with evidence and closely-pondered observations which reveal her mastery of the sources and the tough quality of her analysis.

She belongs to a group of very able women who in the early years of this century refused (in her memorable phrase) to "accept their own lessness". When I called on her once, with several colleagues and graduates, for an informal "seminar" at her house in a Gloucestershire village I was rebuked, with kindness but with great firmness, because none of the group were women.

"Kathleen" extended her father's trajectory, as did her brother Arthur, into the outer educational world. A county scholarship (few and hard to get) took her in 1907 to the King's High School at Warwick; and from there she went, in 1911, to University House, the University of Birmingham.

Introduction

Here (in a post-graduate course in philosophy) she met her lifelong friend—later to become a distinguished educationalist—Margaret Phillips, with whom she now shares, in retirement, their Gloucestershire home. Her work in education has been varied. She has taught in Training Colleges, worked for the Co-operative Union and with the W.E.A., and, in Staffordshire and Cambridgeshire, in an advisory relation to rural schools. (Her first book, *The Country School: its History and Practice*, published in 1929, came out of this experience.) In 1933 she followed Fanny Street as Principal of Hillcroft College, then known as the Residential College for Working Women. This exacting post she held until the War was over, resigning in 1946. But she has always kept in touch with Hillcroft—returning there when she was needed—and Hillcroft and old pupils of the College have been and are in touch with her.

There is at least one more book about to appear from Miss Ashby's pen—a major history of Bledington, the Cotswold village which she and Margaret Phillips have made their home for some twenty-five years. The book has been in the making for nearly as long as that. It will also be about community and about the frustration of community by individualism. It cannot take the same form as *Joseph Ashby of Tysoe*, but it will be about the same problem, seen and researched in a new way.

E. P. THOMPSON

FOREWORD

THIS is the best piece of village history since my friends the Hammonds' *Village Labourer*. With an advantage: it is largely biography and autobiography.

I have the pleasure of having known several members of the family whom this book introduces. Three generations of it have contributed or are contributing to our knowledge of rural economics and history. Apart from Joseph, there was that forceful character Hannah Ashby, Joseph's widow, who lived near me, and their son, Professor A. W. Ashby, of Aberystwyth, successor of C. S. Orwin as director at the Agricultural Economics Research Institute at Oxford, who left his mark on so many students of rural economics. Professor Ashby's son is now working in the same field. Finally there is my neighbour at Bledington, Miss M. K. Ashby, that cultivated and honest writer to whom all who care for rural life in Britain and out of it are indebted for the present outstanding work.

J. W. ROBERTSON SCOTT

IDBURY MANOR
KINGHAM
OXFORD
May 1960

CONTENTS

JOSEPH ASHBY   *frontispiece*

Preface   *page* xv

Acknowledgments   xix

Chapter I   Elizabeth Ashby   1

      II   Joseph: Early Childhood and Education   12

      III Work and Play   24

      IV   Hornton Quarries and Arch's Meeting   45

      V   Court Greenwood Tree   64

      VI   Joining the Methodists   77

      VII Uncle William Emigrates   85

      VIII Friends and Lovers   92

      IX   Husband and Householder   104

      X   Land Hunger: the Promised Land   122

      XI   Vignettes of the Village   135

      XII Sociologist into Missionary   145

      XIII Young Parents   166

      XIV National Politics and Parish Pumps   178

      XV   Young Villagers   198

      XVI Saturdays and Sundays   211

      XVII Village and Education   227

      XVIII Family, Village and Nation   238

      XIX Looking Backward   266

      XX   The War: Coldstone Farm   288

Index   299

PREFACE

At a time when the interest of farmhouse and cottage, field and tool is fully realised and their history is in process of being written it would be superfluous to apologise for a book on the ground that it is the biography of an obscure villager.

I do not claim for this study of my father's life and of his village in his time that it is altogether a work of history; it relies too largely upon memories and oral tradition—on family and village stories, reminiscences of table-talk, of daily life, of speeches heard and occasions shared. Something has been drawn also from writings very slight and intimate in nature, for example childish letters and diaries, and brief manuscript notes eked out by memories. But so far as has been possible such sources have been checked by reference to more massive manuscript and printed documents. Among the former are the parish registers of Tysoe, the vestry minute-book, overseers' account books, minutes of the Parish Council, the School Managers, and the Brailes (now Shipston on Stour) Rural District Council, lists of members of village clubs, etc. It is worth while perhaps to remark how often the accuracy of the oral transmission has been proved. Printed sources include newspapers (*Banbury Guardian*, *Warwick Advertiser*, *Leamington Chronicle*, *Leamington Gazette*, *Methodist Times*, *Daily News*), and periodicals (*Economic Journal*, *Tysoe Parish Magazine*, *Girl's Own Paper*, *Land Magazine*, the journal of the Home Readers Union, *The Church Reformer* and others).

Between 1859 and 1919 there must have been a number of men in English villages living and working in a way very similar to my father's, but in one way he was exceptional—in his powers of expression, which make it possible to set him forth as their representative. He had a gift for talk and a ready pen for many purposes. His conversation had both matter and style; it has proved memorable. His writing was very various, but concerned always with his own local experience and the problems and humours of the rural life he knew. He could never write at leisure, only in time snatched from urgent farmwork and domestic and public duties; his articles could never be so worked upon as his table-talk, hence the paucity of direct quotation from them. They include:

'Statistics of Some Midland Villages', *Economic Journal*, 1893 (written in collaboration with Bolton King).

'Through Warwickshire Villages', a series in the *Leamington Chronicle*, 1893 and 1894.

'Rural Vignettes' and other studies (usually signed J. A. Benson), *Land Magazine*, 1897, 1898 and 1899.

'The Land', a series in the *Leamington Gazette*, 1914.

'A Century of Village History', a series in the *Warwick Advertiser*, 1909, and many other series and single articles in the same newspaper between 1893 and 1914, signed variously or not at all.

I could nowhere discover files of *The Estate Agents' Record* for which I believe my father wrote for a number of years.

Books I have used little or much include:

One Hundred Years of Poor Law Administration in a Warwickshire Village by A. W. Ashby. Oxford Studies in Social and Legal History, vol. III, 1912.

The Passing Years by Richard Greville Verney, Lord Willoughby de Broke, 1924.

Compton Wynyates by William George Spencer Scott Compton, fifth Marquess of Northampton, 1904.

The Comptons of Compton Wynyates by William Bingham Compton, sixth Marquess of Northampton, 1922.

Shoemaker's Window by George Herbert, ed. Christina S. Cheney, 1948.

For the rest, in the unlikely event of any student wishing to follow me along these footpaths through the rural scene, he will find in each chapter sufficient indication of the dates and other particulars of the sources there referred to.

We are now very rich in rural literature of many kinds—histories, tours, reminiscences, verse and novels. Is there room on this crowded shelf for my volume? As I have lived and worked throughout the years in many villages east and west in our southern midlands, knowing their present inhabitants and gathering their history, I have come to feel that some village institutions are not, or were not, as they have usually been drawn. The great house seems to me to have kept its best things to itself, giving, with rare exceptions, neither grace nor leadership to villages, but indeed depressing their manhood and culture. The stress in our country literature on craftsmanship—on hurdles and baskets and wrought iron—appears out of proportion. Surely men and women as characters and personalities should be more to the fore—as they are, so notably, in the incomparable studies of George Sturt. Some of the now superseded institutions, despised by some schools of historians as inefficient, seem to me to have carried out complex duties with much competence. Village Methodism, though now admitted to respectability, has hardly had its meed. If anything could convince one of direct human access to Divine Grace it might well be the example set a century ago by denuded Methodist labourers to all those who claimed superiority over them—an example of forgiveness, restraint and hope.

I do not suggest that this local and individual study deals directly with these large matters, only that it may point the way to some revised thoughts and further studies, useful perhaps to those working now for a renaissance of the English village.

M. K. ASHBY

BLEDINGTON
1960

NOTES TO SECOND EDITION

In chapter 1 I allude twice to the fact that my father's family had 'lost their farm and status' as the result of the foreclosure of a mortgage. I had no family papers which alluded to this event, though I knew the farm. Shortly after the publication of the book a kindly stranger wrote to me that in Jackson's Oxford Journal for March 26, 1803 a notice had appeared that 'The creditors of Robert Ashby of Tysoe, Yeoman . . . . are hereby informed that the first dividend, which will be seven shillings in the pound' would be paid to them at the office 'of an attorney in Shipston on Stour'. (It was after this bankruptcy that the family severed its connection with the Sibford Friends' Meeting). I had not fully realised the importance of the loss of the farm, which a fuller acquaintance with village history has revealed to me.

Throughout this book I have tried to indicate the dialect pronunciation by using a double aa, e.g. *chaange*. The first 'a' should be pronounced like the ai in *paid* and the second somewhere between the 'a' as in *an* and as in *ah*.

M.K.A.

ACKNOWLEDGMENTS

M u c h time has passed since I first made inquiries relating to this book: for that and other reasons my acknowledgments cannot be adequate.

My mother and two of my brothers, the late Professor A. W. Ashby, C.B.E., and William Ashby of Prescott, Ontario, wrote for me some short but most valuable memoirs, as did also Mr W. B. Wells of Tysoe. Mrs T. M. Heron's understanding and appreciation of my family in the early days of a long friendship has been a help to me.

To Mr Robertson Scott, C.H., I am indebted for his foreword and the warmest encouragement. The Editor of *The Countryman* gave a generous permission to use again, chiefly in chapter XVIII, material which has already appeared, in somewhat different form, in his journal. Acknowledgments are due to former editors of the local newspapers mentioned in the preface.

A number of friends in my native village lent me papers and photographs, among them Mr W. B. Wells and Mr Frank Styles. A former vicar, the Rev. T. Elias Jones, entrusted valuable documents to my care. Mr Fred Jeffs talked to me of my father's youth and his own. Mrs Myra McLean will recognise her contributions and know how I have appreciated them. Especial thanks are due to Miss Eva Hutchinson, whose wholehearted encouragement, practical and literary, was most timely. Of the support and criticism I received from Miss Margaret Phillips I cannot write adequately lest this book should appear far too slight a witness to them.

The duty to write about my father's life was laid upon me by my brother Arthur, mentioned above, who died before I had completed my obedience. But for its obvious dedication, I would have wished to devote this work to his most

Acknowledgments

dear memory and to those who loved him and appreciated his work.

I cannot hope that he, or any of my informed friends, would be able to approve in every case of my interpretation of source, fact, or personality. As to that, I have to stand alone.

M. K. A.

ELIZABETH ASHBY

NOT a vestige of my grandmother's handwriting remains, and almost the only worldly goods she left were a row of old books. Could any woman be more obscure? And yet some spoken words of hers have survived more than a hundred years. So clear and meaningful were these brief speeches that from the time I heard them I began to lose the memory of my aged granny in the desire to see the girl and woman she had been. Thus I made out her past.

Late in the year 1858, Elizabeth Ashby, a girl of twenty-one years, unmarried, took her way back to her native village of Tysoe in south Warwickshire because she was expecting a child. Some eighteen months earlier her father, a widower, had angered her and she had left her housekeeping to fend for herself. She had not gone far—only to Idlicote House, not more than five miles away if you took the footpaths. This comely, smallish eighteenth-century mansion was at the time tenanted by a member of a family of very high rank, great landowners in Warwickshire and neighbouring counties. There she had presently become maid to the lady of the house, a childless, unhappy woman. Her husband was the father of Elizabeth's unborn babe.

The girl's situation was bleak. She was 'fallen', as a few years later it would have been expressed, and her family was fallen. Here were her father, John Ashby, and she in a poor cottage of three rooms and an attic, but hardly confirmed cottagers. They had prosperous relatives on a great farm just outside Stratford on Avon, and Mr Joseph Ashby Gillett, head of the old Banbury firm of bankers, was their distant cousin. Like a large number of families, they had stories of far grander connections than these, stories remembered, if not

1

evolved, as a defence against some of the worst mental effects of poverty.

It was not just that the Ashbys of Tysoe had lost their farm and status: they seemed to have lost everything of substance. They had ceased to attend the Sibford Quaker Meeting House, of which they had been members for perhaps 150 years, yet had no dealings with the Church or the Methodists; they avoided all contact with their near relatives at Stratford; they refused such company as the Peacock Inn could offer. In pride, when they lost their farm on the closure of a mortgage, they had parted with every stick of good furniture in order to pay to the uttermost. Worse than all that—a more violent colour in the family aura—had there not been an Ashby member of a gang of cattle-maimers, landlord-haters, in the thirties of the century? No member of my family has ever alluded to this, but I do not think I dreamt it. Villages do not retain for long a live and widespread memory of their most dreadful events. You cannot, after all, tell the worst—such a worst—to the young with their upward looks of weakness and trust. Nor will you readily spoil a bright summer's day or a spell of optimism about human beings with echoes of the most bitter anger. But should some brief allusion to dark things heighten a good tale or talk, then it may be made for drama's sake, and in some such way the tradition reached a little pitcher's long ears.

It was in June 1859 that Elizabeth went to bed for her son Joseph to be born into this poor corner of the world. She was in the inner room upstairs, in a vast bed with four turned elm posts but no curtains. Quite unlike Tess of the d'Urbervilles, and no Hetty Sorrel, she cannot be thought of simply as a wronged or abused girl. It seems unlikely that anything less than an impulse from her own nature had seduced her. Uncommon strength and calm reason mark most of the memories of her. Not all: she had much to settle with an unreasonable father; anger there was at times for a while. From the beginning there was a firmness. No curiosity, no warm

2

interest, ever moved her to confidences relating to her child's father. His identity was never alluded to by her, nor in her presence. Money provided for her and for her son's education remained where it was placed—and later was spent by its trustee before the time when she might, possibly, for the boy's sake, have taken advantage of it. With the birth of her babe her motherly feeling sprang full-grown. He was the first of creatures with her, never a problem, but her vital link with life. She had one other love—her brother William.

Elizabeth's immediate family, then, consisted for the present of her three menfolk. William was not living at the cottage; he had lately married and had a house half a mile away. One friend Elizabeth had in Hannah Soden, William's wife's sister, who had gone Londonwards for her living and recently had married, of all men, a Frenchman of the name of du Rouvray, anglicised to Rouvray. The only sign of Hannah's existence, of late, was an occasional small parcel containing something good—fine tea, or a few yards of good cloth, the only luxuries her friend would ever see.

It was the grown-ups of her family that troubled Elizabeth. There was the uncertainty of their livelihoods. Neither John nor William Ashby had regular work. Both refused to earn wages from a single employer for long at a time. John, her father, sometimes helped his cousin Robert, who had a modest nursery garden and sold plants to farmers' wives. He liked best jobs that used his intelligence; just now he kept accounts, did business, and fed the home stock morning and evening for a neighbouring farmer grown old and sick. William used his great strength, his skill and his endurance on strenuous temporary work—hedging, harvesting, ditching, draining— never staying long on one farm, occasionally going away to do a piece of work at a distance. When father or brother had finished the job of the moment there might be weeks with next to no income.

Then there was Father's poaching. Elizabeth protested

that neither she nor her child was going to be mixed up with it; that sort of thing was all very well twenty years ago. William backed her up: it was fool's work. But, of course, Father had a weighty argument in Elizabeth's and Joseph's presence in the house. Besides, he and the friend he hunted with had built up an interest, almost a hobby; the attic over Elizabeth's bedroom was their tool-room. When the boy Joseph saw it years later, it looked like a small museum of poaching, with neat rows of tools and traps hung on hooks, and nets suspended from the rafters. They had a sardonic amusement from the work too; they poached the farms and coverts of the Middleton who had foreclosed the mortgage, and of old Nicholas Ashby who had so meanly refused help.

Whatever its joys, the poaching had to stop. One day John came home with two magnificent cock pheasants. Possibly he thought their brilliance would dazzle a girl. But Elizabeth's wrath burst out. She ordered her father to 'take those things away', and when he did not obey she took the suet pudding of bacon and late mushrooms she had just lifted from the pot and threw it at him. Wouldn't he learn? Cook those? She would never cook for him again! The poaching ended: the trap-door to the attic was firmly fastened and never opened for years.

William was a greater trouble. The bond of sympathy between brother and sister was such that his joyless life was harder for her to see than for him to bear. His working life galled him. His fabulous strength and speed made his presence in a harvest field worth a bag of gold. There might be twenty workers there, all affected by his method and his rate of work. Tales of these were told so long as sickle and fagging hook continued to be used in Tysoe. But the farmers in Tysoe one and all refused him piece-work; it made men so independent! Let him get used to being a labourer! At home his wife Harriet, pretty, cheerful and genial to others, was proving a profound irritant to him. She could not see why he would not take regular work; she was, he thought, servile to pretentious folk; his one hope for the future lay in emigrating to America, but she would not hear the word spoken.

Elizabeth had a plan to start William towards independence. She had a little money and he could have it to buy a cow and a pig. He did so, but calamity befell the animals, and now Elizabeth had little hope and a great fear—that he would lift his hand against his practical, workaday, undiscerning girl of a wife. Brother and sister each had reasons for silence, a small mental enclosure, and the silence spread. But that made little difference to their importance to each other. While William lived, or rather while he lived in England, Elizabeth had her two beloveds.

In other directions Elizabeth was finding her firm line. The autumn after Joseph's birth she earned money in the cornfields. Would liberties be taken? Would there be allusions to her position, jokes? She took care at first to work with William, one of the three or four who followed him with their sickles, cutting his 'land' of corn, but her own gravity was her real safeguard. She helped in later harvests, but mostly she worked as her father did—using her skill and intelligence in others' emergencies. She wrote letters for her neighbours, helped them to cut out shirts, to whitewash their ceilings. Sometimes she would sit up at night with the sick. Little money passed, but her services were meticulously paid for. Her garden was dug, vegetables and rabbits brought, faggots of wood were stacked against her wall.

Soon after her arrival home, father or brother would find Elizabeth reading the huge family Bible. While she was in bed after her child's birth she read the book, propped between the bed and a heavy chair. She appropriated it and it became her life's companion. Later in the century, village folk took to reading their Bibles in little snippets under the direction of 'Bible circles', as if even a few words had magic influence; Elizabeth read book by book, Pauline letter after letter, as others did too at that time. She was deciding during those days in bed some very important matters, practising thoughts and attitudes to see her through life. She had Joseph baptised at church, breaking finally the chain of family records at the Sibford Meeting House. She came to love the church and its services and became a regular churchgoer. The transition from Quaker ways was not altogether easy, as a famous incident shows. The Vicar had insisted on the duty of taking the Sacraments, and she began to attend the Communion Service. With her large serious thoughts she was not over-sensitive to worldly claims, nor would she blame anyone for expecting her to take a retired place, which was her own intention. But when one Sunday she found herself before the altar among a group of well-to-do folk, and the Vicar motioned imperiously to her to give way to a farmer's wife and await a later turn, her rage boiled up. She stood there before the chancel white and still for a moment and then found expression in a voice as clear as it was passionate. 'You put me aside...? Job says "Thou shalt not even secretly favour persons", and Paul wrote "No respect of persons with God, no distinction between Jew and Greek; the same Lord is Lord of all that call upon Him".' It was the first time that in all the centuries of Tysoe church's existence a woman's voice had been clearly raised in it to utter words of her own choosing, audible to many. This short and simple story is hardly credible to those who know the atmosphere of later Victorian times. But in 1860 the church was still filled with plain light, and plain words might seem less remarkable than they would after the sentimental Victorian stained glass had dimmed it. And perhaps Elizabeth was unconsciously helped—or ill-prompted —by hearing at some time of an ancestor of hers, a puritan fellow, who once stood up in the middle of a sermon in Shenington church just over the hills and said, 'If that thou sayest be in thy Bible, parson, it beant in mine'. But Elizabeth did not intend to be a rebel, and there was no long breach between her and Parson Francis.

How the proud and dominating Vicar came to forgive her there is no knowing. Possibly he traced her pride to her blood; such matters were of interest to one who wished so to insist on rank. One day he came to her door on some slight errand and asked, as it were incidentally, 'Did you ever hear of such and such a House over in Leicestershire, Elizabeth?' 'Oh yes,' she said, 'I think this has to do with it.' She reached down a broken-backed book from the top of her little bookshelf that stood on a big elm bureau and took out of it several papers, one of which was an old print of a coat of arms with the name Ashby above, and below in Gothic letters the motto 'Be just; fear not'. 'Proves nothing', the Vicar snorted. 'No,' said Elizabeth, 'but they are good words; they help me.'

When Elizabeth returned it was not merely to a cottage in the Upper Town, but to her village, where she meant to stay. She could not compare Tysoe with distant villages: I never heard of her going outside her own district. Single visits to Warwick, the county town, and to Leamington, rare days at Stratford on Avon and Shipston on Stour, twice-yearly shopping days in Banbury—these were her longest travels, sixteen miles at the utmost. But when she was a sturdy little girl it was only forty years since the open fields of Tysoe's great communal farms, nearly five thousand acres in extent, could be freely crossed in all directions. Then the vast fields and heaths had been broken up into farms and tiny modern fields. Thus she and her companions were restricted to footpaths; but still for them, as for their fathers, the fairs and shows in other villages were among the chief excitements of summer and she knew every village whose parish boundaries touched Tysoe's, besides those on the roads to Banbury and Shipston.

Compared with all these Tysoe had some high distinctions. It was large, and composed in a rare way. Its trinity of hamlets, Upper, Church, and Temple (or, as the old maps had it, Templars') Tysoe were large groups of houses strung along the foot of the Edge Hills. These, with their minor clusters and lanes, stood on small brooks flowing down

7

parallel courses some quarter or half mile apart. The hills themselves were unique and, moreover, sacred. They looked high and straight, fully their six or seven hundred feet. From their ridge, they are seen to be the edge of a plateau, not straight but a series of curves, forming great amphitheatres, suitable for giant Roman dramas and spectacles, but no one in Tysoe thought of those. For Elizabeth as she grew up, as for many of her fellow villagers, they were biblical hills—steadfast, a glimpse vouchsafed of the foundations God has laid, the bastions he has built; yet sometimes skipping like lambs, while clouds that are the skirts and fringes of God's raiment sweep along them.

When Elizabeth went to church on Sundays in the early days of her return, she had not to run the gauntlet of eyes in narrow streets. She could slip through the fields and then down the street of Church Town, the houses kept apart by a great elongated lozenge of green. The church, between the main street and the lanes, stands a little high on an island mound so that its length and height are well shown. By 1859 a proportion of the villagers had felt so little at home in it that they had built themselves other places of worship. There was not only the Wesleyan chapel, off the street, up the pavement between two narrow green lawns near the blacksmith's shop, but in the Back Lane there was the 'Primitive' chapel, more properly Primitive Methodist. But the church had for everyone its precedence; it was the village's own, the centre of ceremony and emotion where all gathered for national deliverances and Club anniversaries, and were impressed by its physical greatness and its ancientry and dignity. The church was God's house, and the chapels—perhaps at times even more filled with himself—his cottage dwellings.

At the time of Joseph's birth the last stone of a great new building was laid. Across the lane at the farther side of the church the National School rose gaunt and large. A Mr Gilbert Scott, come to give the Vicar some advice about the church, had planned this barnlike two-armed erection with ecclesiastical windows too high for children to see out of and 'Early English' doors too heavy for little children to push. This had succeeded the cottage-like Old School in the street where Elizabeth had learned to read. Here for centuries past twenty boys had been instructed, each for two years, so that in fact many men could read, and then in the early nineteenth century girls had been accepted also. But the new school was intended for all.

There was one other great communal meeting-place, the oldest of all—the green, not one single compact space, but one wide area at the higher end of the street, the lozenge down the street itself, and then the extension below the church— all used at different times for varying public purposes. The babe Joseph was to take early to the use of the pen and one of his first essays to get into print tells what the green had meant. 'It is not so many years', he wrote, 'since the respect- able and substantial inhabitants met here once a year to beat the boundaries of the parish, to see that the boundary stones had not been moved...followed by the court leet of the Lord of the Manor and its jovial associations at the Peacock Inn.' Here too on important occasions like the Wake, bulls were once baited with bull-dogs and poultry-yard veterans were brought to settle long-standing disputes about championships within the limits of a saw-pit which was cleared for the purpose 'and one or two of the very oldest of us may remem- ber such an unpleasant incident as being locked in the stocks for petty offences by our parish constables'.

'Till this day', he writes, 'every propagandist of a new religious idea, a political creed, or a social reform has found his audience and perhaps some of his inspiration on these few square yards of historical greensward.' He might have written also of the folk-dances, the guild meetings, the agitated sessions about smallpox and many another occasion.

Houses—homes—it is thought, are always more interesting to women than public institutions and places. Perhaps it was so with Elizabeth. Perhaps for us all their associations are more intense. Religion, agriculture and politics have their quiet and monotonous times, but homes never. To families and individual breasts every trouble comes home—every loss of temper, sobriety, reason. A happy meal is an ideal achieved, a harsh word a dream broken. So far as appearances go, the homes of Tysoe were much for Elizabeth as they had been for her ancestor who first settled here, late in the seventeenth century; much too as they looked to her granddaughter early in the nineteen hundreds. The comeliest of the houses had been built, or more likely rebuilt in the early and middle years of the seventeenth century. They had still their mullioned and hooded windows but with one or two exceptions not the old handsome doorways, for many houses had latterly been divided. A line of less distinguished cottages had been built in about 1720 along Church Town street between the Old School and the Peacock Inn: the Marquis of Northampton's agent had enlarged and architecturally spoiled some of the bigger farmhouses in the Upper Town, I suppose about 1815, while corn prices were high, and there was one rather absurd neo-Gothic villa, not far from the manor house. A pair of brick and slate cottages had been completed in the Back Lane.

But it is likely that Elizabeth's interest was rather in what had happened inside the houses. From her father's door she saw across the road to the right, Mr Styles's bakehouse in which not so long since an aunt or great-aunt of hers 'had thrown out silver with a showell while her husband put it in with a teaspoon', and to the left, also within sight, in a high cottage, other female ancestresses had kept their father's loom clacking, turn by turn, after he had gone to bed. One kept the heddles and combs moving while the other ran out to see her sweetheart. The manor house and farm at the end of the Town had been tenanted formerly by some of her sister-in-law's folk. These snippets of family lore that I chanced to hear would seem trivial to my serious grandmother. She knew graver associations—which house had set aside a room for a Quaker Meeting House and which cottage had been used

10

for the first Methodist prayer meetings; where there had been bankruptcy, emigration, cholera, alleged witchcraft; and an ancient tale of one family, that an ancestor had been outlawed and had finished his life as a madman in the tree-tops.

What of still homelier matters—children and meals, the gardens and fields and games? From 1859 these began to affect her son as much as Elizabeth herself and we may see much with his opening eyes.

CHAPTER II

JOSEPH: EARLY CHILDHOOD
AND EDUCATION

Two years after Joseph's birth his grandfather died. Elizabeth's need of support was this time met by her marriage to a young man she had known from childhood, a member of just such a family as her own. No word as to his appearance, his thoughts or his character was ever spoken in my hearing. There are memories only of Elizabeth's inability to buy what he needed in his last illness, and of small pieties rendered to his green grave; for after five years he too died, leaving Elizabeth the mother of three children, Joseph Ashby, and George and Annie Townsend.

Charles Townsend had joined Elizabeth in her father's house. Elizabeth and he made few changes in it. The tools and nets remained forgotten in the attic above the trap-door. After Charles's death, the two boys shared a big bed on the open landing at the top of the stairs, where grandfather used to sleep, and mother and daughter slept in the next room. In the 'house' below (this is always the name of the living room in Tysoe, and in such a cottage as this we are not so far from a condition in which one room was indeed the house) a large deal table served almost every purpose. Against the wall stood an old, sun-faded Pembroke table, of which one leaf could be raised, and in the recess beside the wide hearth stood a big elm bureau with three deep drawers underneath the desk and a row of books on top; two old, rush-bottomed elm chairs and one or two wood-seated beechen ones, and besides these nothing but the window-seat. The original fireplace was still there—a low oak beam across rough stone walls—but a smaller chimney had been built within the old one and a small cheap iron grate inserted, with chains for hanging the kettle on top of the fire, and a little oven to the right. To ward off the draught from the front door a papered screen had been set up at right angles to it, and on this was the only brightness of colour, except the fire itself. To please the children Elizabeth had pasted on it one of the new-fashioned trades-men's calendars—a big coloured picture of a fisherman in his boat and his little granddaughter sitting beside him, with a basin of broth in her lap.

A life of great poverty was lived here. The family was largely supported upon eighteenpence for each person from the parish. Thirty years earlier the Poor Law Commissioners had decided that relief must be made painful and even dis-graceful, and the Poor Law had been horribly successful in bringing this about. But it took longer in Tysoe for the widow and the fatherless to regard help with shame. Elizabeth's own forebears had been overseers and had paid out money to all sorts of folk; for example, to farmers like themselves who had suffered catastrophe from fire or flood. Nor was the weekly total of six or seven shillings so much below the income of many in the village. Some men earned as little as seven or eight shillings, and had larger families than Elizabeth's.

Elizabeth was still young and, although grave and sad-dened, she could play with her little children before the fire. Joseph remembered a day when he brought home clay from the banks of the Middle Town Brook and modelled with it gallipots and tools and animals. When he put them in the oven to bake they dried in no time and fell to pieces. His mother, to comfort him, ran out into the garden and pulled lead from an old, small leaded window-frame that lay near her woodpile. After softening it in the fire she made fantastic little men with it. When the three children's prayers were said and she had taken them upstairs, and set the little oil-lamp (oil was cheaper by now than candles) on a table opposite a blank space of whitewashed wall, she held up her long, narrow hands so that their shadow fell clear—as a boat with masts, a hat, a crown, an eagle's head, changing to a duck's. The small boys would try to work this magic for themselves, but little short hands could never be folded to make fine things.

She had stories for them, too, doubtless somewhat later, all out of one Book. As soon as they could read (it was largely she who taught them) she would set them to find within twenty pages of Chronicles the story of the boy who defended his father's patch of lentils, as if, she said, a Tysoe boy had kept an enemy off his father's allotment; or perhaps to find the story of the young Prince Jonathan and his armour-bearer climbing the two crags, Bozez and Sereh. For Joseph the two crags were like small church spires; from these the two young men fell into a crowd of Philistines and demonstrated once for all that there was 'no restraint upon the Lord to save by many or by few'. There is no sign that in early years Joseph felt greatly in his spirit and for himself the pressure of poverty and restriction in this little home. The one thing that we know he felt for himself was the smallness of his family compared with others, and the lack of a father. There were friends enough outside, but he wanted a big warm family within.

From his seventh to his tenth year Joseph became a wanderer and an explorer, gaining his more worldly education. For him and other boys streets and roads hardly existed. They took the shortest line to where they wished to go. Sent on an errand to Church Town, Joseph would slide through a gap in the hedge at the bottom of his long garden and speed through the fields across the Oxhill Road, and was back in no time, free again for play. With other boys he traced the brooks in the upper end of the parish from their springs in the tiny valleys, all the way to Oxhill, wondering at their growing width, sailing ships on them, noting their varying speeds in this field and that, shivering at their desolate looks in winter. A year or so later he knew all the brooks of all the Towns, had visited on Saturdays and holidays every nearby village. The boys had their own news-service, and Joseph went to see every hawk's and moorhen's nest and badger's hole for miles round. Indeed, the boys had a whole body of knowledge, much of which was special to themselves, or shared only with a few men in whose retentive memories boyhood lived and from whom they learned the old names. Until the reading-books in school and the puzzled looks of strangers made the names seem odd the spotted woodpecker was a hickwall, the hedge-sparrow Betty bumbarrel, and the heron Mollyhern. They called the house-sparrow Phil, but nobody it seems had given a pet name to the bright chaffinch, the Chawdow.

Joseph and his companions took, of course, to following the men about their business, especially those whose work was a little exceptional—the thatchers, the builders, the men with ferrets. They knew, besides, the ways of every farmer in Tysoe—who was buying machinery, a fresh kind of drill or chaff-cutter or turnip-slicer; who did well with his cattle and who could grow corn. In February of his tenth year Joseph watched draining operations in a low-lying clay field in Church Town. The old drains, a foot or so deep, filled with rotten branches of thornwood, were being cut across by new ones two feet deep, with glazed pipes laid along them. The Tysoe labourers were as excited as the boys by this operation, calculating the cost per acre and how long it would take Muster Gee to get his money back, some saying he would lose it all: the old folk had known the right depth for drains in clay! Then there was the Lomas's new threshing machine. Its clicketty-clocketty noise and jerky movements as it threw out the straw, and the little buckets delivering the grain, made it far more fascinating than the rhythmic beat of flails on barn floors.

Not all the sights that Joseph saw were directly edifying. One day, when he and some other boys were picking up odd-shaped pieces of wood in the carpenter's shop under the church tower, they saw an old woman issue from a door in a high wall and go tottering up the lane on her stick. 'Let's go and try old Mother Alcock for a witch', cried out one of the big fellows, and he and the other big ones—bigger, that is, than Joseph—snatched up straws and small sticks and ran after her. Getting in front, they laid the sticks and straws crosswise in her path. Patiently the old woman pushed the crosses aside with the point of her stick, and the boys went off yelling, 'Old Mother Alcock's a witch. Stick a pin in the witch!' Meanwhile another boy dashed through the old woman's garden door and presently came out declaring that he had put her scissors under her cushion, 'and when she sits on the cross it'll give her an awful pain'. On another occasion he saw a man on horseback spurring and whipping his nag that refused to go on through a narrow section of a path. A garden thrust out into the path at that point and an old man was working on it. 'Years ago', said someone, 'they'd ha' said it was because old Job Welton's a wizard.'

All this time, indeed since his fifth birthday, Joseph had been a schoolboy attending 'the new school', which he was to leave in the spring-time before he attained eleven years. I do not remember his telling any tales of school until the time when the old schoolmaster left after forty years of his office. Turning out the cupboards Mr Dodge gave my father two old reading-books, the very texts he had read in Standards I and II. As he handled them the doors of this old cupboard of memories swung slowly open, and urged by his children's questions he took out a good deal.

He even remembered something of the infant class. The children had sat together, taught by a boy monitor, Charlie Reason, at the 'bottom end' of the girls' wing, near the girls' door, a great draughty door of the same size and shape as the south door of the church. The chief business of the infants was to learn to chant the alphabet and the numbers to one hundred. In the next class they chanted tables and recited the even numbers and the odd. When the children were unbearably fidgety ('fidget' was the word spoken most often by the teachers), Charlie would tell them to sit up straight; when he could hear a pin drop they should say their rhyme again. He would drop a pin and pretend he heard, through the hubbub of six classes, and then the children would chant all together Charlie's own poem, waving their hands to mark the rhythm,

> Infants never must be lazy
> On to work and up-si-daisy.

There was another recitation Joseph recalled:

> O-n, on; b-o-n, bon; c-o-n, con,
> L-o-n, lon; d-o-n, don; London.

But then the new schoolmaster came and the children said:

> Ride a cock-horse to Banbury Cross

instead of 'Up-si-daisy'. And as Banbury was not far away that seemed somehow important and natural.

Right up the school, through all the six standards (there was a special class of a few boys and one or two girls above this) you did almost nothing except reading, writing and arithmetic. What a noise there used to be! Several children would be reading aloud, teachers scolding, infants reciting, all waxing louder and louder until the master rang the bell on his desk and the noise slid down to a lower note and less volume.

Reading was worst; sums you did at least write on your slate, whereas you might wait the whole half-hour of a reading lesson while boys and girls who could not read stuck at every word. If you took your finger from the word that was being read you were punished by staying in when others went home. A specially hard time was the two 'sewing afternoons'. While the girls were collected together for sewing, the boys merely did more sums or an extra dictation, just the sort of thing they had been doing all morning. As they craned their necks to see what sort of garments, what colours, were coming out of the vicarage basket of mending, they were unusually tiresome to the poor pupil-teacher, losing their places over and over again, or misspelling words they knew

17

perfectly well—forgetting everything. He rapped with a stick; he shouted; he called out, 'Jack, Tom, stay in half an hour!'— a rather effective threat. To remain in school was the thing above all others the children did not want to do. But the most extraordinary thing about sewing afternoons was the quiet that fell on half the school. The girls and their teachers seemed to be talking almost as if they were at home or in a shop, and that made a strangeness in the school atmosphere where contrariwise, the unnatural was customary. The new master, Mr Dodge, had not made so very much difference, though he was college-trained and eager to work. After all, there were a couple of hundred children and he was busy teaching the top class.

Two inspectors came once a year and carried out a dramatic examination. The schoolmaster came into school in his best suit; all the pupils and teachers would be listening till at ten o'clock a dog-cart would be heard on the road, even though it was eighty yards away. In would come two gentlemen with a deportment of high authority, with rich voices. Each would sit at a desk and children would be called in turn to one or other. The master hovered round, calling children out as they were needed. The children could see him start with vexation as a good pupil stuck at a word in the reading-book he had been using all the year, or sat motionless with his sum in front of him. The master's anxiety was deep, for his earnings depended on the children's work. One year the atmosphere of anxiety so affected the lower standards that, one after another as they were brought to the Inspector, the boys howled and the girls whimpered. It took hours to get through them. But the older children looked beyond the examination; the moment the Inspectors had finished the school would be closed. Well, not quite at that moment; time would be taken to open a hamper of great, golden, rare fruit, of which each child would presently have a specimen cupped in his own two hands—oranges! A traditional kindness this, paid for by 'the Marquis'.

Joseph: Early Childhood and Education

'Was there no interest in school?' we asked our father. Sometimes there was. Mr Dodge, the master, might come and take your class for a few minutes, and he was never as dull as the pupil-teachers. He might give you a real sum about some boy's father's garden; it was known that if he gave a dictation he would alter the book's familiar paragraph to catch you out; and he would come out and play, on rare occasions, at rounders, and couldn't he run!—a tough little man, always. There were 'object' lessons now and then—without any objects but with white chalk drawings on the blackboard—an oil-lamp, or a vulture, or a diamond might be the subject. Once there was a lesson on a strange animal called a quad-ru-ped—cloven-footed, a chewer of the cud; her house was called a byre (but in Tysoe it was not); her skin was made into shoes and from her udder came milk. It burst upon Joseph that this was one of the creatures he would milk after school, part of Henry Beasley's herd. He would milk three or four cows, and Robert Philpott, stronger and quicker in the hand, would milk the other six, though in school the latter was a famous dunce, always in trouble.

How dull school was! my father summed up. And yet—no, not *dull*. One didn't learn much but the place was full of feeling. It was so easy to get a beating for one thing. Some boys couldn't get through a day without 'holding out their hands' or a week without a real thrashing. While a thrashing proceeded the school simmered. Would a boy cry? Was the master hitting harder than usual? It might be oneself soon.

Life was uncivilised in school, and yet there was plenty of conscience. For example, the master never caned a girl, no matter how maddening she might be. There was the emphasis on duty. Whatever people didn't know about the children's health or how to teach them, they knew the children's duty. What a tremendous standard was set them! They ought to be silent, they ought to march in and out in orderly fashion, they ought to attend—above all to attend!—to whatever the master or the Vicar or the pupil-teachers or even the monitors might put before them or upon them. The very height of the standard impressed the children. They felt it sincerely pre-scribed by the master (they were not so sure of the others) and that there were sins, such as untruth, that really hurt him. Standards could be very inconsistent: for example, children dared not come late to school, but they absented themselves altogether for every sort of reason. Girls could be kept at home on the weekly washing day; boys would go to every flower-show, every meet of the hunt within seven miles. When the cowslips bloomed both boys and girls would be taken out by their mothers to pick the flowers for wine and for a cowslip pudding. Some families stayed away, too, on all the old traditional festivals—St Valentine's Day, Plough Monday, and on the Club Days or patronal celebrations of villages round about.

School was so unreal. That explained the truancy and the caning and much else, and yet there were only one or two families whose children did not go at all, twenty years before compulsion came. All the parents wanted their children to learn to read, and the National School had put out of business all the dame and gaffer schools, and had absorbed the old Feoffees' School.

Though reality only trickled into school, fate would come crashing. Whenever there was an epidemic some child would die—sometimes more than one, and, on one occasion, several —and the master would be stricken and even the pupil-teachers 'upset'.

Enough about the school! One was always glad to get out of it, my father said. But that was a complex, vexing business, getting out. All the children in a class came out together—or rather in order—to a series of commands. One! and you stood in your desk. Two! and you put your left leg over the seat. Three! and the right joined it. Four! you faced the lane between the classes. Five! you marched on the spot. Six! you stepped forward and the pupil-teacher chanted, 'Left, right, left, right, left, right'. It was agony—you were so

longing to get outside. But if one boy pushed another you would have to go back and begin the rigmarole again.

Life in school—one may sum up my father's account—was rich with frustration. The air was filled with little curses; little chests heaved over broken hearts. But towards twelve and four of every day intensest hope and joy would burgeon.

> Be present at our table, Lord;
> Be here and everywhere adored,
> These creatures bless and grant that we
> May feast in Paradise with Thee.

The verse was sung with unspeakable fervour, eyes tight closed over visions and hands pressed together. Outside school there were feasts indeed.

And yet finally Joseph learned something from school, from one class—the class he was never in. When he was sick of waiting while some classmate spelled out word after word, he would look as often as he dared at the blackboard of the top class, covered with fascinating shapes, and listen to the master's clear, sharp voice explaining how to measure an angle. Or if he dared not look he could listen to what they chanted together—definitions of strange distant things—promontories, peninsulas.

Then, too, he seems to have learned a little grammar, but he may have done this in evening school. And certain it was that he learned a speech or two from Shakespeare. That was after he had left school, but Brother George learned them in his class and taught them to Joseph in bed at night. They would make a tent of their one vast blanket, the old hand-woven one; as heavy as lead it was, not very warm, but an excellent tent to spout fine speeches from.

> By Jove, I am not covetous of gold
> Nor care I who doth feed upon my cost,
> Such outward things dwell not in my desires.

This was the set piece learned in the school; someone must have lent Joseph a copy of the play, for he wrote down one or two

other pieces well fitted for quoting later, on hard and wintry
days.

> We are but warriors for the working day
> Our gayness and our gilt are all besmirched
> With rainy marching in the painful field
> And time hath worn us into slovenry.

One part of the school day was by its nature set apart.
'My Lords' who sent the inspectors had not laid their hands
directly upon religious instruction. The Vicar often came in
during these lessons; then the Master poured out towards the
visitor all his respect and attention, and the children stood
during the Vicar's pleasure. He had been known years ago
to give lessons in the Bible but now he left that to the Master
and the curate. But the catechism he continued to take.

In religious instruction or 'Scripture' everything that had
been turned out from the other lessons came rushing back—a
real book, a hundred books, myth, legend and miracle, poetry
and great conceptions, and a shining Personality. It is true
that the psalms were chanted 'unintelligently', that chapters
of the Bible were read around verse by verse, person by
person, just as other books were, but nothing could keep its
great rhythms from the ear, nor quite all its visions from the
mind's eye. Bible and catechism and hymns alike afforded
mystery and greatness—meat beside the dry bread of the
three R's. When the Vicar and the Vicar's lady taught the
Book they detracted from it, always insisting on its morals.
But the Master and the curate might tell a story so that it
gained for the children in clarity or drama, or they might
illustrate the meaning of a parable in some homely, local
way.

The catechism was almost as full of mystery as the Bible.
Its strange account of the functions of godfathers, its allusions to 'pomp and vanities' and 'sinful lusts' promised for
one a strange and varied future. The mystery slumped and
vanished in the Duty towards my Neighbour, and it was upon
this that the Vicar and his lady laid such stress. Boys and

girls must never 'pick and steal', nor lie, nor have any envy of folk luckier than themselves; they must learn to labour truly to get their own living and order themselves lowly and reverently to their betters. As to what was meant by all these phrases there was no mystery at all; the word 'betters' was especially firmly underlined and annotated. It meant the Vicar himself and the man who paid your father's wage.

But in the Wednesday morning service in church, as in Sunday services, mystery came back. Never mind how or by whom the Psalms, the stories, the Epistles were read or sung, they had their richness and their message; and the prayers bestowed their beautiful and practical phrases. But none of these brought the messages alleged in the Vicar's short, sharp sermon, almost always concerned with some dull and humiliating 'duty to my neighbour'.

CHAPTER III

WORK AND PLAY

FROM the time he was nine Joseph would spend long, lonely days in school vacations and on Saturdays scaring crows off the short, green corn. He had a wooden clapper, but if he saw no one for hours he took to shouting so as to hear a human voice. This method had another convenience; you couldn't cry while you shouted. Another job by which he earned pennies was throwing swedes or turnips to the man turning the wheel of the cutter.

Joseph left school some time before his eleventh birthday in June 1870, and work began for him in earnest that summer. By accidents of weather, haymaking was late that year and yet the corn harvest was full early. Elizabeth took Joseph with her to help with both the hay and the corn on Bald Knob farm, not far from home. For several weeks the two earned good wages. They depended on these harvest moneys, as did many folk, to buy boots and the like for winter. How few now know what it was ninety years ago to get in a harvest! Though the dis-inherited had no great part of the fruits, still they shared in the achievement, the deep involvement and joy of it. In the hay-time Joseph was up sometimes at half-past-three in the morn-ing, and out in the fields with the men half a mile away by four. The mowers worked six or nine in a row, each cutting a swath behind another. Their scythes went singing through the grass, and the triumph of the scythe and the rhythmic fall of the swath continued like a long, slow, sacred dance. Though the men might not have expressed it that way, they felt the drama to the full, as labourers in any village today watch the felling of trees. After a while the men would stop at the leader's sign, and the scythe would sing a lighter brisker tune on higher notes as the men drew their whetstones back and forth along the blades.

Work and Play

The heat at midday—it was half-way through July—
brought thirst-quenching with beer or cold tea, and then there
was the brief, deep sleep. In the afternoon, work seemed
to have settled down to a routine, if the weather were good,
because senses and minds were a little dulled. But under
threatening clouds the work became a battle, with odds
exhilarating or overwhelming!

The number of workers in the fields would seem extraordinary today—there might, in a big field, be three groups
of several mowers, and when about half the field was cut as
many women would come and begin to turn the first-cut
swathes. In harvest, because labour was cheap in this district,
much corn was still being cut by the sickle. A very neat,
small instrument it was; a good worker dropped hardly a
straw where the corn stood up well. A dozen, or maybe
twenty, reapers, largely women, would work in one field,
with men following to tie up the sheaves and another group
to set them in shucks. With the weather a little less hot than
in the haying time there was talk and banter and flirting and
yarn-spinning during the meals under the hedge. But the
great task dominated minds for all that.

Sharing these labours and emotions, Joseph had little need
of myths; his courage grew and his heart ripened upon them,
as other boys' did on reading the *Iliad* and the *Odyssey*. After
the corn had dried in the shucks, and was being carried away
to the stackyards on the yellow and brown wagons, extended
by rafts to carry the great cargoes, women and children waited
at the gate to exercise, in the form of a privilege, one of the
last of the old customary rights of pre-enclosure days. Each
woman, with the children she had been able to bring, took
a 'land' or ploughing ridge, laid out a sheet with a stone at
each corner, and then the whole company began to move
slowly up the ridges, all the figures bending, hands deep in the
stubble, 'leasing' fallen ears. Each gleaner had a linsey-
woolsey bag hanging from her waist. Tiny boys and girls had
tiny bags. Long straggling straws were gathered into the left

hand, while broken-off ears were dropped into the bag. As the bunches grew too large to be held, they were tied and dropped, to be picked up on the walk back to the headland. The family's total gleanings were laid on the sheet and bundled for carrying. Later on, this corn would be sent to the miller and ground, and several weeks' bread might be made from the flour.

In late September the harvest was over. Elizabeth counted her money and surveyed the family's gleanings. She tidied the house for normal life to be resumed, and paid her small debts. Shoes must be bought for the three children, pattens for herself, and some unbleached calico, stout and cheap and warm—you could make almost any garment with it, if you must. Joseph was a wage-earner now; he had left school. You could be proud of him in a field, the tall, rosy, shapely lad, talking and laughing with everyone, quick at the work. Offers of permanent 'places' for him had been made; his new status must be marked. So Elizabeth and Joseph went to Banbury to do the shopping together. Seats were bespoken on the carrier's cart for the return, but eight-pence would be saved by walking the outward journey—nine miles of field-paths to follow, crossing metalled roads only at two points. It was luxurious at first to walk through stubble or grass without rake or sickle in hand, with no heavy sheaves or aching back. Other families had the same errand, and groups passed or were passed by mother and son. When they were within a mile or so of Banbury, Elizabeth made a little speech. 'Joe, I've been reckoning; I've brought thirty shillings with me. The shoes and calico will never cost all that. You've had to leave school, and we can't help it, but you shall have money to spend on books. Here be three shillings. You've read all I've got. It'll do you good to have some new. You shall choose 'em; I won't interfere, my bwoy.'

Nine miles were a long and tiring way, but the astonishing sight of Banbury rapt Joseph out of all his other sensations. Around the Horse Fair and the markets, and Bridge Street and Sheep Street, wherever the streets broadened out, or houses stood back behind a little space, and in the inn yards, stood rows of carriers' carts, hundreds of them, with their hinged shafts turned skywards to make close setting possible. 'Nijni Novgorod!', breathed Joseph as the sight burst upon him. (His last school reading-book had contained a rich collection of descriptions of the world's oddities. There he had read of a giant fair in the Russian city.) His mother went off to do her errands and left him to find his way. 'You go by yourself,' she said, 'and if we don't see one another before, meet me by John Gardner's cart in the Stagyard.' The three shillings filled both minds. 'Buy what seems you good. There's the stall in the market and Mr North's shop in Parson's Street. He preaches for the Wesleyans; he'll not let you buy any harm. You ought to get three books with three shillings, and good'ns too—ones that'll last.' So she went off to the mercer's and he to turn over the books on the stall. Choosing in public embarrassed the boy. That this was a momentous affair the bookseller saw by Joseph's solemn look. 'What sort o' thing d'you want? Not sermons, eh? Not Walter Scott? Borrow them anywhere! Want to larn something?' At the last phrase Joseph brightened. The stall-holder's hand fell on a book with paper covers of heavenly blue and a brilliant yellow label on the back. As he rustled the leaves over, triangles and polygons fell into a procession. 'Top class does those at school, beginning geometry', Joseph stammered. 'Well, that's mensuration', said the salesman, turning to the title. 'Teach you to find out how high the Church tower is; measure everything under the sun.' The books bought at Mr North's shop were perhaps not a success-ful purchase, but they were cherished. I turn their pages now. There were, in fact, three volumes; the *History of Rasselas, Prince of Abyssinia* consisted of two small dark leather volumes, printed in 1759, just a hundred years before Joseph was born. For his mother Joseph bought a little book, also in dark leather, containing recipes for every kind of thing—

for curing diseases, curing children's faults, aiding the memory, making wine, removing stains—John Wesley's book. One is not a sceptic at eleven, and John Wesley was a great name.

Elizabeth never expressed surprise at these additions to the bookshelf. She and Joseph shared, at any rate, the *Rasselas*. Both of them would quote it later, without pointing out their borrowings. 'There are many conclusions in which nothing is concluded', was one of their words. And many years later Joseph would quote with a little pompous fun, 'My curiosity does not very strongly lead me to survey piles of stones or mounds of earth; my business is with man'

It was the book on mensuration the boy lost himself in on the way home. He mastered quite a few pages, for half-way to Tysoe a man left the carrier's cart to take a parcel to a farmhouse across the field, asking Master Gardner to wait for him. Wait he did, till at last the passengers murmured and the truant was left behind. Do all the days in a life have as much significance as this one of Joseph's? Twenty years later, Joseph saw Carrier Gardner balancing a sixpence on his finger-tip. 'I met John Watson just now,' he said, 'and he paid me this. D'you remember a day you and your mother rid wi' me back from Banbury? You were raidin' a book, like the chap you be. Watson got out afoor he paid. Bin tryin' to pay me this tanner for twenty year. Never couldn't find the right minute. He says as I've allus bin busy, or talkin' to somebody.' What a world of slow pace and scruple some folk lived in then.

After the Harvest Home supper at Bald Knob, Joseph became farm boy on another farm, a regular wage-earner. He was to work mainly with the shepherd in the winter and lambing time, and then with the carter and ploughman for the spring ploughing. He had little contact with the farmer, Master Ainge, a sickly, elderly man who left the day-to-day work of the farm largely to the men.

John Makepeace, the shepherd, was nearing sixty-five and looked older. He was shrivelled and bent and dirty, for he lived alone in an old, low-roofed cottage on the edge of one of Mr Ainge's two farmyards. Here he used only one room, cooked his meals on a fire of sticks in a little three-legged cauldron; his smocks he washed once a year, so it was said, in the nearest brook. He had no right to his name, someone told Joseph. An ancestor of his had been born in a ditch, of a wayfaring woman, who had died before the babe was heard crying and taken to the nearest farm. There he grew up in kitchen and stables and became Makepeaces' John, and now his descendant was John Makepeace. Living between Whatcote and Tysoe, he seldom visited either. He had never taken a near view of Compton Wynyates though it was just over the hill. It was half a century since he had entered a church—and this in 1870, when Sabbath keeping was universal. A pagan was Makepeace. Absorbed in the fields, in the animal life and in the murky jobs in his cottage, there was no room in his life for ideal or abstraction. Yet he had his comment on such matters. Periodically the Vicar hunted him down and told him he had a soul to save. 'If I never gus to church I never gus to chapel', was his ritual reply, as if that at least should please the parson.

Something of a struggle went on between shepherd and carter over Joseph. Jasper seemed suspicious of Makepeace, the boy noticed. He himself was fascinated and pleased by the strange old fellow, who showed him hares' forms and taught him how to watch badgers and foxes. There was something very remarkable about Makepeace's knowledge of plants. He knew every one. Of course, he never spoke of their beauty; the plants were 'yarbs', good for this and that, liked by this animal and that bird; and he had Adam's joy in naming. 'Never 'eard nobody call it,' he would say, 'but I calls it "old yellow spiky", or "jumping Jack", "smoky Jinny" or "little yeavy yed".'

John's flocks were scraggy and harsh in wool, but they were a healthy lot, and he knew the ways of each. He could manage any captive animal, tame or wild. He would catch and hold quiet the savage cats and tempestuous kittens born

in the cattleyard. His dogs and ferrets were well trained. On
the whole John was a silent fellow, but at first Joseph did not
notice this. In his constant activity through the long days
Makepeace would be, as it were, half-turned towards the
youngster, correcting by example some mistaken way of
handling a hurdle, drawing his attention without words to a
movement in a pool; or he would stop a moment when some
bird-song was heard in isolation and tap out its rhythm with
wood on wood and simply name the bird. All this was a
form of conversation, but John could also use words. Occasionally he would tell Joseph some long, circumstantial tale,
as we shall see.

Jasper, Joseph's co-master, was beginning to look elderly.
He was tall and a little stooping, with a long face, long hands
to match, mild blue eyes and a slow smile. Sometimes in a
busy season he would join the shepherd in folding the sheep,
or tending the in-lamb ewes, and then Joseph would consider
that Jasper and not John was the good shepherd of metaphor.
He looked the part and acted it too; he would handle tenderly
the 'poor-doing' lambs, whereas John would sometimes sur-
reptitiously finish their little lives.

Jasper was a pious churchgoer, and never missed a meeting
of his Friendly Society, the Foresters' Club. Though he could
neither read nor write, he loved to be read to; especially he
wished to have the Gospels read to him, and on Saturday
evenings, after a fairly early knocking-off, Joseph would go to
his cottage near the Old Tree and read three or four chapters
to him. But Jasper wanted more worldly news also, and they
would turn to the *Banbury Guardian* and read the farmers'
letters in the correspondence column, and (but this was a year
or two later) the reports of Arch's meetings. The best of these
times occurred in the summer. Jasper was never so much at
ease inside his cottage as out in the garden, for his wife
nagged and was a slattern. Inside the cottage a spoiled life
was patiently endured, but outside Jasper had precious
friends and experiences.

Work and Play

Gradually and still rather vaguely, Joseph understood Jasper's suspicion of Makepeace. The latter would watch—and hold Joseph's arm so that he must watch too—a fight of cats and rats in the barn, or a hawk after little birds, a weasel circling a fascinated rabbit, and never show an impulse to save the weaker creature. When the little drama reached its deadly end, his grasp on Joe's arm would tighten oddly and he would give a little cluck-cluck of satisfaction.

Then there were Makepeace's stories. Once Joseph saw Jasper follow Makepeace into a cowstall, in a grimly purposeful way. 'Your taales', he said to Makepeace's back, 'beant fit for a bwoy's ears. If you tells that bwoy...', and then soon silence and presumably some dumb show. But Makepeace had already told a good deal.

During Joseph's second winter on Ainge's farm there was a buzz of talk for miles round. The skeleton of a man had been found in a barn a few miles away. There was a great mystery as to how the skeleton came to be there. The skull had been broken; foul play, but by whom? When?

It was not a mystery to Makepeace. When he was young he had worked for a while in yon parish. (The name of it eludes me, perhaps happily: we will call it Radford.) The parson there had been murdered and the murderer was never found. 'Good reason for why not', Makepeace said. 'Nobody daren't tell o' nobody else. They were all in it, you might say...there beant no naame in Radford the same as forty yurr agoo, bar a laabourer or two. They be all gone, good raison for why.' One after another, it seemed, as they could find another farm or shop or 'public', the families had gone. Did they all know, asked Joseph, about the skeleton? 'Not they; they daredn't know thaat', said Makepeace, 'but there were summat as they knowed.' It took a good part of the day and half the night (they were sitting up with a calving cow) for the whole story to be told. The parson at Radford was newish, a family man and poor. He insisted on his tithes—the tenth egg and fruit and piglet and chicken. 'They were little men down theer, ne'er a big farmer. They couldn't affoord the tithes.' But the man who was always talking about tithes was the publican, better off than any of them. The village grew to be full of hate and agitation. 'There weredn't no Methodists, nor no Quaakers neither, to stop 'em 'aatin' and tell 'em to look to the sky.'

There was a barmy, that is a yeasty, fellow in the village, excited sometimes, often sulky. 'It weredn't saafe to cross 'im in 'is fits—quoiet enough for the mooast.' One day when the parson was walking up the lane from one of his glebe fields to the parsonage, at his usual time, he had been 'knocked down wi' a spaade and killed'. And then the barmy fellow had been missing. That was what everybody had known, but they knew no more, and now the story was forgotten. Joseph asked a question or two and got short answers. Then there was a fit of silence and irritability and, finally, in the dark, the whole story. The skeleton was accounted for. 'If you ever tells', Makepeace said, 'I'll say as you gets silly taales out o' them books as you brings along wi' your fodder.' Talk in the public-house had begun the affair. Two or three men had talked to the barmy fellow, inciting him to the deed, promising him twenty sovereigns. The publican had shown him the money, putting it into a linen bag with its neck in a ring (just like Makepeace's own purse) before his eyes. The deed done, Barmy vanished and the men grew frightened. Barmy couldn't be far away, he hadn't the money; he would tell about the bribe. They had hunted for him and found him skulking in some outhouse. (From this point, Joseph became sure, Makepeace had seen what happened.) The money and more was proffered to Barmy, but on condition that he made off once for all and emigrated. If he didn't go. . . . But Barmy sulked. He wouldn't answer, he wouldn't move. The men went to him again and described the horrors of the court, of hanging, so that he dared no longer stay in one place. But he would not be off. He had slept one night in a dry ditch, and the next night, when the

Sheriff's men were known to be coming, he stole into a
barn. But he had been watched and his enemies followed.
Again they cajoled and threatened. The barn was half full of
corn and beans. There was a heap of sand at one end, and
ploughs, and hanging on wooden pegs in the walls were flails
and other tools. Barmy raved at the men, showing his teeth
like a dog, and then suddenly turned his back on them all and
threw himself down on the sand. Then the publican took the
lead. 'Leave 'im to me', he shouted. 'Goo away all on y'.'
And they all went—except one, a young 'un who slipped back
and clung to a chink in the barn doors. He could not see the
whole extent inside, but heard everything—a thud and a
dreadful groan.

There had been other stories, taking a boy—after all, a
tenderly reared child—back into a hellish world. One other
remained clear in the mind, but was never told in full. It
concerned a shepherd and his betrayal, or supposed betrayal,
of other labourers for poaching, or maybe worse, and the
revenge they had taken after following him one night to his
lonely place with the sheep. They had—can I write it?—
skinned him alive.

It was well, perhaps, that Joseph should know to what
villages had descended, from what they had had to climb up.
Though his own village had known nothing so terrible as
the worst deeds Makepeace could tell of, it was not for nothing
that Tysoe Quakers and Methodists had their rigid exclusions—their objections to song and tale and joke.

The time came for Joseph to be with Jasper. Ploughing
was far harder work than waiting on the shepherd. On
drizzling days, walking beside Jasper's team of three horses,
on the low clayland under Windmill Hill, what 'rainy marching in the painful field!' It was an effort to pull each foot
from the clinging, sticky earth, and one had a hundred feet!
But on the red, light soil of the upper fields work went well,
even with a team of only two. Elderly man and boy would
look out together over the great green vale, telling each other

that it was always changing. Always the light was throwing up some field, or a distant little spinney never seen from here before. More travelled eyes might have found the green expanse a little lifeless, lacking visible water, but for these it was perfect. Its stillness and greenness was its character. But there were days when its staidness vanished, swept away by wind, together with the clouds that seemed almost to bowl along the sky.

When they stopped for bread and lard at half-past nine, Jasper would ask Joseph whether he had any poetry for him, and Joseph would recite his scraps of Shakespeare, always the lines about 'warriors for the working day'. 'The best things be in books, Joe', Jasper said, and gave his little proof. 'Look at the letters you rades me out o' the *Banbury Guardian*. Who'd think there was any sense in Jeff Southerton to hear him talk? But when he writes a letter to the *Guardian* about the waages or the schoolin' he has somewh't to say. He's wrong, but there's a pinch o' sense in it. And they lines you says to me, nobody couldn't *talk* like that. It's the pen, you see.... To think, bwoy, as you can rade the hull Bible. Yoor mother has read it time and again, I'll be bound. But,' he hastened to say lest he should seem envious, 'I knows my pieces. "The Lord is my Shepherd; I shall not want; He leadeth me beside the still waters...."'

The two shared some outstanding experiences. There was the late February day of dreadful windstorm. They had taken a cart up to the windmill with sacks of corn. On their way back they had to pass a little farmyard, derelict since the enclosures. The smaller buildings were already roofless, but there was still one high, ancient, thatched barn. It looked majestic to eyes which had seen so few buildings of height. That day as they came down towards it, they saw pale patches on the near side of its roof—the top straw had been blown off and left unweathered straw beneath. The edges of the patches were fringes blowing in the wind, inviting it to take them. Then it was dreadful to see the wind lift great gobs and gouts of thatch and fling them sodden and heavy far across the yard. The skeleton of the roof began to show. For an old reason the two were compelled to watch. The scene stood for age and uncomprehending youth, for the fragility of the created thing before primeval force. They tried to express the symbol. 'A sick 'ooman', said Jasper, 'losing 'er locks.' 'An old man grieving.' Neither could murmur 'Lear', for they had not read of him, but when Joseph did he would see the old barn in its trouble.

Jasper remembered Joe's lack of a father. He was the first person to speak to him about his own powers. 'Dooan't you stop a laabourer, bwoy, twun't do for a lad like you. What be schools for? Ever thought about them chapel folk? They rades and they says their thoughts. I dooan't want to be a chapel man, but, bwoy, you goo and see what they doos. Parson Francis be middling good, but he dooan't know what goes on in yoor yed, and dooan't want to, and he wun't help you.'

In the conflict between the two ways of life, Makepeace's and Jasper's, the latter gained Joseph's mind. He presently completely forgot Makepeace's ugly stories; they only returned to him long after when his mind was preoccupied by the past.

There were some social occasions on the farm, even in the winter. Sometimes the midday meal would be taken down at the farmyard in Jasper's little harness room beside the stables, with horses' collars and harness hanging round. Here Jasper and Joe would meet the other labourers on the farm—the yardmen, the second ploughman, and Makepeace might be there too. A little brick chimney had been run up through the shed, and each man would carry in a piece of dry, rotten wood, and they would frizzle small pieces of raw bacon. The shelter and warmth were heaven. Talk often fell on old times, old sports and farming ways, and especially on food.

The old amusements were the topic on happier days. Those

which had totally disappeared were the favourites—cock-fighting and bull-baiting. Some of the men had seen cock-fighting and told how the cocks were fed and trained. The cock-pit had been on an island of village green near the home of one of them. He and Joseph went and looked for traces of it and found them very clear. Pitch-and-toss gambling was only lost to view, being illegal but easily hidden. The men said Methodism had killed the sports because the best sportsmen had been converted. But Jasper said it was due to a change in the Church too; the clergy and the gentlemen-farmers had ceased to be spectators. Altogether, the matches had lost interest.

One old sport survived still—wrestling, generally between two wrestlers, but still occasionally pick-a-back wrestling in two lines. Joseph himself had seen this. It was an accident that he saw the very last match of another kind, for his mother would have objected had she known. Two men who had a quarrel fought it out in a crude duel, with bare fists, but in a regular way, with a few rough rules—times fixed and seconds present to see fair play. Unfortunately, there was trouble. One of the men died of exhaustion on the field, and presently his opponent was tried for manslaughter. After serving his sentence he went off to New Zealand, and thus came to an end the old rough sports.

The meagre diet of some years back was mentioned often. Men used to start the day on a breakfast of bread soaked in hot water, salted and peppered. Bread and onions had been eaten in the fields at dinner-time. A man's wage would not buy bread for a family, let alone any meat. 'No, nor it wun't now', said Jasper, 'if there be any childer.' Someone told of an occasion when a family of parents and nine children had shared a single bloater at Sunday dinner. Cabbage had been a great standby. The young children, they said, had lived on cabbage and lard. 'My old 'ooman', said one of them, 'says cabbage killed many a babby, but kept the next biggest alive.' Now in the seventies the men brought a bit of cheese

as well as an onion. When they ate at home they might have
suet pudding with scraps of bacon rolled in it and mushrooms,
too, once or twice a year, and then it was the richest of
dishes. Usually this talk was cheerful; times were not so bad
as they had been, but sometimes a darker spirit ruled. Life
was hard laabour abroad, squalling babbies at whum, and
the workus at last. The workus was hell, but a cold un. And
all, mark you, in a land of plenty. There was nothing to live
for.

Ainge's farm itself was talked of. Fifteen years before it
had had a plough-team of oxen—old Gloucester long-horns,
with horns a yard long. Blacksmith made cow-knobs to stop
their stabbing one another in the sheds. It had been the last
farm to make the shallow, pale Banbury cheese, the last good-
sized farm to thresh with the flail, and now Makepeace's
sheep were the last of the old sort. As to the value of the new
ways, there was no proof of more profit.

One day an adder was killed in the woods beyond Sunrising
Hill, and there was some excitement. 'What a to-do,' said
one of the men, 'adders used to be as common as 'ares on th'
'eeaths. Badgers be gooin' too. And what ought to goo, that
be Raynard, but 'e dooant.'

The heaths? Where were they, Joseph asked. 'You better
goo and talk to old Tom Lynes; 'e sin the first 'edge planted.'
Jasper took Joe to old Tom. Tom was ninety, but strong still.
He did not look like a labourer, for he had a massive frame
and well-formed features, not wrecked even now. He had
been born before the worst of the famine years. On his fore-
head were tiny white hollows; when he was six, Tysoe's last
great epidemic of smallpox had occurred. All his family had
been ill; his mother had been carried on a stretcher to the
pockhouse at Westcote, two miles from Church Town. Tom
had been sixteen when the first hedge had been planted along
the top above the Red Way. He could still walk through the
three fields on to the lower slopes of Old Lodge, and from
there he named all the fields within sight. It was as if the

hedges shrivelled, and the natural country revealed itself. Along the hills to the east of the parish were 'moors' and 'heaths'—Westcote Heath and Mere Hill. Over Old Lodge in Shenington parish were the First, Second and Far Barnacombe Fields. Barna, then, must be the name of the tiny stream that flowed through them, thought Joe, though no one ever named it now. 'Barna'—like Hook-a-Norton—barn, bourn! Burns; burn! Why, it must mean brook! Lynes as he talked named every path and spinney. Small things and great were alike to him each with its name or its past. Did Joe ever see that loop in yon hedge? A grett tree had stood theer and the hedge was planted round it. He could explain, if you waited long enough, some very strange names—Duffus, on the Manor farm, was where the dove-house used to be; Tithekers had to do with tithes, he didn't remember quite what. On the flat clay land, all newly enclosed in Lynes's time, the names were taken simply from the shapes cut out of the common—the Picked (or pointed) Ground, the Three-corner Field.

Jasper and old Lynes discussed the days before the hedges. The lower slopes of the old heaths were very tolerable grassland now, where they had grown only furze; thyme and harebell could only be seen now on Bald Knob and the hill walks. Enclosures would have done good if ther had been justice in 'em. 'They give folks allotments now instid o' ther rights—on a slope so steep a two-legged animal can't stand, let alone dig!' In the old days you could walk all through the parish and all round it by the balks and headlands and cut wood on the waste, if there was any. 'And what can you do now, Jasper?' asked Lynes. 'Make a farmer mad and you be done.' Fall on evil days then, and your own parish looked after you. 'This bwoy 'ere now, wi'out a dad, 'e'd a bin prenticed to any traade 'e'd a wanted, a bright un such as 'e be. Now they 'as that noisy grett school and pitches 'im out on it afore 'e 'as begun to learn. A good bwoy should be under teachin' till 'e's nineteen, at a good traade, saame as I could 'a bin only

I wanted to be out on the land. But dooan't you taake no notice of us old fellows, bwoy, we be only meahnderin'.'

All that arose out of Joseph's work. All the children then spent more time with the men and women than they would later, for no one thought of school as carrying the real burden of their training. Besides, when the men and the youngsters came home from work they had not earned the wherewithal to live, only part of it. Wood had to be collected and dragged home from the lanes, water drawn from the well, gardens dug and planted. When the diphtheria epidemic at Brailes had horrified the district, purer water must be carried from standpipes, two or three only in each town. The children shared these jobs and chopped sticks, picked fruit, ran errands and went mushrooming. The better the home, the greater their responsibilities were.

When the men had big works going on at home, building or thatching a shed, maybe, or cleaning out the well, or emptying the privy pit, boys must be there to fetch and carry, flying like the wind for the tools or wedges or nails the men had need of. Looking on, a boy would get absorbed in the men's skill, yet not beyond a certain degree, for it was a boy's deepest disgrace to fail, when a crisis came, to see where his weight was needed to supplement the men's, or when his smaller hand must be thrust in.

Some of the labours were communal. As a biggish lad, Joseph carried his mother's corn to the Upper Town tithe barn near the Old Tree, where several men were already threshing with their 'stick-na-halfs', as they called flails. The boys would be allowed to take short turns while the men shook themselves free of the horrid, pricking dust and slaked the thirst it gave them. The call to share work was so frequent that where a job was concerned men and boys came to take all the world for neighbours. They would put shoulder to a clogged wheel if it belonged to Old Nick himself. In accident there was no doctor, in calamity no fire brigade at call; squeamishness and fastidiousness were lower than crime. If a labourer's boy had not the courage or will to throw himself into the breach, the word went forth that he was of no account. In such labours and crises it was perhaps not the more imaginative lads, such as Joseph and his young brother, but some boy more silent and slow who got the accolade, 'You be near a man, you be'.

One part of the neighbourly training in these out-of-school and after-work hours was done by the women. Elizabeth would send her boys to carry some old woman's water, or to chop her wood, or dig her potato plot—not usually very welcome work, but wise old women had always some small treat for the boys when the job was done—some bite or sup within doors, a hot roast potato or a glass of metheglin, though sometimes they would be taxed to find anything. It was not labour that hurt even the very young; it was the insufficiency of the harvest when gathered—the low feeding, the lack of clothes, the draughty houses. It was always one of the most moving experiences to young Joseph to see inside another house, like peeping into another world. He was too young to 'observe', but a fresh eye registered on its periphery what would come to its clear notice later. He knew exactly how and what the cottage women cooked in the one big oval pot, with also perhaps a little old bronze, three-legged cauldron to seethe the potatoes in their skins. Into the boiler went everything else—the bacon, the greens in a net, the dumplings of flour and fat which were taken out as the first course, blunting the appetite so that the meat could be decently shared. As for his own meals, they were not quite so limited. His mother had one of the small stoves, with a little oven. He was aware that only the raven gave his mother the wherewithal for the better meals—the gift of pieces of chine after pig-killing, the rabbit left inside the kitchen door. There were a few sad sights in the houses—the two idiots, a child and a man, and a poor invalid 'in a decline'. Out in the street, he saw old Mrs Wells's heavy ancient pewter dishes carried along home, after their grisly use, to restrain the bloating of some corpse; and his mother, making broth over her fire, exclaimed about the horrible messes offered to the dying.

Of course, there were homes different in kind. Joseph went on errands to his Aunt Hannah Rouvray. Her cottage, a fine large one, was furnished with rosewood and mahogany. There were many small pieces of china, with hand-painted flowers and moulded fruits. The path from her garden gate to her door was bordered deep with flowers, from snowdrop-time to the last tiny yellow chrysanthemum. If you visited her, she offered you a glass of French wine on a painted tray. The only work Joseph ever saw her do was her fantastic patchwork, and such gardening as could go with wearing of a full, black silk dress. Just inside Hannah's door hung a tiny, deep rosewood frame containing a print—the certificate of Adolphe Rouvray's admission to the Chairmakers' Guild. Could chairmaking have provided her with the mysterious sources of her living? The village thought not. But it had no grounds at all for its thoughts. On her little fortune in the Funds the widow lived very completely to herself. She was not very neighbourly, but she was good-natured, kindly-mannered. Altogether she was good for something in the education of young boys—for a little vision of comfort and leisure and propriety and for a streak of colour.

But, of course, there was sheer play at times. There were 'ducks and drakes' on the green—a good, slow play for fine evenings when there were the air and the scene to enjoy. Cricket itself was coming; the fame of Surrey and Wiltshire county cricket had reached Tysoe, and the boys were making home-made bats and bowling along the smoother bits of road. Every year, in the lengthening evenings of late spring, the echoing cries of a race of giants filled the village. The eleven- and twelve-year-olds had need to be giants—they were getting so strong and yet not growing into men. Joseph and his brother, George, liked this play well and made stilts every springtime. Their posse of playmates would act the beginning of half a dozen stories on their stilts. One boy would suggest some stronghold to be attacked, and they would start on their way towards it, and then someone would shout, 'No, no, tisn't fun; I know what we'll do'. Half a dozen starts would be made, two or three evenings spent in elevation, and then the boys would feel the need for speedy movement and reality. The stilts were thrown down, all magic gone from the clumsy sticks, and soon they were broken for the fire. We have one clear, momentary glimpse of Joseph himself at play. It is a verbal photograph, often handed around long after the event. The scene was the village green at the south end where it widens into a rough square, on which in the seventies the speeches and out-of-door sermons took place. As late as the fifties the old games used to be held here, and in the sixties the boys played their version of them. Two long lines of boys, each with another on his back, stand ready for a pick-a-back battle. The riders will wrestle together till one line is riderless and the other has won. There they stand ready for the fray. Round the corner from the Back Lane comes Joseph running, a rider on his shoulders—a donkey foal's skin stuffed with straw. He joins his line and makes for his opponent; the little grey head wags and wags, and the little form moves so comically that onlookers and wrestlers are all undone by helpless laughter, and the battle is off. That was Joseph always—a serious fellow and yet merrier than the merry.

But it was not always spring and summer. Amusement and information came in the winter, as also to a lesser extent in other seasons, from the lighter side of religious life. The Church especially, and Joseph was a Churchman, hatched out and gathered under its wings many minor groups—an Insurance Society, a Band of Hope, a penny bank, penny readings, the list changing with need and fashion. It was from the missionary meetings and leaflets that Joseph gained his early introduction, all in exotic mode, to the world beyond the seas. Melanesia, India, Africa would always have a more homely, familiar feeling for him than France or Germany.

There was, for example, the visit of Mr Florin, the missionary from Norfolk Island. He drew back curtains from a wonderful scene. Passion fruits, pineapples, grapes made the mouth water. In the big, cold barn-school, the warmth of the Island was felt and the cliff-bound coast vividly seen.

Tysoe had adopted a Melanesian boy, Buha, but he was no longer in the mission school. At twelve years of age he had been sent home for a time, but he returned with a girl to be his wife. Then her relations had come in boats to rescue her and presently Buha had gone away too. The natives, though tractable and lovable, had their customs. Give offence to a chief and you must expiate it by an offering of human heads. Thus had perished some young officers of a British naval vessel; there had been no hatred in the slaughter, only necessity from the Melanesian point of view.

What impressed Joseph equally with the foreign warmth and wealth was the missionary's justice of mind. His first picture of India was less happy. The Vicar allowed his mother to read a letter from a lady-missionary who had been governess to the Vicar's daughters. She was so tired, she wrote, of Ahmed Jugger—'Those unmelodious voices dinning incessantly' in her ears were more than she could endure any longer. She would go to Calcutta, the Bengalis were well educated and understood English. She had been at the Cathedral at Bombay; the organ sounded heavenly in contrast to the yelling natives she always heard at the Marathi services. She was trying to buy land for a school, but it was difficult to get a safe title; the natives were such rogues—they cheated at every turn!

Then there were the 'treats'. The Vicar was at his best on festive occasions such as the Church Sunday School treat. It was a very fine affair. First, the afternoon service in the Church, with the Vicar and curate officiating and four clergymen from the neighbouring villages in the procession. Recitations in the school followed and then tea on the Vicarage lawn. There was cake at this tea—a wonderful change from bread and lard. Games on the slope of Old Lodge, the beloved familiar hill rising behind the Vicarage, finished the day for the young children. But on one occasion Joseph lingered to see what the grown-ups did during the later hours. At six the Vicar's own friends, four or five other clergymen and their families, came spanking up in gigs and dog-carts. Mrs Francis led off with one of them in a country dance and the big village children looked on till, after cake and lemonade, they were despatched home. But Joseph sat among the branches of a tree and saw Chinese lanterns lit and hung among the green-black leaves of the laurels round the lawn, making great blobs of colour, glowing yet pale.

Many of these experiences of my father's early days come back to me in his own voice, but of murky stories and the uglier hardships I heard nothing directly from him. He kept them in his mind to correct what might have become a rose-coloured vision, and though not to be recounted in his home they could be charmed from him in outline by my brothers working with him out in a field.

CHAPTER IV

HORNTON QUARRIES AND
ARCH'S MEETING

W HEN Joseph had spent two years on Bald Knob and Ainge's farms and was thirteen years of age, he emerged into a wider fresher world. Of this time he would like to tell, laughing at the foolishness of a lad taking work at the Hornton quarries, three miles from the Lower Town and nearly four from his home. Sometimes he had to walk the whole way through the Towns and then turn up the Red Way, diagonally climbing the hills, but on other days he had lifts.

Joseph and his heavy carthorses and carts with foot-wide wheels took loads of stone from the quarry to any site within nine or ten miles where houses were being built or roads made—for the latter purpose the soft mud-producing yellow-brown stone was still being used. My father never spoke of this experience as hard. The elder workmen were accustomed to training the young and never left him to lift stones of excessive weight. Getting safely down Sunrising Hill when loads had to be taken to Hardwick sent his heart into his mouth, for the staidest horses dreaded the twists and turns of the hill and felt the dangerous camber towards a cliff hidden by hedges, but they learned soon to trust him to slip on the braking-shoes in time. Arrived on a level stretch, if his load was a few great flags of the blue ragstone that occurred in some strata he could sit tolerably at his ease on a folded bag, to see the world and ponder on it.

But on his early journeys from Hornton his thoughts were still often drawn to his own village. During the last discussion he heard at Bald Knob, in the harness room, Jasper had mentioned a meeting, held some years ago, concerning the

Feoffees' or Charity Estate, which he said ought to be called the Town Lands. A day or two later, from inside the cottage door, Joseph overheard an exchange between his mother and the Vicar's wife. 'Goodday, Elizabeth', said the latter, 'The Vicar has sent you the New Year's present from the Charity Estate. Just as usual, six and eightpence.' 'Thank you, Mrs Francis', was the reply, 'The Town Lands money.' 'How do you dare correct me, Elizabeth? And it is insolent to use my name. Can you not say "Ma'am"? The Vicar excuses you too much.' 'If it is charity, I cannot take the money. I have no need. If it is Town Lands money, I can.' Mrs Francis reached past Elizabeth, laid the money on a chair-seat and was gone. The listening boy said, 'You didn't say ma'am, Mother'. 'No', she replied, ''Tisn't the old Quaker way. But it is manners—for servants.'

There had been another incident a day or two later. A ripple, a rustling and a cackling of amusement had gone through the village. A labourer's wife, whose husband had just taken another job in another village, received a parcel from the Charity Estate of several yards each of unbleached calico and scarlet flannel. She had wanted to cut up the calico, which must first be well washed, but then she had put the red flannel through the water too, and hung it on her line just where the neighbours and passers-by must see it.

'Sarah Ann, what ha' you bin doin'?', they asked, 'washin' that new flannel?' 'Why, I bin washin' the charity out on it', she said. And there it hung, a long scarlet banner, pure of charity, and the three towns laughed.

So Joseph worried Jasper to tell him about the Town Lands Meeting. 'Yoor Mother were theer', Jasper said; 'You ask her'. 'I don't think she'll tell me much', Joseph had answered, 'she talks more when you come.' So Jasper dropped in. 'We maaks a muddle of a yarn', he said to Elizabeth, knowing how to make her talk. 'We were beat about the Town Lands, but never ought to ha' bin. You tell 'im. As well be told right as wrong.' Many times the long

story of the Town Lands affair was told in our home; always
in my father's best style; humorous and yet clearly intended
to convey points. His mother had been at the meeting Jasper
spoke of, but rather impatiently refused to give her son an
account of it.

'Now Jasper'—Elizabeth spoke to him in the local mode,
otherwise using her book language—'be it any good to tell
the bwoy all that? Unjust, I daresay it all were and be, but
mind my words, ther's a bigger unjustice every time a man
'olds out 'is hand of a Friday night for 'is wik's waage. What
be the Town Lands? A couple o' 'underd aacres and a fyow
housen. Why, ther be nine or ten farms in the parish as big
as that; mind you what 'appens on them: dooan't think o' the
parcels.' Then she spoke mostly for Joseph. 'The town lands
business was tangled far back. Neether the Fayfees nor the
folks understand it. They can't twist and turn ther minds fast
enough to follow lawyers' talk. Parson could, but he's obstinate, the world knows; a crumb of grace and goodness 'ould
solve it. And what then?' She turned to Jasper. 'Naamin'
a few shillins different, do it stop starvation? Or spendin' a
couple 'underd pounds different on 'underds o' folks?...
Emigraate—might be good in that. Too few men in far parts,
too many here. The school is stuffed wi' childer and where'll
they get their bread?...Jasper, you looks well arter my
bwoy and I be beholden to you, but dooan't you larn 'im to
waaste 'is thoughts on what dooan't matter.'

That was all that day, but Joseph had a chance to question
a friend outside his family circle. He was sometimes sent on
errands to a well-to-do farmer in Oxhill, who had once
farmed in Tysoe. He was at leisure, being a late case of gout,
and also fractious. Joseph, the bright lad, having been sent
in to 'amuse the master' told the little tale about the red
flannel, and asked the frowning, groaning patient whether he
knew about the Town Lands. Well, said the farmer, it had
been one of those disputes in which everybody was wrong;
had he felt better he might have said in which they were all

right. There seemed no doubt that the estate was parish property, but now the Charity Commissioners were responsible for all public property of that sort, and under them the trustees. His own father had been a trustee some years ago, but when he died the others (they were a self-recruiting body) had not chosen himself though he was still in the parish, but another Middleton. Three Middleton trustees now, he believed. Not quite right that! But all the same the inquiry had shown that they were within their legal rights. But you can be that and still behave damned badly.

The fact was the world was going to the dogs. Charles Dickens was dead now, and there was nothing for him to read, nothing for him to do, sitting with that accursed leg up.

But Joseph still wanted to hear the story. He couldn't see how Charles Reason and men like him could possibly have made speeches and stood against the Feoffees, all farmers and employers, and the powerful, unapproachable Vicar, with their laws and their Commissioners. Look at Charles now, driving his muck cart to his couple of fields, a little shrunken, down-looking man.

One evening Jasper dropped in to ask Joe how he liked his new work. Elizabeth bade him sit. 'Joe's still botherin' me about that Town Lands meeting. Better tell him once for all. You stop a bit, and tell what I miss out.

'The to-do began with the Vicar and his lady; instead of paying out the Town Lands money in cash to the poorer folk and the sick, they took parcels of stuff. Reason given, that the men used to spend the money at The Green Man and The Peacock. The Vicar, being a temperance man, hated the public-houses. But only a few men ever touched the money at all; mostly the wives took it at the door and spent it too. And many a man never drank, in or out of the public-house, except beer at harvest. So it was false, they said; the Vicar grudged that ordinary folk should have any money at all. He'd like 'em all paupers. Odd!, the Vicar said that money pauperised the folk, and they said the red flannel made them paupers. The money was theirs, they said, so it couldn't pauperise, but you have to be a beggar to take red flannel you hadn't bought for yourself.'

'They did taak it', put in Jasper. 'Pity us ever did.' 'I don't know, Jasper; the Vicar would have given twice as much to them as would take it, doubled the temptation. And flannel's warm! Red petticoats be clothes by day and bed-covering at night. There are houses in this parish without one blanket in 'em.' In a moment she went on, 'It wasn't only the parcels; they said in time gone by the folk had decided what was to be done with the money. The Feoffees made a plan for the Vestry, and if the folk met at the Vestry didn't like it they changed it. Townsfolk's money spent townsfolk's way, so they said. The man who talked most was Charlie Reason. He wasn't a labourer, so he could afford it. His aunt had left him his house and a bit o' ground and fifty pound too, a year or two afore.'

'He knowed', put in Jasper, ''ow to goo about things a bit. 'Ad to 'ave a solicitor about the bit o' property. If you han't got nothin' you don't larn nothin'. So 'e said 'e'd goo and see a lawyer. An' so 'e did, an' paid 'im too. An' the lawyer said there must be a petition. An' it were drawed up and took all round the towns.' 'Yes, not only cottagers signed; you might say everybody did', Elizabeth carried on, 'except the big farmers and anybody who depended on the Vicar. A hundred signatures.' 'There's nine hundred folk', said Joe. 'You don't suppose that babbies signed? 'Twas only house-holders', said his mother. 'And then there was the meeting. The fact is, there were two, but folk run 'em into one. A man was coming down from London from the Charity Commissioners to hear what everybody had to say. An Inspector. The meeting was to be held in the Old Schoolroom. Of course, that is where the Town Lands School used to be. A school for twenty boys, two years' schoolin' each. That was another thing; the Feoffees had given the master's money to the new Church school, and the Methodists said that was

wrong; why should everybody's money go to the Church
School? But not so much was said about that. There was the
allotments question. The men wanted good big ones. Master
Francis had given them ten-pole allotments, but not enough
of them and so small. The Town Lands farm was in the best
place, right in the middle of the parish. Leaving out the hillside land it would make eighty or a hundred one-acre plots.
But that nobody dared be known to say; it was more than
your job was worth. The farmers hated a man to have so
much as a pig; and to keep pigs and get a bit of meat, that's
just what the men wanted land for. You couldn't get near
telling the parson all that. Ah, Jasper, what folks wun't hear
you can't say. That's why my tongue's getting stiff. I could
have a lot to say but silence becomes me best.'

Jasper resumed, 'They reckoned the laabourers 'ouldn't
lose their arternun's money to goo to a meetin'. But ther
were a crowd round the old school door by three o'clock;
a crowd o' women in their print bonnets and aaperns, all with
their knitting sticks twisted in their aapern strings. Just afore
three, the men come runnin' up. One arter another they come
pantin'. I come meself from the windmill, tearin' down.
'Twer laate when the parson and the Commissioners' man
come. A tall silk 'at the Inspector were wearin'. I mind
me thinkin' he must ha' brought it in a box. Couldn't ha' druv
from Kineton in it.' 'When 'e sin the crowd the parson
frowned and chuttered. We all 'ad to troop to the new big
school. They sun rigged up a taable; th' Inspector sot in the
middle be'ind it with the parson and the Trustees.' 'Dooan't
forget the lawyers', Elizabeth put in, 'nor the reporters.
'Twas county news, that meeting.' 'Ah, I pretty near forgot
'em. But funny they looked, grett men tryin' to write in the
childer's desks. The Fayfees' wives sot in the front seat, in
fine clothes, and behind them the laabourers' wives, all knittin'
so fast, till the talking started, you couldn't see their hands
goo. An' back of all were us fellows. Charlie Reason sot in the
middle, close to th' 'oomen, to be heered if he should spaak.'

Joseph loved Jasper's details; he built from them the picture that so helped his memory of events, but they tired Elizabeth, whose mind moved quickly. So she took up the tale.

'The Inspector started off. He was sure everybody wanted what was right. Then the petitioners' lawyer said all the same things as were in the petition, but Charlie Reason thought he didn't sound strong enough; but Charlie wasn't used to speakin' so he didn't make much of a job of it either; too busy tryin' to talk so the London man 'ould get 'is meaning. All the time the Inspector was coughing and blowing his nose, looking sorry for himself. Then old George Padbury got up—worked on Gardner's farm, Wesleyans, or maybe he wouldn't ha' dared.' She left this speech to Jasper. '"We've 'eerd our fathers say as the Trustees talked in the vestry, in the chancel o' the church, everybody theer. Now it's the Vicar and a handful o' farmers. They taakes our own from us and wun't listen to nobody. Who be they? Three Middletons, two Godwins and two Waltons. And two Waltons han't one tongue between 'em."...Folks didn't like that: naames shouldn't be naamed. So Charlie got up again. "Us all wishes", said 'e, "nothin' but what's fair and raisonable." Everybody said 'ear, 'ear. George himself shouted, "Right! Right! We wun't say nothing agin em."'

'The Trustees' lawyer', said Elizabeth, 'was very short. I remember the very words. They "knew nothing of any rights but their own in disposing of the Charity Estate rents". In the end the Commissioners' man said he felt so bad he'd have to go. He couldn't see any grievance. But our lawyer held up the petition and said, "There were the grievances and no answer had been made to them". Then the young man said he'd go fuller into it all.

'It was months before he came again. Then it was worse than ever. The young man talked 'em all dumb, same as you talk me. Fact is I wasn't there, but I read it all in the *Banbury Guardian*.' Then she drew from the table-drawer a folded piece of newspaper in black, furry print on fibrous paper. 'He kept on talkin' about the Petty Bag Office and Dugdale's History an' "enfeooffments". But it's simple enough to read. As far back as Henry VIII the estate was the common property of the inhabitants of the towns of Tysoe and should be spent by the inhabitants. And then, when Elizabeth was queen it was "the best and sufficient part of the inhabitants then resident" as should spend. After that it was always "the chief inhabitants". Believe me, he didn't stop then. He told how the money had used to be spent, as if the folk couldn't ha' told him. The school, apprenticing boys, buying a poor man a horse when his died, giving a man the money to go and spend Christmas with his daughters. The parish brewhouse was paid for and an orphan girl was fitted out with all her clothes. He talked about a "peckled handkerchief".' Jasper was excited. 'So he did,' he cried, 'and didn't the folk groan at last! A peckled kerchief! You allus tells folk to be patient, not to maake a to-do, but beant the folk too slow? Talkin' about allotments, Duke Middleton got up and said the Feoffees weren't a-goin' to make little farmers o' the poor, an', can you credit it, our lawyer got up and said 'e quite agreed. What could we hope wi' a lawyer like that? Poor folks can't even find a lawyer to look arter 'em, y'see.'

Elizabeth hurried to the end. 'Charlie went over all the ground again, stuck to it champion, everybody said. The trustees since that other meeting had been spending three hundred pounds on a farmhouse, while the Feoffees' cottages were reekin' with damp. Folks livin' in housen like pigsties, he said. But he always finished with "nothing but what's fair and reasonable".'

'But did the Parson and the Feoffees budge?' put in Jasper. 'Not one ell! They 'ouldn't stir towards the folk; they 'ouldn't show a sign of goodness. The Bible talks o' charity, but there were none o' that sort, only the sort that goos wi' bootlicking. Beg pardon, Elizabeth, I knows you dooan't want that sort o' thing said to the bwoy.'

And afterwards, said Elizabeth, a notice was stuck on the

church door to say that the rules of the Charity Estate were changed. Henceforth payments to the poor must be paid in kind, among other rules. When Jasper said quietly, 'The poor were beaten and kicked too', she only asked him, 'What's the good o' you and Joe reading the Gospels if you be gooin' to talk like that?'

'Then why, Mother', asked Joseph, 'did you have money at New Year if it's against the rules now?' 'I tried', she said, 'to get the Upper Town women to refuse the parcels. I thought, not havin' a man as could be refused work, I'd better take the lead. I said to the Vicar, "Please not to send me a parcel. I wouldn't have one inside my door." "You must have it", he said, "for the child's sake. It's against the rules to give money now." "They that makes rules can unmake 'em", said I, "you wunt tell me as you didn't make that one." And I said, "Is it against the rules, Vicar, to give to God the things that be God's and the folks the things that be the folks'?" And since then I've had money. But nobody followed me and it's all settled down now more or less. An' now Jasper, it's long past this bwoy's bed-time, seeing he gets to Hornton bi ha' past six.'

Jasper gone, Joseph had one more question. 'Why were the folk so good, Mother? Why didn't they burn old Duke Middleton down?' 'That sort o' thing's been tried', he heard, 'and, besides, they couldn't believe in such unjustice. 'Tis in their blood to expect fairness. I don't know why, but it is so.'

But Joseph was interested now in the district he was seeing. Three things came to him in this period; some idea of how events elsewhere affected his own home and village; some knowledge that other communities produced other manners and other men; and then the sense, to describe it as best I can, that under the wide acreage of grass and corn and woods which he saw daily there was a ghostly, ancient tessellated pavement made of the events and thoughts and associations of other times. This historical sense he shared with many of the men he met about his work. Their strong memory for the past was unimpaired by much reading or novelty of experience, and yet their interest had been sharpened by the sense of rapid change.

Once a week a neighbour gave him a lift on his cart as far as Sunrising. Philpott's talk would come round to roads and vehicles: his own grandfather had been the first man in Tysoe to have a spring cart when the roads had been improved after the enclosing of the fields. Grandfather had been Waywarden of the Lower Town when the parish was cited for not repairing the road past Brixhill Farm, an old enclosed place belonging to the Spencer family, and had had to go all the way to Warwick Quarter Sessions—sixteen miles—and with him the Lower Town constable. ''Twas a shame, but just like the Brix'll folk, saame as they be to this day. They could ha' mended the road therselves, for nobody never used it but they. But no, they would have folk go and work on the road all the way from Tysoe because it had been the custom since the devil knows when.'

Twice a day, going and returning, Joseph crossed the ancient British road running along the top of the hills, past the Rollright Stones and away westward. Each time he took loads by the Kineton road he crossed the 'salt track' by which salt was carried on packhorses from Droitwich to London till about a century before. The packhorsemen had always rested at Hardwick Farm, and their horses, the wise things, always drank at a little stream there of chalybeate water.

There were the folk jokes, scores of them. On the lower road to Kineton a stranger had met a Tysoe lad. 'What is your name, boy?' 'Tysoe, sir'. 'Where do you come from?' 'Tysoe, sir'. 'What is your dog's name?' 'Tysoe, sir'. And then presumably, a box on the ear. In this field the owl had hooted and drunken old Robert Benson had replied. The dialogue varied in the telling. But all the jokes are slight; they fade on paper.

Shutford folk, hearing that Joseph belonged to the Quaker

Ashbys, showed him the ring in a wall where a great-uncle of his used to fasten his pony when he rode up to Meeting. Later generations of Ashbys, they said, couldn't stay Quakers, their tempers were so high. 'If thou dost not hold thy peace', one of them had been heard to threaten, in the diction of pacifism, 'I will pick thee up and throw thee over into the New Pool.'

Often Joseph looked down on the battlefield of Edgehill. What a little time since the Civil War it seemed. He heard of the very words men had spoken on the day of the battle. 'Which side be you on, fellow?', cavaliers riding from Compton Wynyates had called out to a youth leaning on a gate. 'Parlyment! Parlyment!', he answered witlessly. Instantly one of the riders fired his musket in the air and off rushed the terrified lad up to the hills among the gorse and hawthorn bushes, and there stayed two days. There were lots of little stories: he even knew that Dame Wells had got up earlier that day than Dame Colcott, and that the riders from Compton had come in and seized her fragrant hot bread. One day he had to wait in Oxhill before his stone could be unloaded, and he went sightseeing. In the little Norman church a flat gravestone on the floor of the nave bore an epitaph on an Oxhill gentleman who had followed King Charles at the battle.

> When I was very young I ventured life and blood
> For my King and for my country's good.
> In elder years my care was chief to be
> Soldier for him that shed his blood for me.

'Shed his blood'! 'Soldiers of Christ'! The gallant Royalist sounded like an Oxhill Methodist. Brave Christians on both sides. Thieving Cavaliers, silly Parliamentarian lad. Things had a complex look.

At the back of Sunrising House, so Joseph wrote some years later in the *Land Magazine*, old Henry Parkman, once 'boots' and later postillion of the inn, sat in his cottage, always in his old, tall, silk hat and a smock with fantastic stitching and stiff bulging folds. His thin, silvery hair hung loose about his face. He had seen the celebrations for Waterloo and known the one Tysoe man who had been with Wellington in the Peninsula. It was natural that his thoughts should go to the French Wars: France had been at war again, and Tysoe women had knitted and sewn for besieged Parisians. Now Henry sat with the *Saints Everlasting Rest* lying open in front of him while he told a boy stories of his life. 'Did you ever drive any famous men when you were postillion?' 'Did I? Well, for one I druv Lord John Russell from Sunrising to Stratford. He were all for repealin' the Corn Laws; I'd ha' druv 'im to Lands End wi' pleasure.' 'Did he speak to you?' 'He put 'is yed out o' the winda an' said, "Get on as fast as you can, Postillion. I must get to Stratford by two o'clock." The next time, with th'orses gooin' as fast as I could drive 'em, 'e just put 'is yed out o' the coach an' said, "Ride on, Postillion, ride on!" An' I bin ridin' on, mi bwoy, ever since.'

Joseph found on his travels that villages have their special ways and dispositions, as men do. He skirted Upton every morning, either passing by vehicle in front of the Park gates or walking through the fields past the estate houses. There were ten times as many tons of stone (he thought now often in terms of stone) in Upton House as in all its dependent hamlet.... The Upton men hadn't the Tysoe men's talk and jokes. Cautious fellows, they wanted to know what the other man thought before they spoke. The Ratley men, working in the section of the quarry to which he most often went, were silent old-fashioned fellows, lost in their heavy, skilled work. Their village at that time was a strange, poor, hillside place, with, it was said, only three surnames among the families. But the men had great knowledge of their stone— in what year this and that part of the valley had been cut, and which of the great houses scattered over Oxfordshire and Warwickshire had been built with it.

There were churches also of the rich, brown stone— Banbury's new, that is eighteenth-century, church had been built of it, and stone was still being sent to Birmingham for a great Catholic church there. One of Joseph's tougher jobs was to take vast stones—so they seemed to him—to Radway where a new steeple was being added to the village church. They each filled a whole wagon, but once fixed in their skyward position looked quite tiny—though, after all, it is only a toy spire. Here at Radway he met the rector, Mr Sanderson Miller, descendant of the architect of that name, who had built Radway Grange, a small version of a Palladian mansion, and the mock ruins on the Edgehill battlefield. Joseph heard of the great folk who had stayed at the Grange in its distinguished early days, but the only name he had ever heard and could remember was that of Fielding, who had read aloud one of his novels there.

Banbury was Joseph's metropolis. He would drive his cart on to the bridge over the Cherwell and look down on the traffic in canal, railway line and road. Traffic was a modern note; old crafts were still carried on there—the weaving of plush and of girth-webbing; coopers were making barrels for the two breweries; there was a rope-walk, and makers of bespoke footwear displayed in their windows little ladies' boots of patent leather and cloth, and the high riding boots made for Lord North. The new age was indicated by Samuelson's factory making agricultural machines—mostly horse-drawn or driven—turnip-cutters, rollers or harrows, cake-crushers and threshing machines. They stood in a great yard, all brightly painted, as exciting as boats in a harbour.

But it was at home in his own village that Joseph felt for the first time that history was being made before his eyes, and that he felt a strong current of action pull upon himself to come along to take a part. That was in the summer of 1872, only a few weeks past his thirteenth birthday, but the event etched itself on his mind in detail, so that in 1899 he gave a full account of it in the *Land Magazine*, whose yellow pages yield me detail now.

A wonderful thing had happened. In February, at Wellesbourne, a village some thirteen miles away, a labourer had led a strike. In eloquent speeches, and accurately and moderately, Joseph Arch and a handful of men who had begged his leadership had told their tale of low wages, tied cottages, tyranny and arrogance. Arch was known to one or two Tysoe men. He was like themselves; a leader, only more powerful, such as Charlie Reason had been in the matter of the Town Lands. He was a champion hedge-cutter, a travelling piece-worker like Joseph's Uncle William and a Methodist preacher like Josiah Smith. Only he had wonderful advantages—he owned a good cottage, bought by his mother with tips flung to her from carriages as she held open the drive gates at Warwick Castle. And he was physically strong, not merely to endure but to act. In the *Banbury Guardian*, while the Editor's comments were strictly impartial, much space was given to the threatening letters from farmers and moral censure of the labourers by the clergy. Those were to be expected; so was the dying down of the movement. The labourers were uplifted because a few score of their own sort had shown themselves men and one was a prophet, but they expected the prophet's voice to be lost in the wilderness. An open struggle was sweet in idea, but it couldn't be successful. How could families be kept even for a fortnight when things came to a strike?

But they, and farmers and parsons too, had reckoned without the young reporter of the *Daily News*. Now Tysoe labourers bought and read a London paper for the first time. Joseph and Jasper had between them half a share in one. The labourers saw their own case mirrored in the minds of the towns, and the picture was sharply and excitingly drawn. Up to now it had always been the labourers who were the cynosure—their fecklessness and lack of sobriety—but the rural picture of the *Daily News* included the farmer and parson, and an unhandsome part of it they formed. There was a national aspect of the trouble. Arch began to talk of large matters—votes, emigration. To vote for his own Member of Parliament—there was a prospect for a boy!

Though Barford, Arch's home and the headquarters of the Trade Union he was forming, was only eleven miles away, it was late July before the prophet visited Tysoe. The weather was set fair for the meeting, timed for seven in the evening. Some farmers were still haymaking—Joseph gave these details in the *Land Magazine* some twenty-five years later— but the men laid down their tools in good time without a by-your-leave. On the green, by six o'clock, labouring men and women began to arrive from neighbouring villages, Oxhill and Whatcote, Brailes and Shenington. They saw no evident preparations for the meeting. The usual platform was a farm wagon, but no farmer could be asked for a loan in this case, and none was offered. Towards half-past six four or five labourers collogued together with an air of heavy responsibility, and then went off down the street to the smithy, whose owner was a trustee of the Wesleyan chapel. Soon they came hurrying back carrying great heavy boxes—sections of the Sunday School platform. The crowd grew immense. A group of total strangers appeared—a set of rough, loud young fellows. The word went round that these were navvies building the new railway from Stratford to Fenny Compton Junction. A few minutes before seven, farmers began to appear, not only Tysoe men but several from miles away. That was a portent— for farmers to attend a meeting in another village.

Joseph had secured standing room on a hillock on the edge of the green by the road, and could look down the broad village street with its immense island of grass. The houses were turned a deep, rich gold by the rays of the sun, and their chimneys of red brick and blue brick stood out violently. Suddenly new sounds were heard, as moving as the skirl of the bagpipes—a distant brass band. The hymn-tune ceased and Joseph heard the footsteps of the band's little escorting crowd, men from Barford and villages on the way. As they reached the beech tree half-way up the street the band burst into 'See the conquering hero comes'! The hero, Arch, and two or three others detached themselves and joined the Tysoe men on the platform. Something was discussed and settled: a Tysoe man was to chair the meeting. All would be well then. Josiah was a Primitive Methodist lay preacher and one of the chief pillars of his chapel. The meeting would be orderly. The group on the platform, wearing corduroys and mopping themselves with red handkerchiefs, looked grotesque in that situation to Joseph, and still more so to a small group coming quickly up to the fringe of the crowd—the Vicar and his wife and the Marquis's agent. The Vicar's disapproval of the meeting was known and the young agent's face was all contempt.

Josiah Smith opened the meeting. It was his own life he told of—a hungry childhood, no schooling, a crowded cottage. In thirty-five years' time will his sons have the same tale to tell? It looks as if they will. For the labourer things have stood still. What of other folk? Farmers' wheat prices have risen; the Marquis's rents have trebled. Yes, trebled. All Josiah's facts were local; he mentioned no names, but would stretch out his arm in the direction of a cottage or a farm as he mentioned this and that. It was his bit of rhetoric to cast his matter into the form of questions. His audience knew and gave the answers. 'Did y'ever hear of a little un dying o' wakeness? (Ah, that we did.) An' what's t'other word for it? (Starvation.) And did y'ever hear o' the red ribbon took from a little gal's hair, and her told to tell her mother not to dress her above her station? What do they pay a lad of fifteen, fit t'eat an ovenful of bread as a lad is then? Give him a man's work and half a man's starvation pay.' The farmers looked disturbed and sheepish, but then Arch rose and they recovered from their embarrassment. Arch was stockish and robust-looking. He had never suffered starvation! That was true. For him this was not a protest about his own conditions; he could earn his living anywhere in England. No, he spoke of the misery of his fellows, the unnecessary misery; the work-house future, the denial of manhood to labourers, the down-thrusting of their children...it was time the labourers stood firm for their rights.

The example was before them; workmen of the town had shown that unity is strength. Farmers agree together day in, day out. Their Union meets once a week, in Banbury market place, and round the table at the Black Bull. Let the labourers follow their example. They must have a Union. Further, they must have the vote and men in Parliament to speak for them. For their children the way must be opened here in England or they must be helped to emigrate.

Arch had no poetry, no rhetoric, but his voice was full and clear, reaching far beyond the limits of the crowd, thrown back now and then from the houses and even from the hills behind in a fine echo. Joseph, more or less on the edge of the crowd, was completely lost, absorbing every fact, every note. When a horse or gig came up the road, forcing the people to press forward on to the green, it seemed an outrage that anyone should have any purpose but to listen. Arch went on. There would be opposition, there would be threats. Wives would think it hard to see twopence a week go to Union funds. But let injustice be all on the other side; rely on truth; believe that God would aid the right.

He had finished, and immediately the Vicar called out to him. He demanded to be allowed to speak and walked up to the platform, followed by the agent. Arch made way for the two men and called to the crowd to hear them, but the navvies shouted, 'Duck 'em! Duck 'em in the pond!' and pressed forward, looking as if nothing would stop them from dragging the Vicar to the pool across the road. But the Tysoe men closed in round the platform. The Vicar began. Arch and his like were stirring up mischief. Some of Josiah's facts he admitted (the stranger's speech he would ignore). He himself, some years back, had paid eight shillings as a wage. (Shame! groans the audience. 'It didn't pay the baker', called a shrill woman's voice.) But things had improved; wages had gone up by a shilling a week. The audience groaned again. 'I my-self', he said, 'have obtained allotments for you.' A voice went on with the Vicar's sentence, 'At two pounds an acre, and

let them to you at four'. Whether or not it was fair play for
the Vicar to use the platform, he was doing the cause no
harm. Then the Compton agent spoke. It went without
saying that no Union man would be employed on the
Marquis's estate. 'Wait and see. Bet you! Bet you!' was
murmured around. The steward was a young man and furious.
How could Compton get on without Upper Town men?
And the Marquis would never be so shabby.

Arch closed the meeting by announcing that men could now
enrol as members of the Tysoe branch of the Agricultural
Labourers' Union. He left the platform and lingered by the
group who were receiving names. Meanwhile the bandsmen
took up their instruments and grouped themselves ready to
march. It was good manners on such occasions to escort
a visiting band to the Middle Town brook beyond the church,
and a good crowd now followed in a rough column of fours
or fives. The tune for the march was a new one:

> Ho, my comrades, see the signal
> Waving in the sky,
> Reinforcements now appearing
> Victory is nigh.
>
> Hold the fort for I am coming
> Jesus signals still,
> Wave the answer back to Heaven,
> By Thy grace WE WILL.

These 'Primitive' fellows and their fathers and mothers—
such was my father's view—had held the fort of civilisation,
not without losses, through the attritions of a hundred years.
Now they had made a sally. But they were troubled about
the shoe-leather they would lose as they trudged six, seven,
ten miles home on the roads, some parts of which were now
mended with the Hartshill stone, broken into hard and sharp-
edged nuggets.

Joseph's deep excitement about Arch kept him and his
mother from their beds a long time that evening. Elizabeth
listened with unusual patience and commented a little.

Emigration, a fresh start! That was best; it was the only way. Not if there were leaders, Joseph said. Men who could be leaders, his mother replied, could rise in life; they ought to, to feed their families. Yet it was impossible to lead poor labourers unless you stayed near them.

Then Elizabeth did an odd thing. She took some old papers from the bureau—those from among which she had shown the Vicar one or two. 'Did you ever read these?' she asked. Joseph had looked at them, he had meant to look again soon. 'Well,' she said, 'we'll say goodbye to 'em. Rake the ashes out.' She dropped them one by one into the fire, each making its bright flame. When Elizabeth's mind was clearly made up, as now, its suggestive force was great; impossible for the young lad to do anything but watch and follow. The last paper had turned to black ashes and Elizabeth still watched it. The clock struck eleven, and when his mother stood up Joseph stood too. For now he was tired and quiet, thinking how early he must get up. But Elizabeth said, 'Wait a minute' and went upstairs. She came back soon, carrying a little bundle of white papers. They were covered with handwriting —one could see that, though they were wrapped round with a piece of white paper and tied with a bit of green string. Joseph had never seen these and had no notion what they were. He raked the ashes from the grate again, and Elizabeth threw the little bundle on the embers and drooped her candle over them so that the grease fell on a tiny flame which reared itself high and warm, consuming the papers.

'That's done', said Elizabeth presently. 'You join the Union as soon as they'll let you.'

The ceremony was impressive but not portentous. Elizabeth was not taking the liberty to dedicate her son's future. On the contrary, Joseph understood, without words said, that his mother had given up some thoughts about himself, some ambition possibly; had said, as it were, 'I see; this is your place. Fill it, then.'

CHAPTER V

COURT GREENWOOD TREE

AFTER two years of stone-carting, Joseph was fifteen years old, a great lad, as tall as most grown men, taller than most labourers. It was time that he should have, again, a larger wage. A firm of builders buying stone at the quarries noted the likely lad and offered him work at Compton Wynyates where they were putting up a house for the Marquis's agent. As yet, Joseph had no special plan for himself, and the pay offered was fair.

Compton Wynyates is about a mile from the Upper Town, over Windmill Hill, lying in a wide round hollow. On his way to work there each fine morning Joseph had a perfect view of the ancient mansion from the top of the hill before he ran down the steep and tussocky further slope.

He was moved by beauty now, even more than by stories. Built of small rosy bricks, and roofed with lichened stone, from which rose delicate spiral chimneys, the house lay there as the rose and gold centre of a green corona of hills. Around it were pools, the remnants of a moat. On cloudy days they were like the brown-black stains at the base of the green petals of hellebore flowers. Compton was modest as well as lovely; there was nothing to overawe a lad and set him at a distance, as an eighteenth-century mansion would have done. It was the first great work of art and time, other than books, that had gone home to Joseph's mind, and it was one of the loves of his life, a love his children caught from him. It is natural to remember all he told of Compton.

As to the work he came to do there, that was no great matter. He ran nimbly on errands, carried drawings and tools after architect and foremen and provided an extra pair of hands wherever they were needed. No breath of architectural adventure or excitement stirred among the workers. The house was being built mostly of brick, of a crude modern kind; it was to be embowered with trees so as to be invisible from the mansion. Joseph's workmates and masters were genial folk and he stayed with them till the work was done. But their talk and their ways had little significance for him.

Compton, on the other hand, belonged to his life. There was a many-stranded relationship between Tysoe and its neighbour parish—parish not village. It was said, and there were plenty of signs that it was the truth, that there had once been a village of Compton, but now the house and estate depended on Tysoe for labour. On the other hand, the Compton family owned most of the farms of the Upper Town and many cottages there, including Joseph's Aunt Rouvray's, and also part of Church Town. The Marquises (that is how it was usual to spell the word then) of Northampton were Lords of the Manor of Upper and Church Town; lordship had been important not so long since. They were great folk, of course, but had never overshadowed and alarmed Tysoe, doubtless in part because they had never been sole owners and had been beneficently absent as landlords; of four lordships in the parish they had never held more than two. Their stewards had been efficient, sensible men whose power in the manorial courts had been well balanced by custom, by numbers and by the independence of Tysoe's thirty stout forty-shilling freeholders.

The great family had besides a genial liberal tradition. They laid no claim to the blood of conquerors, but on the contrary believed themselves to be of pre-Conquest Englishry. Nor had their blood turned blue in the course of centuries; they had perhaps replenished it too often by marrying the daughters of Lord Mayors and Cotswold wool merchants.

If Joseph did not as yet know quite all that, he knew the air he breathed and felt free to wander around the house and to venture once or twice into the small courtyard at its centre, with its tiny, enclosed lawn and old rose trees. Every side of the house seen from the high field walks was different, even though at this time the walls were ivy-covered. To the south was a gabled front with black velvety oak glowing in gables and window frames; on the east side were the great stone windows of the chapel and the hall; at the back an ancient brick tower, the nucleus from which the house had grown. Here, also, were some windows of Queen Anne's time, and under them carved in stone the words of the Compton motto, 'Je ne serche que ung'. The meaning of these words Joseph had tried to discover in an old book he had come across. *Chercher*, to seek; seek but one? Which one? God? But to seek God is saintly and Marquises are hardly saints. A better motto for feudal lords would be to serve but one; it is easier to serve God than to seek him, to obey laws said to be his than to try, like Job, to know him.

One day, while Joseph was cogitating about the house, a voice asked him, 'I've seen you here before; you are working with the builders, aren't you?' This young man, on a stout pony, was Lord William Compton, eventual heir to the Marquisate, but now a student of history and a budding diplomat. Although he had the quick, wide glance of an awakened mind, his face had a homely look, with its short nose and slightly prominent eyes. It was Joseph who had the tall form and high brow. Out here on the hillside alone, their social inequality was not an embarrassment; they were gazing at the same beloved object. They talked of the Civil War, of Compton in the hands of the Parliamentarians and of the young Comptons' attempt to wrest their home from the puritan Colonel Faithful's two young sons. There had been gallantry and dash on the Comptons', the Royalist side, against determination and doctrine on that of the rebels. 'Rebels?' The word offended Joseph. 'Well, shall we say "Parliamentarians"? You would have been with them?' 'I expect so', said Joseph, adding hastily 'But there were Tysoe men for sure with the Comptons'. But there had also been Puritans in Tysoe, Lord William said, just as there were Nonconformists now.

The talk ended on another note. The heir was going to make changes; his elders were allowing it. There would be more gardens—an Italian garden on a broad terrace. Yew hedges and box and cypress would throw up the colour of the house when the ivy had been stripped from it. 'Oh, not so many evergreens in the garden!', said Joseph. 'Avenues of pears and apple trees in bloom!' Lord William laughed and rode off.

Whenever it was possible to go to his work by the fields, up over the hill, Joseph liked his morning walk. The windmill on the top was the ancient mill of the Compton manor, and here the Upper Town corn was ground. The miller's family had been feudal tenants of the Comptons certainly for hundreds of years, and perhaps ever since the latter had become lords of the manor not so long after the Conquest. One of the most antique figures Joseph ever knew was one of this Styles family. Occasionally as he climbed the hill in the early morning Joseph caught up the miller or walked behind him. Others thought the old man's gait very peculiar, for he walked always with his body twisted and eyes turning continually to the right; but Joseph found that he himself had a necessity to look back from the hill over the vale, to keep his eyes on the distance and off the steep hillside so close to one's nose. The old man was dull of sight and deaf. To his more youthful period a little folk anecdote, doubtless far older than the miller himself, had been attached. A stranger had remarked to him that all honest millers had a tuft of hair growing in the palm of the left hand. 'Ah,' said the miller, 'and here you be', as he stretched forward his spread palm. The stranger was surprised, but managed a little bravery. 'You don't qualify, you see.' 'Hair be theer all right', said Styles, 'But it takes an honest man to see 'em'. Of deeper interest it was to think of the old man's life dominated by the wind, the mill and the hillside. On winter mornings, reaching the hill at seven o'clock, Joseph might find Master Styles had been at work for hours by the light of a couple of hurricane lanterns because, after frustrating days of stillness, the wind had sprung up in the night. How moving it was to see him with a mere small iron bar change the angle of the great sails so that they caught the wind; to see the wheat dribbling down between the circling mill-stones, as large as cartwheels, and the thin stream of flour pouring out below. And later to see the sacks of flour standing at the door awaiting the horses and heavy carts climbing up the slope, each sack a symbol of many labours and final triumph. But sometimes as he saw the miller struggling up the hill, getting daily now more short of breath, the latter would seem for a moment a Sisyphean symbol for the endless struggle of life.

For the old man himself his mill was a symbol. From a certain point on the hill the two could see the skeleton of the old barn that Joseph had seen stripped of its thatch. 'It should ha' bin built round', said Master Styles. 'My mill 'll lose its sails one o' these days, like the ships, but the tower 'll last 'undreds of years; wind nor wet can't get a hold on it. As one wind wets', he said, as though reflecting on the wide world, 'another dries.' At the mill in a few years' time Joseph's own corn would be ground as corn had been ground for so long, but then in a few more the sails would be locked fast to the tower, never to swirl again—at least so it seems.

Most of Joseph's education came of itself through work and village life and incidental talk, but a year or so after Arch's meeting a few of his elders had aimed some instruction at him and other boys. He was fourteen at the time, a very usual age for initiation.

Every year in July came 'Club Day'. On the Saturday preceding the Sunday of the church's patronal festival, two or three booths were set up in the street, selling gingerbread to the children. These were the last crumbs of the old fun fair on the green. In the public-houses the old men were asked to sing the two folk-songs that still lingered, and on the Sunday morning a special sermon for the day was preached in church:

after that, at Sunday dinner, spiced raisin pudding was eaten in every house. Possibly the whole festival, service and pudding and song, went back via the medieval village guild and the founding of the village church to a pagan midsummer feast. Certain it is that the festival was felt to be the whole village's affair, although the 'Sick and Provident' chose this time to recall its founding. It was for this week that Tysoe men and women came back from the towns to see the old place and the home folk. Neighbours from villages around, who had used to come on the Sunday for the gaieties of the church festival, came, in these Sabbatarian days, on the Monday to 'the Club'.

The Club was not Tysoe's only Friendly Society. There was also Court Greenwood Tree of the Foresters', a good many years older and as large, but the Club had had this excellent idea to adopt the old festival time as its own.

The Day was strenuous from the beginning, for the cottages were full of visiting relations, and the women had to prepare an immense meal, while the men hurried through the essential jobs on the farms, to be able to attend the Annual Meeting before dining on boiled bacon and beans and raisin pudding. Public festivities began precisely at a quarter to two, with the brass band of the Tysoe Temperance Society issuing from the tithe barn by the Old Tree. Awaiting it were all the boys, ready to fall in behind the official procession. Immediately after the band came a group of three men—the Vicar, a man of height and breadth, and two other burly, well-clad gentlemen. These were the Trustees of the Club. Next, carried by two young men, came the Club's banner, proclaiming 'God is our Help', and behind that the body of members, sixty or seventy labourers walking two and two, each wearing a scarlet and white rosette. They were, young and old alike, dressed in corduroy trousers and cloth coats. The men's gait had a touch of the absurd. While the three Trustees in front swung along like the free and the well-fed, the older members of the rank and file shuffled and lunged and plodded while the younger ones, stiff enough too, took short steps to accommodate themselves to the older members. But for all that some fine, thoughtful faces gave tone to the group. While the men walked in procession, the women hurried through the washing-up and the toilet of the younger children and then ran through lanes parallel to the street to be at the church to see them file in. Then they followed them into the sacred atmosphere, with the visitors and the doddering old folk. A visiting preacher talked of labour and thrift as great Christian virtues and of all the blessings they bring. After the service, the procession formed again but more loosely and turned into a field half-way between church and Upper Town. The band's work was now done, for the merry-go-rounds supplied music more blaring than brass, and everybody was absorbed in the gaiety of movement or scene as the swingboats and the stalls with frail and gaudy toys and the coconut shies started business and the women set out the tea in the open.

On the Club Day just after his fourteenth birthday, Joseph paid almost two days' wages, that is a shilling, for his tea and then swung up his young cousins, Hannah and Dinah, in the swingboats. After that, as he stood idle, the Vicar came up to him. 'You're a great lad, Joseph', he said. 'Time to join the Club. It's your duty to your mother. Best to join young—you'll see that if you can understand the tables at the back of the rules. Join your own village club; there's none better.'

The book of rules the Vicar handed him contained dozens of regulations. The actuary's tables had a mathematical symmetry and clarity. The club had been founded in 1857 and boasted of being a purely Tysoe affair. Local clubs were always failing, but the Tysoe Club had such large investments that no absconding treasurer could ruin it. So flourishing was it that smaller clubs at Oxhill and Whatcote were linking themselves with it. One could be proud of that.

It would be interesting to find out what some of his old friends would say if he were to join: he knew they were

Foresters! On his way home latish that evening he saw
a little group of men sitting on the steep bank opposite the
Old Tree. At the cottage doors were other men waiting for
the twilight that favours talk. Joseph sat down with another
boy or two, humbly, on the edge of the seated group, and took
the book of rules out of his pocket, half expecting to be told
to get off home, time for youngsters to be abed!

But the pamphlet had the right effect. Old Master Blunn,
the saddler, had seen it. 'Here, Sam Gould, and you, Josiah,
come and stop this bwoy joining the Club! What be Foresters
doin', never puttin' out a hand to get the young uns in?
Master Francis 'll get the lot on 'em.' Hearing a spirited tone,
the men from the cottage doors gathered to the bank; the
topic for the evening was settled. 'Look here', said Blunn,
turning over the leaves, 'the Club's got to be run by Trustees
and they're always to be drawn from the honorary members,
paying a guinea subscription. As good say a labourer's got
no sense. Why can't the members manage their own money?
If you can save your month's payment out of ten shillin'
a wik, you're clever enough to put it out to interest.' Some
of the Club members, still wearing their red and white favours,
were warmed by the Foresters' superior air. The Tysoe Club
was independent; what did they want with help from outside?
As for the Trustees, of course they had wider experience than
labourers; what was the use of gainsaying that? The prosperity of the Club was due to it.

Wider experience be blamed! The Trustees didn't intend
the labourers to have wider experience! They paid a guinea
a year and never drew a penny. Call that brotherhood?
Foresters called it wanting to run the show. As for prosperity,
that was due to the Marquis's subscription and an annual sum
from the Feoffees' Estate. Besides, the boys wouldn't be in
Tysoe all their lives. Go where they might, there would be a
Foresters' Lodge, and their membership would be transferred.

Presently, as usual, the talk became reminiscent, not to say
historical. Court Greenwood Tree had been established in

1842, more than thirty years ago. The Tysoe Club began so much later because it followed the old dividend club. 'Sick and Divvies' those clubs had been called. Annual phoenixes they had been. Every December the money remaining from the relief of the sick was divided among the members. Then in the New Year the clubs were re-formed and fees began to be paid again. In all the yearly clubs there was this annual division of remaining club funds. ''Twere a bit of a gamble wi' all on 'em', said a member of the village parliament. 'But us all likes a gamble, wicked or no.' The final reason, some-one said, why Tysoe folk, led by the Vicar, had decided against the old type of club was its refusal to accept old men or anyone whose poor health was known. Men who had paid into the Club decade after decade would find themselves refused at last, just when help was becoming necessary. Ah well, came agreement before parting, plenty of room for both clubs. It had been a bit of good work, give Parson Francis that, to get rid of the 'Sick and Divvy'.

As the men got up to go home in the darkness, Saddler Blunn grasped Joseph's arm and drew him along. He disappeared into his small dark house and came out with a book in his hand. 'You read the pages I marked when I read this. You'll see why folk must do things for themselves. Can't make everything plain to a lot of folk.' Next day Joseph stuffed the stout old book and the tract of Club rules into his rush dinner-bag. The book—I have it by me now—was a bound set of 'The Labourers' Friend Magazine' for 1835, full of reports of Labourers' Friends Societies. The boy read them entranced; here were titled folk and clergy, landowners and estate agents discussing the lot of labourers and with pretty full knowledge. He had had no idea such people troubled themselves so. They had a remedy for the low wage —thrift, especially the thrifty cultivation of allotments. In print, progress from extreme poverty to sufficiency is painless; talk of bread and beer, crops and pigs and gardens has perennial charm. Joseph read of allotments provided by great lords, seeds and tools bought by bishops for the poor to start work with. But he turned back to the date—1835! Why, the book might have been published yesterday, it was all so true still. Then he looked at the marked passages.

'In the first place, Sir, I have been told that land allotments would lead to diminution of the employers' profit, and that the labourer will be made independent of the employer. I deny that the employer will be a loser, for if he lose anything by not supplying the poor with wheat and potatoes in the market...he will save a great deal more...by the reduction of the rates....'

'An objection, Sir, that I have heard made to the allotment system is that a man's strength is exhausted at the end of a day's work if he has done justice to his master, and therefore he has no extra labour to bestow on his allotment.' (But no one said, 'Then he must have a good wage'!)

So bad consciences were not bound to make very generous minds. Dukes and bishops and farmers wanted labourers fed, but not independent. Labourers must lie very low before they could be helped. Gifts might be ropes to tie you down. Joseph saw what his lesson was. Arch had shown that. This was just interesting corroboration. He would join the Foresters when he was ready. Labourers, any set of people, must find their own way out of their difficulties. They must never trust another class to do justice without having to. But after all, wasn't that right enough? Resistance could be a debt you owed.

It was a year or two later, just before his Compton work came to an end, that Joseph became a junior brother in Court Greenwood Tree, and thus was qualified to wear a beautiful forest-green sash at Jubilees and Coronations and Hospital Saturdays that lay in the womb of time. In his first year he received a brief, impressive lesson in the need for good Forestry. An old labourer, almost stone deaf and bent absurdly, dreadfully double by rheumatism, had hanged himself from his house beam. His coffin was carried to a grave in unconsecrated ground under the yew trees in the churchyard by half a dozen dejected Foresters in their green sashes. It was, of course, a day of shame; the brethren had not penetrated through old Jeff's manifold imprisonment—his loss of hearing, movement, speech and of the household decency so dear to good folk. But it might be that Forestry need not fail. It could not often have done so in Court Greenwood Tree or Joseph would not have treasured his sash ever after as he did. Presently he would be doorkeeper of the Court and then secretary and treasurer (though he had no liking for accounts). Later he would alternate for some years between the offices of Trustee and Chief Ranger. After that he declined such positions. Office, he realised, had done something for him: let it do something for other young men.

After he had been some time a member Joseph wrote a record of one meeting, published in the *Land Magazine*. It was a dark winter evening. Members steered themselves along the street by the bright light that sliced the darkness from the Old Schoolroom to the New Pool. At the inner door of the School stood the doorkeepers with green clubs, ready to raise them if anyone came near them before the signal—the call 'Time, brothers!' from within. The brethren pressed past the green clubs. Change of raiment was not exacted; the men were collarless, wearing their corduroy and bagstring. On the whole, too, after they had solemnly answered to their names, they spoke in their everyday conversational way. Yet there was a certain formality.

The Chief Ranger rose, put his watch on its steel Albert chain back into the pocket of his soft velvety corduroys (he was John Parish, carpenter on the Compton estate) and read from his ritual book. 'All is to be done in order, with dignity and in mutual respect.'

'We have met tonight, brethren, to decide about the investment of five hundred and sixty-five pounds we have in the Post Office Bank. The money has grown apace, and it is

felt we should have more than two and a half a hundred on it.'
A proposal had been made to the court on this investment.
The proprietors of the Black Bear Inn at some village beyond
Ratley had written asking for a mortgage of five hundred
pounds on that house. While the Treasurer was reading their
letter a certain brother, an irascible total abstainer, broke in,
'Surely us yent agooin' to lend money to a...'. But the
Chief Ranger threatened a shilling fine and the fanatic sat
down. The Treasurer gave some details. As the brethren
knew, the Court had already a mortgage of three hundred
pounds on the Black Bear. Interest had always been promptly
paid and now new money was wanted for extensions. The
village there was growing, for the hill behind was being
quarried for iron-stone. Also there was now a railway station.
An enthusiastic brother rose to speak, but to what effect was
never known, for the men to right and left of him knew he had
difficulty in checking his weekly wage and firmly pulled him
down, while the company smiled.

Then someone asked for the letter to be read again, and
this time a statement was noticed that if the Court could not
comply with this request notice would be given to repay the
previous loan. 'Oh, will it?' called out several brethren, and
there was a general groan. The threat had gone against the
Black Bear. A group of serious brothers who had sat quiet
now arrived at a conclusion, ''Twunt do, Brother Chief
Ranger. We wunt lend 'em no moor.'

By now the teetotaller brother had decided on a serpentine
mode of serving his cause. 'The neighbourhood of yon
village, Brother Ranger and all brethren, is poor farming land;
there be at this minute two vacant farms within a mile of the
Black Bear.' Iron-stone, he continued, had been quarried
there for fifty years past at intervals; there would be intervals
again, or perhaps a final stoppage. Where would the Court's
money be then? The devil Alcohol had not been mentioned
and the meeting applauded both the self-restraint of this and
the sound points.

Next a brother rose and told the tale of a visit he and two others had paid to the Black Bear when the original loan was under consideration, how they had joined the company in the bar, asking questions about the quarrying as if they might be thinking of asking for jobs. They had looked all about outside, peered up the stairs from the passage, had had drinks in the kitchen as well as in the bar and made the landlady fry them some bacon for their dinner. For several years past the company had known these details and many another, and that the deputation had liked what they had seen and drunk, and just how proud they were of their astuteness and cunning. 'Without moor bother', asked a Brother, his patience all paid out, 'is the Black Bear worth the money?' 'Not', said another, 'if you don't count the licence, there's no farm to speak of.' A third Brother, possibly the young Joseph, put that point with a greater command of words. The value of a licence depends on the licensing policy of political parties and the conduct of the licence-holders. Court Greenwood Tree should have its money on a solider bottom than any one or two public-houses could afford. He moved to reject the request, and the Abstainer fell over himself to second. 'Motion carried', the Chairman shortly announced, but before the words were out of his mouth murmurs arose. 'Theer, you've done it—throwed away a good chance, Brother Chief; that's right, a good chance!' Then came counter-murmurs. 'Why didn't you say so and vote money to the Black Bear like men? You be fair bet. Let be and 'old your tongues.' The Chairman tapped with his mallet for Wheelwright Styles to be heard, a quiet fellow known to do well with the money that he made by his fine craftsmanship. He moved in formal words that the Trustees be given instructions to consider the best means of investing five hundred pounds and to report to the next meeting.

So novices learned not to be awed by hundreds of pounds or even thousands, and other lessons.

CHAPTER VI

JOINING THE METHODISTS

SOMETIMES, when I was a small child on the way to chapel with my hand in my mother's, I would catch sight of Elizabeth's, my grandmother's, bonnet nodding along Saddlers' Lane, near the church, and only very dimly wonder why she went one way and we another. But when I came to ask myself how it had happened I found that I had heard of all the steps: it was not difficult to arrange them in their series.

Between his fourteenth and fifteenth birthdays my father began to worship with the Methodists on a good many Sundays. He accompanied his mother to church in the mornings but claimed freedom to wander in the evenings, visiting the 'Primitive' and 'Wesleyan' chapels in Tysoe and sometimes going off across the fields to chapels and churches in other villages: only religious adventure and exploration was permissible on Sundays.

Joseph's mother never welcomed his leanings towards Methodism. Her attachment to her church was growing, perhaps with her increasing submissiveness, for the women even of remote Tysoe were becoming humble and retiring wives and widows, yielding though late to the strong Victorian current. On one occasion Elizabeth went with Joseph to a special service at the Wesleyan chapel, but the flat square walls and the near, clear view of all the congregation oppressed her, and she missed the words of the liturgy. One might have expected Joseph to feel with his mother; he loved order and continuity. But he could not give himself within a church whose leaders in and round his village hated his older friends' crusade for the Union. His mother sympathised here: she agreed that clergymen had no business to take sides with landlords and farmers; she too hated the demand for servile manners. Nor would she defend the Vicar's contemptuous sermons and writings in which he accused the Methodists of ranting in their missions of salvation, but she told Joseph that he would find extravagance and unkindness in every camp. The old Quakers had not been so very attractive; the stories about his own ancestors would show him that, though they were always told as jokes.

Joseph's first visit to the Wesleyan chapel had taken place on his twelfth birthday. On that day the Wesleyan Sunday School was also celebrating its anniversary, a highly success-ful type of festival which the Wesleyan Church had invented. Joseph so liked the children's service in the afternoon that he insisted against his mother's wish on going again at six in the evening. The hymn-sheet used that day was one of the little bunch of papers he put, during his childhood, into a small oaken box that his Uncle William had made.

That early summer Sunday was the children's own. Expected to keep small and silent as a rule, on this day they were allowed to expand so as to fill the chapel. They wore their best clothes, new or freshly washed and brightened, and sang their very own hymns, some of them newly written, which they had especially practised to burst completely novel upon the grown-ups. So the young Church lad, Joseph (on weekdays, of course, a family wage-earner) heard the fervent songs:

> 'Tis sweet to think of Thee
> When earthly friends may fail,
> When sorrow, grief and bitterness
> Our wounded hearts assail.

> 'Tis sweet to think of Thee
> When on the bed of death,
> When sorrowing friends around us stand
> To watch each shortened breath!

Such verses would seem highly unsuitable in the twentieth century, but we have to recall that the children died then in the cottage beds. A few months after this occasion ten of these very child songsters died of whooping-cough. Well enough the children knew that death might happen; maybe to combine the thought of it with the impression of a happy day was sound enough.

Then there were the passages expressing the children's perennial pleasure in sunshine and flowers.

> Tender herbs and lovely flowers
> Hail the sun and drink the dew;
> Grace divine like sunny showers
> Can our youthful hearts renew.

The later century would enter into a conspiracy of silence about true child nature, persuading every child that not to be angelic of temperament was to be a monstrous exception. Perhaps the child of 1871 could profitably and even comfortingly pray 'Subdue my sins and passions wild'. At all events, the rhythm of the hymns lent itself well to childish and adolescent fervour:

> Lord, I would come, a little child,
> And ask Thy daily care;
> Subdue my sins and passions wild
> Shall be my constant prayer.
>
> Thy love and goodness claim my praise
> Nor shall it end in death;
> For when the grave shall hush my tongue
> In gloomy silence sad and long
> My soul shall sing the enraptured song
> > In Glory.
>
> I cannot of Thy goodness doubt
> I cannot but Thy praises shout
> I cannot, must not, be shut out
> > From Glory.

It was rather more than a year after this Anniversary that Joseph Arch had come to Tysoe and young Joseph Ashby had his first inkling of the relation of religious sects to the simpler, the economic aspects of life: the labourers who could and

79

dared make claims for themselves and their children were Primitive Methodists. Perhaps that was why he went at first mostly to the 'Primitives'. Here some of his older friends of the fields and the roads were preachers and trustees. Here, too, were proofs of the power of religion, something very interesting for a boy to contemplate—men who had been drunkards and wife-beaters, brutal fellows whose lives had been changed. There was a frank, brotherly attack in the sermons on all sorts of simple evils—drink and gaming and strong language. One old brother would scold about a game of football, thinking that the old brutal sports might be coming back. Once Joseph laid up in his memory an expression of the attitude that enabled labourers to read a deep lesson of restraint to their neighbours in the higher walks. 'Men are not equal', said the preacher, as making a quotation. 'No! but they are brothers! Our neighbours on the farms and in the great houses be lucky and selfish and proud, and they expect you and me to put up with a lot of nonsense, but they be our brothers. Bitter in our hearts we are, but we can remember it; they and we be brothers.'

A village after all is very like a tribe. Jewish wisdom could be very directly applied to it. These mere shepherds, carters, and odd-job men never forgot that Christ himself was shepherd, carpenter and countryman. The original Methodists, John and Charles Wesley, had spoken the Christian message afresh for men as lowly and wretched as themselves. The hymns they wrote—and there were few by writers other than the Wesleys in the Methodist hymn-book of the day—stressed the essentials of Christian dogma hardly more than they recognised the needs of the flesh of downcast folk. Now here in the eighteen-seventies were some of the same conditions that had been seen among the miners the Wesleys had preached to and written for a century before—men without money or hope or respect and no prospect of them. But they had the gospel that brought them not merely respect but love and wooing.

> Love divine, all loves excelling,
> Joy of Heaven, to earth come down.

In their depression they had triumph:

> His Kingdom cannot fail;
> He rules o'er earth and Heaven,
> The keys of death and hell
> Are to our Jesus given.

In their services they could admit their own condition without humiliation:

> Disdain not, Lord, our meaner song
> Who praise Thee with a faltering tongue.

> Hear Him, ye deaf; His praise, ye dumb,
> Your loosened tongues employ;
> Ye blind, behold your Saviour come;
> And leap, ye lame, for joy!

Even the need for mutual help had been understood—for the Friendly Society, the pig club and Arch's Union!

> Help us to help each other, Lord,
> Each other's cross to bear,
> Let each his friendly aid afford
> And feel his brother's care.

They prayed to be lifted above their economic circumstances to the high graces of civilisation:

> Make us of one heart and mind
> Courteous, pitiful and kind.

They could join, too, in spirit with all the followers of Christ:

> One family we dwell in Him
> One Church above, beneath.

The class war was not for them; a man was a man for a' that—for all that his imagination failed him and his self-interest blinded him.

But the grace of God, the love of Christ were the central themes. These were praised and adored till the chapels were full of happiness. Faces glowed as the people left the little brick chapels, and some of them developed a permanent saintly warmth of expression.

All the same, it was the Wesleyans Joseph joined. Sudden conversion is a difficult idea for a rational temperament, but yet in any undertaking there has to be a moment of decision. Joseph would occasionally refer later, in the course of a sermon, to his own conversion. What he indicated was the story Charles Wesley had told:

> Yield to me now for I am weak
> But confident in self-despair.
> Speak to my heart, in blessing speak
> Be conquered by my instant prayer.
> Speak or Thou never hence shalt move
> And tell me if Thy name is Love.
>
> 'Tis Love! 'Tis Love! Thou diedst for me!
> I hear Thy whisper in my heart;
> The morning breaks, the shadows flee.
> Pure universal Love Thou art.
> To me, to all, Thy mercies move
> Thy nature and Thy name is Love.

The 'Primitives' were on the whole men of one Book, but Joseph was a man of many. There was a tradition in his new church from John Wesley himself that learning was important. 'Every voluntary blockhead is a knave,' he said, 'he defrauds his benefactors, his parents and the world, and robs both God and his own soul.' In his opinion learning would seldom be found without religion; the labour required to be a scholar was 'seldom united with light views'. He had taught his lay preachers that it was essential to read the best books and had helped them to possess some. Ministers and lay preachers alike were expected to be able to expound their matter well, considering it from various angles and suitably illustrating it, whether from books or life. Sermons were important to hungry minds, having the function of adult education before a specialised movement was developed for it. Sometimes they would be half an hour long, which gave time for thought.

Always in the end the preacher came to some central Christian teaching of theology or ethics, to the grace of God or the love of Christ. The Vicar's statement in his magazine that the Methodists were blown hither and thither by every wind of doctrine was very wide of the mark. If there was any swerving it was from John Wesley's Pauline outlook to emphasis on the Christ of the gospels, on Christ the Healer, Christ the ever-present friend—

> What a friend we have in Jesus
> All our sins and griefs to bear—

rather than on him resurrected and ascended and returning.

Almost from his conversion Joseph hoped he might become a lay preacher. To his shelves of books he added commentaries and a concordance; he read what he could of the history of Methodism. From his friends in the chapel he drew stories of its development in his village and district. The Tysoe chapel had been founded almost a century earlier by a group of three men and one woman, the ablest among whom was William Geden, tailor (if I have his craft correct) and shopkeeper. The little group had at first held prayer-meetings in cottages, leaving the door wide open on the street as an invitation to passers-by, but it seemed that these were annoyed by the Methodists' excited 'converse with God', declaiming and praying about Divine Glory and 'the Lover of Souls'. For these early saints there were terrific moments in life; light broke at the time of salvation on each convert as if he were on the road to Damascus. In their last illnesses they would see visions and sink to death exclaiming, 'Glory! Glory! Glory!' William Geden was the first tradesman in lax days to close his shop on the Sabbath, refusing rigidly to 'oblige'. It was merrily and admiringly told to Joseph how he would publicly tackle drinker and Sabbath-breaker about his sins, were the sinner poor or wealthy, high or low. But the sinners had retaliated. Time after time young men, the sons of Belial, had rushed into his meetings to scoff; they had waited for him after services to beat him and he had been obliged to slip away and hide in outhouses, or lie in a hedge behind long mowing grass.

The story most frequently told was of the Tysoe men who had walked thirty miles to see John Wesley. Everything that had happened in their brief interview with him was still recalled—how he had inquired after the health of their souls and of their Society, prayed with them in his cosmopolitan way for the whole wide world and led them in the singing of a verse. Sixty miles afoot had, it was evident from the detail of the story, been a small price for such a meeting.

These tales were told the young with smiles, but Geden's founding and cherishing of the small Oxhill Society was treated in impressive tones. For thirty years he had walked summer and winter in all weathers across the open fields to the Sunday evening services there, and then again to a class-meeting on a week-night. When he was over seventy he was still to be seen setting out, stout stick in one hand, a lantern in the other.

In the early years of the Tysoe Society quite a number of its youthful members had gone into the Ministry. Among these was Geden's own son John, who later became a tutor in one of the theological colleges of the connection and a noted theologian. His old age was as active as his father's; in his eighties the Reverend John had helped with the great Revision of the New Testament. And finally, not to be regarded as minor heroes were the poor labourers, lay preachers, who walked fabulous distances to preach three times or even four on a Sunday.

Thus went the story of Wesleyanism in Tysoe. Tradition is no mere matter of the long passing years; it depends for vitality on the courage and energy that makes a mark. A few persons, even one man or woman, can create a tradition. His new Society was well able to offer Joseph the exemplars youth needs.

CHAPTER VII

UNCLE WILLIAM EMIGRATES

THE early part of 1876 brought another of my grandmother's griefs. Her brother William had been growing steadily more sour and moody. In 1874 and 1875 the prices of farm produce had slumped alarmingly and forecasts were gloomy: Tysoe farmers skimped the hedging and draining, refusing to pay for piece-work. William would be reduced to taking a weekly wage. His wife, who to others seemed bonny and kind, had become more enraging to her husband by her lack of imagination and refusal of sympathy. Once during the previous year he had threatened her rather alarmingly and she had gone to confide in Elizabeth. In an ill-advised moment of trust in his office, if not in himself, Elizabeth mentioned the family anxiety to the Vicar. He bade her wait a little; he would consider what might be done. To Elizabeth's surprise and agony, William had been caught like an animal and taken off to a madhouse. Within a few weeks William was at home again, but he could not forgive either his wife or his sister, though in his heart he knew them innocent of responsibility for his experience. Some years before this—no living memory can establish the date—a couple of Mormon propagandists from Utah had stayed a few days in the village trying to gain converts and emigrants. Strange views and polygamous practice, as his later life showed, had not attracted William, but he had talked with the two men about the vast, wild, half-desert territories of Utah and Arizona. Now the postman began to bring him letters and pamphlets from the United States. It was evident that his mind was on emigration.

Meanwhile depression was general among the Tysoe labourers. Week after week, during the bad weather of 1875, the men had lost time and brought their wives home only

five or six shillings or less. Some of the farmers claimed that
they paid men wet or fine, but the time they paid for had to be
spent on the farm. To get his wage a good man must choose
between 'making work', 'hanging about', and working out
in the rain in clothes that were sopping wet in a matter of
minutes, so often he came home. The Union had brought
fresh interests to every lively mind. There were new goals—
parliamentary votes, parliamentary action to get larger
allotments, radical policies in education, Free Trade. Earthly
hopes and interests had grown. But now farmers were
suffering losses; forward moves in wages, which alone could
help at once, had become impossible. Whatever their wives
said the men kept up their subscriptions, but the Union could
do little for them now except to give advice. A few miles
away, at Priors Marston, labourers went on strike in June
1876 for an extra shilling a week, but the Tysoe street-
parliament, having adjourned out of the pouring rain to
resume talk in the blacksmith's shop, decided that the
Marston men must be mad. The weather was nearly as bad as
the year before. Autumn corn had not been planted, spring
corn was late in being set because of iron frosts; now the hay
would be ruined. The farmers' faces were nearly as long as
the labourers'. Farm rents had gone up a few years ago and
had not yet come down. There was little English corn on the
market, yet the price paid for it was lower than in 1874 when
crops had been fair. The men had over the reasons for this in
the smithy and Joseph, now seventeen years old, was present
at the debate. The French and the Americans had recovered
from their wars, it was said, and nobody wanted English
wheat. On the other hand, the foreigners had it to spare.
Trade was slackening in the towns; there was unemployment
already in the north. The English couldn't afford to eat their
own wheat!

The parliament was always a full one now, for the women
at home were nagging and miserable. No sooner had the
children recovered from one ailment than they contracted

another. First there was an epidemic of jaundice; then measles and scarlatina and mumps, and some cases of smallpox. The school was seldom at more than half strength, and the master spent even more time than usual nagging about attendance. Three times that year he wrote the name of a little child in his log book and set round it a frame of four crosses in heavy black ink. One of the children died of 'weakness' and so did others in the next spell of years. A number of grown-ups contracted English cholera, which was worst of all judging by the fact that it continued to be alluded to years after the other plagues had been forgotten: in my childhood a quarter of a century later, it was still being mentioned. Still, nothing slew so many children as the whooping-cough had done a few years before; the black crosses would become fewer from now on. Had that anything to do with the fact that the open drains down Church Town street were abolished at this time? Anything to do with the building of the infants' room at the school, so that the classes could be spaced out a little? It would be fanciful, no doubt, to suppose that tripping round in action songs as the babes began to do in their new room reduced the power of the germs, but that and the sewing cards and the sticks and peas certainly made them happier. Another cheerful note was struck, very literally struck, by the new church clock in the tower. Now there were so many meetings to attend, so many folk were catching trains; punctuality was more and more a virtue and a necessity. The old clock lost and gained according as the weather was warmer or colder, but you could set your watch, as you still can, by the new one.

But cheerful notes were few, and sad events were on the way. William Ashby had completed his preparations to leave for the States. A day or two before he left he sent for his nephew Joseph and handed to him his sickle, his favourite corn-dibber and one of the best of the small oak coffers he had liked to make. He also gave Joseph a job of work, to feed his tame badger and his dog till they should be fetched by a friend. But he sent no message to Elizabeth. William left for ever his wife, a large family of young children and his village which had refused him everything, little as he had asked, and finally degraded him in his own eyes. One slender link with his home he retained. From time to time he wrote short letters to his eldest daughter, his trim girl Hannah, only once or twice giving an address. He never married again or made a home with a woman and many years later he bequeathed to Hannah the property he had acquired in Arizona on condition that she, too, left England and Tysoe; but by that time Tysoe had changed somewhat.

The departure of William Ashby turned many a mind towards emigration. It began a deal of talk about Tysoe men who in earlier years had gone by ones and twos. Weavers and whitlaws, finding no work at home in the thirties, had carried their skill to the States. Within the memory of old Henry Parkman parish rates had been used to ship a family of nine to Canada. Emigrants then had to take their own food for the voyage, and the neighbours had given, one a cheese, another a well-cured ham, or a pan to fry their bacon in on board, as the way was then. Agents of Canada and New Zealand were advertising in the local papers. The Union was advising young men to accept the offered assisted passages.

In 1877 and the following years Elizabeth found herself brought into closer contact with her neighbours. She had been writing letters for Upper Town folk for a number of years. It was natural that when the young men made up their minds to go to Canada they should come to ask her to write to the Canadian agent for them. They could read well enough, but had never handled a pen since they left school. Such visits usually ended by Elizabeth telling the men what to say in their letters and how to state the case to sisters or aunts in 'service', for once again these must help. Often the men would go off only to come back a few evenings later asking for a letter to copy. Gradually Elizabeth became well-informed on the opportunities in various countries, the ports the ships sailed from, the cost of the voyage, the help that might be obtained from charitable sources for boys who were members of very large families.

It was not that Elizabeth encouraged men to go; they would not have allowed a mere woman outside their families to do that. But she would discourage! One evening Joseph, having his wash in the scullery beyond the 'house' heard in the dialect and in the heavy tones that went with it, 'I wun't write nuthing for you, mi bwoy. You be yoor mother's last man. Goo from whum if you will, but not bi deed o' mine.'

The cottages had been recovering a little from the denuded-ness of a generation before, but now they were stripped again to give the emigrants blankets and sheets and towels, brushes and knives. They had to possess these before they could embark, besides specified clothing. Elizabeth had patterns for the shirts and jackets and waistcoats, and helped with the cutting out. After all the efforts it was a little flattening to spirits when one man came home again from Southampton, pushing his painfully gathered outfit on an old wheelbarrow, but it did not stop the outflow. The men and boys who left tended to be the more forceful and bright characters, the darlings of the families. For the village to say goodbye to ten, twenty, thirty good fellows seemed a calamity. It 'would never be the same again'. Looking back over the years it could be seen that emigration had taken several of the ablest families. Maybe Tysoe has indeed never recovered.

After 1877 the exodus became slower but did not cease. Letters came from the emigrants speaking of 'free-growing fruits' in Vermont; of the 'land of liberty', the States, 'where every man can speak his thoughts', of Australia's plentiful meat. Sometimes the men in Australia would comment on the wasteful, unskilled farmwork they saw—it wanted more of the Tysoe men! And the Tysoe men went, though only by twos and threes after the great exodus.

Unemployment had had its surgical cure, but the corn receded further down the hill slopes till it grew only on the very best clay land in the vale, leaving the signs of ploughing in the ridged and furrowed fields. There was no improvement in wages, but the low price of corn, ruinous to farmers, gave the bread of physical existence to the labourers' children.

No doubt it had been well for William Ashby to cut loose from a situation that was driving him crazy, but he left his family in great hardship. In spite of her large brood, however, his wife was not given to worrying. Whenever Joseph was at home he acted to some extent as the man of the family, but the one to feel most responsibility was Hannah, the eldest child. She was fifteen when her father left for the States. With the stern uprightness of the very young she felt very severe towards him, but the same quality caused her to tidy up his affairs with the utmost scruple. What she chiefly remembered of that, later, was what took her longest—the gathering up and gradual payment of his debts. She had already been earning her food and a trifle of money for three years. First she had worked each morning at the schoolhouse, and then had gone to a farmhouse some miles away where she found herself not only carrying wood and coals, cleaning all the rooms and cooking meals, but also skimming the milk and making the butter. Hannah had, even at thirteen, indomitable pluck and health and could work at all these proper tasks from June dawn to June dusk, but her mistress required her also to brush her hair! Even Hannah jibbed at this addition, though she had all her life the least complaining mind, the greatest readiness to render up all she had to any claimant.

Presently she thought it her duty to get work in one of the great houses in the locality: you could earn more money there because you could rise from scullery- or between-maid through several grades. But Cousin Joseph, now a man of eighteen years or so, declaimed against 'the bare idea'. Go to spend the whole day in a scullery or brushing stair-carpets—that's what it would mean. Houses with two centres, 'room' and 'servants' hall', were monstrosities like double-yolked eggs!

Of course, if you were silent and servile in the one you were a termagant or a vulgarian in the other. And then, such houses unfitted girls for a 'sensible' life in a cottage or on a farm. All this, though expressed in Cousin Joseph's furious words, was a view held by many villagers.

So Hannah sought work in a more modest type of household and in fact went to Warwick, whence she could get home the sixteen miles for a few pence by carrier's cart, and where, if really necessary, her younger brothers and sisters could go to see her. She became house-parlourmaid, one of a staff of two, in a kindly, well-connected family. It was a very limited life: if father's debts were almost paid, she still had to send money to keep the young tribe. With next to nothing to spend and a life of indoors and subordination, her bright intelligence had little stimulus. She became unduly resigned to serving all those to whom service was due. It took all Joseph's persistence to keep her looking a little outward, and he was handicapped, had he but realised it, by being himself ready to accept too much from the hands of Hannah.

CHAPTER VIII

FRIENDS AND LOVERS

WE reach, now, a time in my father's life that is more familiar to me. My mother comes fully into the story and I and my brothers knew many of his friends of this period. There was much in his life from now on that he liked to tell us about, during the long slow drives behind nag or pony, when he took one of us to bear him company.

So it was that I came to hear about the time he spent in Surrey, during, I calculate, the year 1876. I had just begun to see our Warwickshire countryside as (to use a word I did not know then) landscape, and said something childish about its beauty. Then my father spoke of seeing the pinewoods on the sands of Surrey, the darkness of their foliage and the brilliant colours of the trunks and of the soil they rose out of; they had seemed to him quite foreign; our grass and elms were homely beside them. It seemed that he had spent some months in the southern county, with the firm who had built the steward's house at Compton. His work seems to have had little interest for him, but Surrey as a neighbourhood had left many impressions. The rich gardens of some of the cottages had pitched far higher for him the attainable degree of fertility of soil. But especially he had learned, to his astonishment, of the wealth of England. It had been a fact to be digested. Everywhere in the eastern parts of Surrey builders were erecting large houses, many-gabled, with architectural features such as towers and great porches, and set in vast gardens. Sometimes they had conservatories, hot and damp, filled with palms—little tropical islands—or they had galleries for works of art, or even small theatres; and sometimes all these features. Such paradises were not being built for a handful of aristocratic folk, or merchant adventurers and magnates, but for hundreds, thousands, of manufacturers and shopkeepers and men returned from un-explained business abroad. This was a strange, rather unreal country; the new houses belonged to no town and the small villages were swamped among them.

After a few months Joseph had left the firm of builders and the distant country to spend a short period at home. It was at this time that he concluded his local preacher's test. That done he was free to return to wider reading and to look around for new work. He was nineteen years old when he obtained work that pleased him well for several years. He seems not to have been touched by any fretful ambition; his duties were simple enough. The Ordnance Survey of the country was being revised, and Joseph accompanied a group of surveyors, carrying instruments for them and taking the simple measurements, thus following up his small boy's interest in mensuration. His group worked in Warwickshire and the neighbour-ing counties, so he was able to get home fairly frequently. Cousin Hannah was working in Warwick where he some-times lodged, and the two saw each other often. Good lodgings cost most of his earnings, and there was his mother to be helped; nevertheless he began to buy books and clothes. The clothes had to be of good material for protection against the weather, as he followed the surveyors across the fields; thus he discovered his taste for fine cloth and elegant cut. With his full height attained (six foot two was not so common then) and now his well-cut coats, his boyish beauty changed into the attractive manhood that now and then opened doors to him and helped to warm acquaintance into friendship.

Often—so his friends told us—his handsome face and form expressed a youthful melancholy and sternness, but when talk began he was never for long merely serious but often broke into fun and humour. Solitude in his lodgings and reasonable hours of work gave Joseph the opportunity to read a good deal and now it was, I suppose, that he gathered his surprising range of fact and his insight. Novels, poetry, history and stray volumes of science all came his way. His books were a haphazard series, for there were no public libraries and he could not afford the guinea subscriptions of the literary clubs of Warwick or Banbury. But his excellent memory and his plentiful time for reflection while he walked with the surveyors enabled him to place his books in relation and order his thoughts.

One constant and lifelong taste Joseph shared with great numbers of country readers. People who were not at all literary, who had not read Fielding or Scott, needed no introduction to Dickens other than the infectious laughter and smiles of his readers. His books were the favourites at the penny readings, and passages from them were read and recited in the 'public' and on religious platforms. So all sorts of folk became Dickensians in their degree: the hopeful young like Joseph, farmers, magistrates on the bench, the clergy, all read at least three or four of Dickens's novels. Even the children read them. Not to have your mind touched by Dickens was to remain a relic of the early nineteenth century, or maybe the eighteenth, as after all quite a number were. Dickens exercised the muscles of laughter and practised the imagination. If the Vicar preached one of his pre-Christian sermons, or a lay preacher's language was unequal to his message, or a mean mistress locked every cupboard although there was next to nothing in them, or a shopkeeper watched his scales over-sharply, or his local lordship was unbearably patronising, the risible muscles stirred before the frowns. All the tyrants and fools could be transmogrified into Dickens characters, and once you had smiled at your enemy you could think the better how to deal with him. The best of it was that everybody benefited. Lord Willoughby de Broke found a Dickens name for everyone he thought tiresome as easily as did Joseph. Thus Dickens affected the community life. The New Testament taught the principle of forbearance and Dickens supplied the technique of it. But Joseph and his like did not learn mere charity but rather an economy of indignation; it was saved up for the big things and kept turned in the right directions.

A different kind of reading Joseph shared with a very few friends, notably Fred Jeffs, who had an intellectual concentration quite unlike Joseph's inclusiveness. Fred's young frustrations and heart-sicknesses had been exceptionally severe: he was an orphan and to poverty had been added a gloomy home. Now he was pulling himself out of and above the worst of his circumstances. On his errands in Stratford on Avon, selling cabbages and the like, he regularly devoted a florin to the purchase of a book. His hardships and griefs became tolerable as he saw them schematised in political literature, and read of plans for social justice. Mill's *On Liberty* he read and passed on to Joseph. Then they both read Paine's *Rights of Man*. The latter part of this, with its proposals about taxation, narrowed Fred's line. He would thenceforth follow any radical movement, walking always on the left of it, always chiefly interested in its economic teaching. Presently he would be Tysoe's most convinced Single Taxer. He read and re-read Henry George's *Progress and Poverty* in a state of intense excitement, though he had to do it at night by the dimness of his bedroom candle. This book was the real determinant of his fixed economic interests. In due time he became the only Marxist in his village. When I saw him last in the late forties of the next century, his remaining fire was being spent upon unswerving admiration and defence of Stalin and his Russia. Joseph was sufficiently interested in Henry George to go with Fred to meetings and dinners of Single Taxers, but he could not long credit the idea that any exclusive theory of social organisation would be the world's salvation. Mill's *On Liberty* had suited him down to the ground, but there was nothing doctrinaire or monopolistic about that.

Towards the end of his time with the ordnance surveyors Joseph gained a friend whose talk had new content and qualities for him. While the surveyors were working near

Lighthorne, a dozen miles from Tysoe, a young man came up to the group. He had the air of ease and welcome that comes of hospitable ownership: the surveyors were on his father's land. Bolton King had recently left Balliol College. What Joseph's situation afforded not at all, King had had heaped upon him—an established family, high social status, comparative wealth, the best tutoring and travel. At Oxford he had had the crowning luck to be one of a group of keen young intellectuals—Toynbee, Nettleship and others—who had found a purpose proper to themselves and important to the world at their moment—the study of social philosophy and practical work in social reform. King had already decided that his own section of this work should be done in the countryside. He had also another aim—to be one of the historians of Italian unity. Thus the talk between him and Joseph ranged over many exciting topics. Perhaps it helped friendship that King was somewhat the elder. His intellectual breadth could be displayed by him and made use of by Joseph without any shame. But in any case Joseph could put much into the pool. Especially he could help his new friend to that close grasp of rural problems, the lack of which was about to be very expensive for him.

Mr King had not yet shed all the romantic idealism of his youth. He had fallen in love—so I heard, surely—with a grazier's daughter and sent her away to be educated as a preliminary to their marriage. When Joseph met him he had recently bought a farm a few miles from his home and made arrangements for it to be co-operatively run by its workers. Already, after a short time of working, there were difficulties. King rapidly planned that Joseph should go there and help to make it a success. But Joseph said no! He had other views for his future. Would he, then, accompany Mr King and consider the experiment on the spot? No, to that too; but he would go by himself. Arrived on the co-operative farm, he made friends with an already exasperated manager and walked and talked in the fields with the labourers. On his return the conversational leadership changed sides, and the pleasing genial Joseph delivered one of those blows that on rare occasions surprised his friends as well as his enemies. 'The thing is a good idea', he said. 'It is all right except that the farm is the wrong one, not fit for intensive working; the men are wrong and the scheme of management is wrong. Take the men,' he went on, 'I walked round the village and made a few inquiries. There is not a friendly society in it, only a "sick and divvy"; no chapel, not so much as a pig club the men have run themselves. Is there a man on the farm who has ever had such a job that the boss could not take his living away at a week's notice? To co-operate, day in, day out, you have to be independent and generous too: what practice have they had? They know your manager cannot dismiss—you told them—and they are sulky to him. They called me "Sir" because I had a good coat on, but they don't give their manager a name at all. Just a symptom! The Tysoe men call the farmers "John" and "Giles" in the street, but on his own fields the farmer is "Master" and so is his bailiff if he has one.

'Your "partners" don't even grasp that they have to make the farm pay! Every wet day they stay at home, don't even go and clean up the yard buildings before they give up: they've heard that union men demand pay for wet days, work or no work. Because a carter has to get up earlier than other men, they take that job in turns. Consequence, your dear-bought horses are beginning to look sick.' He talked of the relevance of the village's past—a "closed" one—land till lately all in one ownership, innovations discouraged or for-bidden, minds overawed, no sort of independence even for middle-class folk.

The failure of the experiment would not be a knock-out blow, though very troubling, for a person of so many resources. If the job could be done at Tysoe, said Mr King, let Joseph and himself find a farm there. 'But it could not', said Joseph. 'I can hear the men say "Twunt do! Twunt do!

Us can't fraame to that!"' Tysoe men, Joseph said, had their own idea; what they wanted next was allotments. Good cottages with large gardens, and other fairy gifts, of course! But they felt they could do something themselves towards getting fair-sized allotments. Those they were absolutely ready for. Co-operation was an excellent idea and so was independence.

By now, Joseph's favourite cousin Hannah had become his sweetheart, his affianced. As to knowing my mother I had the advantage of a daughter's intimacy, and beside that there stretched between us a resonant string so that I felt with her and often I seemed to see through a very clear glass into her thoughts—and still I see her meagrely. But it is useless to regret. Women of her time and sort (and how many were different?) took seriously, if not literally, the story of Eve's creation from Adam's rib; they accepted their lessness. They might be all to their children in the uncorrupted years before the patterns of the time affected them: but from that point mothers were the source of comparatively little in their children's minds.

Hannah had been working as house-parlourmaid in a tall house under the high graceful tower of St Mary's church, living in the kitchen regions with Emily, the somewhat older cook-housekeeper, waiting upon a small, elderly, kindly family called Malory, connections—says a quite stray memory—of the Lucys of Charlecote. Joseph dropped in often, welcomed by both the young women, persuading Hannah to go to chapel with him on Sundays instead of to St Mary's, which—with other advantages—secured him time alone with her. It was when Hannah's ageing employers decided to move their household to the mild climate of the Isle of Wight and the new, small resort of Ryde that she and Joseph became engaged. He was leaving Warwick and encouraged her to stay in a 'situation', as the word was, where she was contented and even a little cherished. To Hannah it seemed a great distance to go, but Joseph said she would find familiar things:

he had somehow heard that Mr Gilbert Scott, who had drawn the plans for the Tysoe schools, had built the new church at Ryde. There would be links; but also the island was beautiful.

As to my mother's life in Ryde, there is evidence. Her book of recipes is a record of what Emily taught her to make: marinaded rabbit, cakes, rhubarb marmalade and furniture polish. She went to parties and sang 'The Lost Chord' and 'I'll be all Smiles Tonight': the words are written at the end of the 'receipt' book. The theme of the time was preparation for wedlock: her friends helped her to make her little trousseau of 'three of everything'. She could not afford to buy more calico, cambric, and flannel than would make so many for she had also to save money for a sewing-machine— a Jones made of iron and steel, which fifty years later was still capable of use. She acquired also, at a cost of about a third of a year's wages, the only beautiful object she ever bought for herself—a watch of chased silver, with fine gold scrolls and figures on its face. In 1960 it keeps time still. For her watch Joseph bought her a long gold chain. That also was unique; she would never have from him another present that was not in fact for their household. These few things she would cling to—cling it seems unconsciously to signs of a time when she possessed herself and was sometimes for herself alone an object of consideration.

Meanwhile of course the postman brought letters from Joseph. For good manners' sake, her own and Joseph's, his news was shared with Emily but she went out to the sea-front and along the esplanade to read the verses he sent her and wrote them in a manuscript book when she could get a quiet moment. The marbled green and gold paper of its cover and the leather back and corners of the book are still fresh, for it was always kept in Hannah's bedside chest and never joined other books on shelves, though it is a real book, indexed as well as neatly written. Perhaps it did not deserve to join Cowper and Gray: verses were not the best expression for Joseph's measure of the poetic spirit; they are the work of a youth whose life, perhaps, had only the intensity of good prose. Yet they show us the hues and forms of this young mind, so typical of his time and kind. They were not mere supplements to letters.

There is no need to linger over short poems that might have been written by any young countryman hopeful, intelligent, and pretty well read—on, for example, the first glow-worms he ever saw

> Climbing the ripening grasses bent
> Or close beneath the groundsel leaf;

or the verses headed 'We all do fade as a leaf'. Leaves are seen

> Faded, fallen, lying silent
> On the earth for swift decay

and ageless response is stirred, that was being expressed by another poet about this time:

> It is the blight man was born for,
> It is Margaret you mourn for.

Such verses as Joseph's are mere daisies in the poetic meadow. But there was something about them special to these two lovers and something also that belonged to their generation as perhaps to no other. Joseph was looking to the future, dreaming of it but thinking also, expressing his conceptions of husbandhood and wifehood. He was already, to use an expression of his own, 'a steady spirit, regularly free', knowing that law is the condition of freedom. He and Hannah had already decided to return on marriage to their own village, where they would have to begin life on small earnings, little more perhaps than a skilled labourer's wage of ten or eleven shillings. Nevertheless, it was to be a life considered, not to say planned. We gather Joseph's feeling for Hannah—devoted, thoughtful, kind, rather linked with other, wider, loves than altogether concentrated on a lass. He is trying to discover true love, and sees it, I think, as a draft upon the parents' feeling for the young; as nothing if it does not spread in widening ripples to give at its limits fellowship and mercy to all; as a small matter if it be not a symbol for the love of God. As another said:

> Love refines the thoughts and heart enlarges, hath his seat
> In reason, and is judicious; is the scale
> By which to heavenly love thou mayst ascend.

Was Hannah critical at all of her sweetheart's thoughts in the ballad 'A Maiden Fair'? The maiden has rudely rejected a lover, but falls into her accustomed deep sleep on her pillow. A year later she is alone and wretched, for her parents have died. Her patient, faithful lover returns and she repents. Ever after she is a humble, faithful wife. The husband is, we gather, to be loving and fatherlike and the wife loving, admiring and resigned. And so it came about; Joseph's attitude to his wife was precisely that of Milton's Adam to his Eve and Hannah responded to him as the admiring, innocent Eve to her Adam.

One of Joseph's subjects that is markedly of his time is the damned thraldom of drink and rescue from it. 'The Navvy's Street Prayer' is the kind of poem that Masefield brought to a climax and an end many years later in 'The Everlasting Mercy'. That poem, so swift and dramatic, so densely set with imagery, is an historical novel: Joseph's verses express a terror not past, but gripping still. The navvy prays in the street for his drunken, disbelieving fellows:

> Lord God, my ways have sinful been
> Full of sin my days,
> But Thy mercy I have seen
> And learned to sing Thy praise.
>
> Now forth, Lord Jesus, I am come
> To tell my fellows of the love
> Which bought for me a heavenly home
> (I'll dwell with Thee above).
>
> Sinful their ways Thou knowest, Lord,
> Their hearts as millstone hard;
> But Thou canst save them by Thy word,
> Draw them by love's own threefold cord.

> Their days are fleeting onward fast,
> Their end it soon must be.
> Help them their sins away to cast
> And give their hearts to Thee.
>
> I once was their companion, Lord,
> In ways of death and sin.
> I heard Thee whisper 'I am come',
> Swore not to let Thee in.

And Masefield in 1911, in his swan-song of romantic evangelism went on with the story:

> The bolted door had broken in.
> I knew that I had done with sin.
> I knew that Christ had given me birth
> To brother all the souls on earth,
> And every bird and every beast
> Should share the crumbs broke at the feast.

'The Navvy's Street Prayer' was not Joseph's only poem on drink. Drunkenness and the cruelty and lewdness it released (Joseph had seen them) were the darkest blot on the villages. It might be that all this was the result, undoubtedly it was, of loss of status and self-respect. Never mind where the fault lay, the vice was in the sodden men. With his pen now, with years of work later, Joseph does what he can about this evil.

> See how the homes are wrecked and spoiled
> Once the monster enters in:
> Peace and virtue quit the threshold
> Love and truth give place to sin.
>
> See that loving, truthful husband
> Cease his home and wife to love,
> And the solemn promise broken
> He'd a guardian to her prove.

'A guardian'; the last line contains a part of Joseph's plan and promise for the future. His lass need not fear that he had not thought of dangers! There is the nineteenth-century chivalry of the good husband, *de haut en bas*, too closely enveloping, but perhaps a comfort to Hannah. She had known a broken home; she knew the sadder sides of village life and she as well as Joseph was a Victorian.

An aspect of evangelical sentiment and perhaps of Victorian feeling in general, almost past imagining now, is the trustful one which gave repose to spirits:

> They ne'er are wrecked who closely watch
> Their chart and inner guide,
> And never anchor till they reach
> The golden shore, the Saviour's side.
>
> Who trusts not in the Sailor's skill,
> The vessel's strength and might,
> Sees the storm ere the cloud arise,
> And darkness ere the night.

The last verse sent to Hannah was brief and hurried:

> Our hearts are sighing this goodbye,
> So heavy with the load they bear,
> But we'll meet to bless each other
> With faithful love and care.

And so they did. Every promise made to the future in these youthful verses was kept. And fate granted, whatever her exactions, every hoped-for joy.

CHAPTER IX

HUSBAND AND HOUSEHOLDER

A DOZEN years or more after my mother's wedding day my sisters and I teased her for details of her wedding dress. On several occasions quite late in my own life aged friends who had been present spoke of the day and the ceremony. The weather on 8 April 1885 was fine and the hours precious for work in the fields, but the Wesleyan chapel was full of friendly witnesses. There was more here I fancy than a tribute to charm. Joseph had not been expected to return to Tysoe, but now it could be hoped that he and Hannah would support the chapel and other causes.

By the privilege of brides, Hannah's appearance is best remembered: Joseph was dismissed as looking tall and severe and romantic. Hannah beside him was much shorter but so very neat and bonny. She was dressed in grey with dashes of brightness, and under a little hat her dark hair was coiled magnificently. Her jacket as she described it to her little girls was of finest serge, fitting closely at the waist and having a wide basque; the lapels were turned back from collar to waist and the shaped cuffs were bordered with cherry-red velvet ribbon. She had rather wanted to have an over- and an under-skirt, but Father, that is, Joseph, when she showed him the drawing in the *Girl's Own Paper* had frowned on the artificiality of that. So she had merely had a full skirt with a cane run round it six inches below the waist to carry the fullness of it and to show off the jacket's basque. Her hat had had a high crown and a small brim with a bunch of cherry and grey ribbon at the front. Such a hat must have set off the breadth of the face and the large keen eyes. Never again would Hannah be so well-dressed; life became so full that minor questions of beauty and taste were crowded out. By the time her daughters asked their questions they had to wonder that their mother could have looked so beautiful as they had heard, for they had seen in their father's eyes that she sometimes bought them frights of hats and coats.

The groom and bride had been promised a good small house in the Back Lane, by old Retta Maria Gould, a fellow Methodist (Hannah of course had joined her husband's church), but as matters fell out they had to wait seventeen months for it. They were forced to take refuge in a cottage in 'the Dock', an old houseless farmyard off the street. The 'Dock' had gained its name in the eighteenth century, when coal was coming to be a usual fuel, and had been bought by the Overseers of the Poor for sale to small buyers. A barn there had been used as a 'Wharf' for the unloading of the coal. Later, the barn and its nearby smaller buildings had been turned into cottages. There had been several, but whenever one of the poor old places was left vacant awhile it crumbled.

We have to imagine the bride coming from a pleasant, comfortable house, with all the freshness of sea-views and breezes, into the wretched place. From my parents, though I learned something of their life in it, I heard no details of the building, but when it stood empty and disintegrating their eldest boy played in and out of it a time or two. The curiosity and photographic memory of eight or nine years enabled him when an ageing professor to stumble through the old place at will. It had two small rooms on the ground, one with a rough stone floor, the other a floor of beaten earth. Upstairs were also two small rooms, the sills of their tiny windows flush with the floor. There was almost no garden and the pit closet was over-near the house and in view of neighbours.

Joseph said it was perhaps good that they should live as others had to and in fact a little good came of it. Hannah had no range for cooking, only an open fire with a shallow oven of seventeenth-century pattern under it. Yet here she managed to cook, preserve and store. Other cottages nearby were worse off: the housewives could only boil and fry.

Some official visitors to the village (who could they have been?) in their report girded at the improvident and limited cooking of the cottage women. Joseph and Hannah were incensed and with his wife's clear demonstrations as a basis Joseph wrote letters to the *Banbury Guardian* describing the worse-than-medieval limitations of cottage hearths and the lack of facilities for cleanliness and storage, and adding an attack on the state of housing as a background for children's lives. Like the youth he still was, Joseph contemptuously derided the critics for knowing so little of how and where to direct criticism. His fellow cottagers were delighted by this spirited defence: who could the anonymous writer be?

In years to come the furniture and utensils with which Hannah started housekeeping could be pointed out among the family effects. There were the six good elm Windsor chairs, locally made and left raw for Hannah to finish with linseed oil and beeswax; a large deal table which scrubbed to a beautiful pallor; three orange-boxes covered with cretonne of salmon and orange and green held 'the tea-things'. Joseph's special possession and contribution was a large book-case painted crimson, with glass doors. By chance its colour matched the crimson band on Hannah's best tea-cups (almost a service, given her by her mistress). And so even in that ramshackle cottage colour called to colour and made brightness and beauty.

How did Joseph hope to maintain his family? Certainly in part by using his knowledge of surveying to measure stacks for farmers and land for piece-workers. He would get occasional crowns and half-crowns as reporter for local papers. He would presently obtain an allotment and grow a good deal of food. One of his first pieces of work took him again daily to Compton Wynyates. Much work was to be done there. Lord William Compton had recently married and Compton House was to be prepared for his bride. Not only that, but the whole estate was to be put in order. Joseph was especially engaged to lay out the new Italian garden, but when he first arrived the field was not even levelled for it. Part of the moat was being filled so Joseph joined the men in cleaning the moat-ponds and filling one of them. That is remembered partly because he brought home eels and required them baked in a pie. The oven under the fire would not serve, but Hannah begged the use of a neighbour's brick oven, and to justify the use of two or three faggots of wood she made and baked pastry for several housewives.

Soon Joseph was able to turn, at Compton, to his more skilled work; he marked out on the ground the complicated plan of flower-beds, circular, crescent-shaped and rectangular. He staked the spots at which yew- and box-trees were to be planted, ready to be shaped presently into statues of Henry the Eighth and ladies in full skirts and ruffs, or into peacocks and bears. Among these were to thread alleys of pleached and pruned pear and plum trees. When he ordered these did Lord William remember a talk between himself and a lad ten years before? He sometimes came now and talked with Joseph and his team in the garden. As manager of his family's estate in London he had experience of practical matters. He had just become Liberal candidate for the Stratford division of Warwickshire, an entirely rural constituency. Bolton King's views and enterprises were known to him and he discussed them affably with Joseph.

Meanwhile Hannah reconciled herself to the necessary extent with her surroundings and learned to manage her primitive apparatus. Coping with the wretched cot intensified her power to concentrate on practical problems and to wrest order and efficiency out of mean materials. Her neighbours benefited by her presence; her Jones sewing-machine and her ability to cut out clothes for any size or shape of woman or child and even to make a shapely jacket for a lad brought them to her. She cooked admirably and in this one region of life could be adventurous, ungoverned by even the most respectable conventions, for she had the gift, said to be rare in women (but that may be a Victorian slander) of a very fine palate.

Under her husband's vivid appreciation of her dishes she discovered how to use it.

As for her power to enter into wider mental realms, her Adam promoted it so far as seemed desirable in his Eve. He was himself both a stimulus and a discouragement. He took flights of thought so easily, like a sparrowhawk rising from Old Lodge, whereas she was a beautiful domestic fowl, keeping close to her mental pabulum, taking what came, not surveying the fields to find it. In the matter of reading Joseph gave Hannah good guidance. He brought her the best novels and would not allow her to read the *Girl's Own Paper*, the periodical taken by all the good and aspiring young women of her sort at this time, calling the articles and stories 'sentimental-sensible'. The heroines of the *G.O.P.* were not beautiful but only comely as any girl might be. They were often governesses or clergymen's daughters, portionless girls of good birth, who would eventually marry modest wealth and position, never penniless fellows or working men. Joseph would read aloud short extracts and then toss the paper away. 'No English gentleman would approach a lady in the street unless she had first bowed to him, after which it would not be impermissible for him to speak to her.' Yet though it ministered to dreams there was an undercurrent of good sense in the paper; in spite, for example, of its lithographs of gorgeous clothes it always showed how fashions might be simplified and how much material a 'neat yet stylish' dress would take. But gentle ridicule banished both sentiment and sense. However, there were the best novels. Hannah's extremest luxury and pleasure would always be to spend an hour with Scott or George Eliot, but she would never greatly develop her literary taste or any other intellectual quality, for it seemed her duty to be perpetually poised for swift service—to husband, child, animal, neighbour and the chapel. Her delicate senses and vivid emotions were under the severest control—no job too hard or dirty, once its necessity was seen; the most innocent tastes were permitted no indulgence; no strong feeling was allowed to break through her resignation to heaven, husband, and fate. And so, naturally, she passes into the background of her husband's and children's lives, not often to emerge.

At last the house in the Back Lane was ready. Its ancient stone roof had been stripped off and blue Welsh slates now covered it. It stood next to Retta Maria's own cottage—the two together had been once a small farmhouse. The new home was, in one of my mother's prudent, soothing sayings (they were meant to be soothing), 'sufficient for the time being'. There was a large living-room and a small kitchen; a wash-house stood detached. The garden, or rather the yard, was big enough for pigs and fowl and perhaps a cow or a pony with space enough left for a 'junk' playground for boys and girls; simple enough, but worlds away from the Dock.

I myself remember this Back Lane House; several of my mother's children were born here. My first memories are of a few sensations, formless and wordless. There were big gold flowers growing under the wall all round the house, roses of Sharon we called them, their great bunches of gold stamens threatening the eye of a child taking her first staggering steps; there is a hot smell of iron on calico—Caddie was goffering our white summer bonnets; there is my mother's face, just as it was later—to a child's sight which notes nothing but attitude and feeling—full at the same time of severity and careful attention.

Later memories are clear enough, for example baths before the open fire in the 'house'. The greatest luxury in life is non-existent now—a bath between a hot fire and the draughts from three doors! Exquisite to turn a shivering shoulder and feel glorious warmth on it, and to smell soap and have some grown-up given up to oneself, to towelling and comforting. It was not always my mother: she had a series of thirteen- or fourteen-year-old girls to help her with her children, till the elder ones could tend the younger. In later years when friends have spoken of their nurses and nurseries I have thought of these girls practising their mother-feelings and mother-

109

knowledge on us—on me; coming between a babe and a vexed mother when drawers were wet; carrying a heart-broken child from some scene of catastrophe, nettles perhaps; or goffering a bonnet instead of merely ironing the frills, to make us feel fine and to do credit to the holiness and beauty of Sunday. Perhaps the everlasting arms when I have felt them have been really by origin Caddie Woodfield's; she was never in a hurry as my mother had to be.

Other things for me at the Back Lane house were the hand-some looks and grand strutting of my father's Homburg fowl and at some other time the Polish ones, with their glossy black coats and white crests; and presently the beautifully marked bantams he bought especially for us, to teach us to like our job of watering and feeding the fowl. What were these fantastic fowl doing in our yard? Certainly illustrating a little trait in my father: in small matters he liked a little style and extravagance. They probably meant too that he had had some small luck in earnings; he would never throw away a bit of good fortune on dull purchases. And then as to the inanimate contents of the yard there were the old tricycle and 'penny-farthing' my brothers careered around on, chopping-blocks turned into seesaws and the rest.

For young children there was little wrong with the house; we could make an Oslo breakfast there, ready for life's day, with all the vitamins of love and play and responsibilities; but it sufficed less well for grown-ups. The smell of corn and toppings hangs about the house for me because my father was forced to take a larder from the living-room for his animals' food and for sides of bacon, constricting my mother's space. My father lacked a room where he could call small meetings, and my mother tired of his callers coming while the room was littered with damp linen or her sewing.

Joseph was earning a better living than immediately after his marriage. Simple surveying was coming his way, a Leamington newspaper had recently been bought by a group of Liberal politicians and he was regularly sending reports of village affairs and beginning to write notes on politics from a rural angle. He had as many animals as his yard and his allotment would support. Could he but have rented an acre of arable or a small meadow—or, as they said then, the moon!

By this time the new Warwickshire County Council had taken the roads in hand. Hartshill stone was being applied on almost all of them. It gave the roads a new quality, made them hard and, for those days, quick drying. Half-way through February the roads would shine like long white ribbons, when the old brown ones would still have been ankle-deep in mud. The stone brought new economic chances for some folk. Local men with a cart or two contracted to convey it from the railway yard and tip it beside the sections of road that were due for mending. Many were anxious for this work: fewer made bids to break the stone. No skill had been required to break the Hornton stone but 'Hartshill' was close and hard and yet not brittle. Besides, a stone-breaker must be prepared to work at a distance from home, and find lodgings. The advantage of the work for Joseph was that you contracted to do it by a certain date and then your hours were what you chose. It was seasonal and the seasons for it, autumn and early spring, came when Joseph's little harvest was over, the mensuration done, and before the animal births in his yard had begun.

Some men tried the work and gave it up, but Joseph and his assistant experimented with tools and methods till they settled upon hammers with small, almost tiny heads, and long stales of thin pliant ash, and found the stroke that split the stone. The two men worked together, one on each side of a heap, their strokes alternating rhythmically. Three or four months of this work each year gave a little stability to Hannah's budgeting, for during the other months the family income was precarious.

In some seasons there was no road-making anywhere near home. Joseph would have to go away twenty or thirty miles for a week and leave Hannah the animals and the allotment to

111

tend as well as the house and children. But he bought a penny-farthing bicycle so as to ride home on Saturday evenings, and sometimes he would sacrifice hours of work to be at home for a meeting on a 'week night', for interesting matters were working up in the village; and then would mount the penny-farthing again at dawn.

Being a tall fellow, Joseph found the road-work rather back-breaking, and it soon became monotonous to a lively mind, but the roadside life had charms like those of an inn. When he worked alone wayfarers seized the chance of greeting and talk, as his account of one day exemplifies. He was working on the Southam road on the day of Banbury Fair. Innumerable carriers' carts went by on journeys of from three to twenty miles. Pedestrians in their best clothes 'streamed along'. The experience was of an ancient sort and Joseph's record uses old phrases: 'all sorts and conditions', 'not only Hodge and his sweetheart', 'a motley stream'. There were tramps smoking their 'guinea gold' cigarettes or small cigars called 'seignettes'; young 'strappers' too, getting their first taste of tobacco from new clay pipes purchased so that their owners could go to the fair as men. Old men and old women passed who assured Joseph that they 'hadn't missed a fair for forty yurr' Said one 'I shall know I be an old man when I can't get to Banbury Fair'. Well-to-do farmers 'tore' along in fashionable set-outs, that is, in high, polished gigs, behind well-groomed spanking mares, 'as though Banbury were one of the best markets in the world'. There was one clergyman, 'just one gentleman of the cloth', who stopped on his way home and talked to the road-mender about the twopenny shows he had seen. Not a bad sign, Joseph thought; such a parson might understand the younger and simpler members of his flock and be of use to them.

Road-mending allowed of much meditation, and life in Tysoe was giving Joseph plenty to think of. In December 1884, a few months before his marriage, he had been present at the planting of Tysoe's Franchise Tree. I saw so many photo-

graphs of this event that I came to feel that I had stood in the
crowd and seen Lady Compton with the spade in her hand,
and Mrs Cobb, wife of the Radical member for the Rugby
division, standing beside her. One copy hung over my father's
writing table and another in the Vicar's study. It had been a
curiously harmonious occasion, seeing that it celebrated the
enfranchisement of labourers. What could have brought the
superior folk of the village to approve of this? Disraeli had
enfranchised town labourers: could any villager admit, then,
that it was wrong for Gladstone to do the same for country
workers? The Liberal sympathies of the young Lord William,
now become Earl Compton, who was landlord and patron to
farmers and Vicar had not, evidently, gone unnoticed.

All those facts did not convince the Vicar that labourers
could use the vote in a rational way but he recognised their
new status. He urged, now, that they should not congregate
at the back of the church during services, out of sight behind
the new carved wooden spire that hung over the ancient font,
but should come forward and let their responses be heard. If
he advised them in season and out of season about politics, that
meant that he spoke with them on subjects he had previously
deemed to belong to a world above theirs.

It was about 'the vote' that Joseph and he had what I think
must have been their sole longish, amicable talk. How
could men of such narrow experience have political wisdom,
the Vicar asked? Question answered question: was wisdom
required of other voters? Or displayed by all the members
of any other class? It was certain that country labourers had
information and experience that could counter the bias of
men in other situations. Little schooling? Well, they had had
some very fine teachers out of school. They had learned once
for all that if they did not look after their own interests, no
one would do that for them.

Thinking of the good old friends of his boyhood and of
some of his contemporaries, Joseph carried further his
thoughts of these political teachers of theirs. First, there

was bread. It was no good, for example, to lecture the labourer, though it was often done, on the identity of his interests and the farmer's: bread had shown that for a false, idyllic notion. No good to tell him that import duties on flour, however small, would not affect the price of his loaf. Mr Jesse Collings was admired for his knight errantry but not for his policy. 'Three acres and a cow' to every cottage would not do in Tysoe. A fair weekly wage and a good-sized garden—yes, one could do on that or on a little farm of thirty or forty acres. Three acres were too much or too little—either a waste of good land or a perpetual anxiety added to perpetual work.

The Bible—even that must come after bread—was the second of their trio of teachers. From this they had learned their basic point of view. They were on the side of the Prophets, rather than of the Kings, the institutions. The grounds of self-respect their fathers had lost in England they found afresh in Palestine. There were no two nations of the ancient Jews and there should be no great cleavage among Englishmen. They had read the injunction to the King of the Jews that 'his heart be not lifted up above his brethren'. The great men of Israel were but farmers like their own cousins and ancestors. David had been a shepherd, Amos a herdsman, Christ himself a carpenter. For the more imaginative, the gorse bushes on Old Lodge could be on fire with the flames that do not consume. They could imagine the Saviour walking on the blue brick causeway the Feoffees were laying along the street, and were certain that saintly followers of his had walked and would yet walk the Tysoe lanes.

From their third teacher, the village, they had had lessons in human nature, especially about character. They tested every man's views by his actions, by his carriage of himself on all sorts of occasions. They knew the effect of interest and class, and how in some cases these were the whole mould of mind, and in others far otherwise; and would ponder on what kept a man's mind in part unbiased and free to think.

Time showed in fact that Tysoe men could not be won for
vast schemes; they wanted this wrong righted, that foul spot
cleared, and reasonable scope for a man's activity. They had,
the best of them, wise inherited attitudes outlasting the
occasions of learning, knowing for example from their grand-
fathers who saw the enclosure of the village fields that a
procedure or a plan could be proved up hill and down dale
to be profitable and fair, and the result go roaring of itself on
a career of injustice. But though they were sceptics, they
saw that there were good men in all ranks and grades, and
moreover, that in all but the worst time, everybody, just
and unjust alike, contributed something: the foolish amused
and the wicked instructed. They saw men as members one
of another.

In the street-and-smithy parliament every contemporary
problem was discussed. Among them were men of information and reason. At that date an intelligent man was not
lonely in their midst: he would not be hampered by a sense of
apartness. Fred Jeffs, burning, as he expressed it to me,
'hundreds of candles' over *Progress and Poverty*, had a critical
audience for his exposition of the doctrines he loved.

But of course there were the weaker brethren. Perhaps it
was by chance that my father discovered both just how weak
they were and a means of strengthening them. Pig clubs
were quite an old institution in some villages. Joseph himself was a pig-keeper—insurance would help him as well as
others. Pigs were not his best object of contemplation but
he could simulate the passion some men felt. It is difficult
now to appreciate fully the pleasure it was to these to lean
over sty doors and sympathise with a grunting sow nuzzling
under straw for food or shutting her eyes happily under the
scratching of her owner's stick. It was no gross love;
thoughts of bacon did not impede it.

Although a pig was essential if a labourer's family were to
have a fair diet, it was an undertaking to save out of the wage
to buy even a small pig and a bag of meal. On the other hand

if you could prosper with a pig or two, you had money for clothes or to manure and stock a second small allotment. But pigs are or were subject to sudden and fatal diseases, and the breeding season was risky. To lose a pig after investing in it the savings of months and getting the toppings 'on tick' would be a terrible discouragement. So the Pig Club filled a blank. No need in this case of influential support! Ten or twenty men subscribing a penny a week and half-a-crown for each pig insured could start it, given one good season. As time went on, the compensation could be raised until, if epidemics were avoided, all losses could be met. Every sensible man could do good work in the Club, inspecting pigs proposed for insurance, advising young recruits on sties and on tending and feeding. There is nothing like advising others to ensure that one's own standards are high! Rules had to be thought out to make sure that losses due to carelessness should not fall upon the Club, and that boars and sows and porkers should all be satisfactorily covered.

Pious youthful Joseph, Chairman and Secretary, noted the reforming influence of pigs. A man who would turn sulky at a hint about his family duties would halve his visits to the Peacock once he grew fond of his pig. Joseph found his office of Secretary brought him intimate knowledge of members' affairs; he found himself in a situation from which it was natural to make himself useful. Years afterwards my brother would hear how he had lent a man the money to buy a small pig or to replace sour corn, and arrange for the debt to be worked off—the kindest stroke—not in cash, but by doing some job on his allotment or by a bag of potatoes. The Pig Club daunted no one, not even silly-simple Jack Brown, about whose name the jokes clustered; who when his donkey died said ''Er ahn't ne'er done that to me afoor', and who was credited with having once set out to drive a couple of ducks over the hill to Shenington. The Pig Club could both serve Jack and men like him and make use of them. It showed how far down the scale (whatever scale you took) there could be real citizenship, if only the framework of life was right.

My father found this work worth doing: I remember seeing the Club's account books on his table at least twenty years after its first meetings.

Another attempt at self-help on the part of labourers was being made at this time. The Tysoe Labourers' Charity Lands Allotments Committee had been formed in March 1883 a year before my father came home to stay. The brief and ill-written minutes of this Committee are among my treasured possessions: it is deeply pleasant to follow the sustained attack made by nearly illiterate men on an entrenched position! It was known that the lease of the Town Lands would expire in a year or two: the Committee was to try to get a part of the Estate for small allotments. They studied the Instrument of Government of the Charity Estate, obtained copies of Acts of Parliament, and corresponded with the Charity Commissioners. My father's hand appears in the book: he had given help in writing letters and the like, but he was never a member. Why not, he had asked, recruit men who wanted more than an acre? Why not wait and bring up bigger guns to attack the fort? The vote was coming, had come. The Committee made its tender to the Feoffees, but the farm was let as a whole to a farmer.

An opportunity to vote occurred during the year after the planting of the Tree. Overseas there was evil weather in South Africa, in the Sudan and in Ireland. In home affairs there was controversy about Ireland, disestablishment of the Church and Land Reform. It was Gladstone's and Chamberlain's home programmes that chiefly at this time interested the new Tysoe voters.

These rejoiced in their new status and did not harbour cynicism about it: did not someone hang a Union Jack on the Tree on every anniversary of the Planting till the First World War?

The Vicar's fear that they would be all for the disestablishment of the Church was something of a turning of the tables between him and them, but in fact they showed only a transitory interest in that project. They had to see to it, so far as in them lay, that landlords dropped their refusal of smallholdings, that the Town Lands came back to the village and that there was no interference with the cheap food that had begun to arrive.

Nervous folk had feared that there would now be more political dissension in the village, more excitement about elections. The dissension was more visible but perhaps less grim. From now on for many years, as great questions arose they would be expounded and debated on the green or on the strip of greensward down the street where it was widest, between the Peacock Inn on the north-west side and the blacksmith's shop opposite. The innovation seemed shocking to those who felt themselves superior to mere prejudiced villagers; but had they felt it consonant with their dignity to see and hear for themselves they would have found the audiences sufficiently sceptical and that new hopes kept the meetings from the grimness of the old days, though it might come back. Tom Gardner, a young farmer, an enthusiastic 'Primitive', ran the first of the meetings. Tom was constitutionally fervent; just now he had adopted Chamberlain's Radical Programme for his own. Joseph, who opened the meeting for him, was not so sure: free schools, allotments and smallholdings, security of land tenure—yes. Home Rule for Ireland? Yes, to that too, so far as he could make out; but disestablishment? Was there something doctrinaire about that? Nobody in Tysoe grudged the Church its endowment or its prestige, not even Tom (its exclusive control of the school was another matter). What always troubled Tom was 'the principle of the thing', but he made few converts from Liberalism to his more radical notions.

Joseph had one early turn as chief speaker but we know only the general line he followed. Tom Gardner and he took their stand on the old wagonette in front of the smithy just when the men had finished tea and some of them were beginning to drop in at the Peacock for their evening talk and drink. Tom raised his powerful voice, exercised at 'camp meetings', and called the men together. (How was it, their critics wondered, that these two men could always get people to listen to them? They had not noticed the Pig Club, for example, and did not know how the two had 'seen' families through periods of unemployment and illness, and mostly did not come to hear the oratory they despised.) With one hand Joseph waved a sky-blue paper and in the other he held a book. Everyone knew that the Vicar had written in the Parish Magazine an angry paragraph about the meetings. The speakers were 'pothouse swaggerers, parochial wiseacres, full of prejudices'. Joseph referred lightly to the Vicar's words. Why need a respectable inn be called a pothouse? Or when had he or Tom or speakers on other evenings been seen with a beer mug in hand? Everybody knew Tom for a teetotaller, and most of the others too. As to being parochial wiseacres—well, what else could they be? To learn all you could from what went on around you—that was what every man of sense did. It was better to learn day by day as a grown man in a village than to close your mind at the end of the best schooling and college! But, he said, the Vicar had given his audience one bit of good advice—'Go home and read a good book'. Here was a book for them, by a Tory, too. The subject of the meeting was Home Rule and the book *Realities of Irish Life*. The author was an Irish landlord and estate agent for far greater landlords. Quoting from the lively and fair-minded book Joseph showed the condition of Ireland; extreme poverty, men ambushing agents and landlords, good men committing terrible crimes, suffering for them and ruining their families. All that on the one hand, and on the other government by an alien race, money taken from Irish estates to spend luxuriously abroad, on keeping up the standards of wealth and position.

Did life in Tysoe and around make those conditions intelli-

119

gible, the speaker asked? Did his audience know anything of
land hunger? They ached for allotments and smallholdings.
Did they know of the effects of land monopoly on the life of a
village? A Tysoe man would never take a job that meant living
in a closed village. No! He'd go to Birmingham, rather, or
cross the ocean. Did they know how wealth from over-large
estates gets misused? They'd heard of great estates being
enclosed in the past by removing villages (there was an old
example not so far away): of Compton House being emptied
and the old place in danger of being pulled down to pay for
bribes and oceans of beer at an election. Did not the old folk
know of starvation and crime here in the old days? Those had
not been due to lack of corn in England. In a certain chapter
of *Irish Realities* they would read the proof that deaths in the
so-called potato famine in Ireland were not due to lack of
food in the country. The food was there—the deaths were due
to the impassable gulfs between classes and to a 'governing
class' which did not know how to govern and was not in a
position to find out; and yet would not let the people learn
to manage their own affairs. In Ireland the gulfs were
deeper than they had ever been here—conqueror ruling
conquered still.

Now there was the Home Rule Bill to let the Irish improve
their own country, take their own problems in hand. There
were to be safeguards and compensation. Those were right
enough: over-sudden and over-drastic changes meant trouble
and loss always.

Joseph held up the book again. It had been printed seventeen years before, yet conditions were still the same. Why?
What stood in the way? Who stood in the way of Tysoe's
small desires for betterment? Who whittled down the Allotments Bills? Who threw out bills to give farmers security of
tenure? And all the bills ever drawn up to allow a village to
have a real village school? Who prevented villages two years
ago from gaining a reasonable court of appeal from decisions
of Feoffees of Town Lands and the like? The House of Lords!

And the House of Lords would throw out the Home Rule Bill.

Let Tysoe men never forget it: what worked for well-being in Tysoe would work in other communities. What went seriously wrong here would go wrong there. You can't, he said, turn the Home Rule Bill into an Act: but it was the duty of all village wiseacres to vote for it.

CHAPTER X

LAND HUNGER:
THE PROMISED LAND

THE main subject of this chapter was too plain a tale, too little lightened by any humour or success ever to be told as a whole in a family circle. But though I never heard the story in full I gathered its outline; its events affected the childish lives of myself and my brothers and sisters. They helped, for one thing, to form our economic background. They must also have had a certain influence on my father's outlook—not too large an effect on a mind so naturally large, but they must have sharpened its political edge. Locally, the events had their publicity. By 1896 my father was writing occasional notes for the *Warwick Advertiser* and counted its editor among his very friendly acquaintances. Mr Lloyd Evans was a Radical and a warm-hearted spectator of village struggles. So it came about, I infer, that Tysoe affairs were well ventilated in the county paper.

In the election just passed, of 1885, Gladstone had been returned to power but, as everybody foresaw, his Home Rule Bill was thrown out by the House of Lords. As a consequence, there was another election in 1886 and this time a Conservative majority was returned to the Commons—but the Tysoe labourers had the satisfaction of knowing that their spirited member, the Radical Mr Cobb, still represented the Rugby Division.

The Liberal programme had included the promise of an Allotments Act and now there was no chance of it. True, the new government hastened to promise an Act with the same title but it would not have the same nature. It would permit and even encourage ten-pole allotments, which the Vicar already permitted, and would do Tysoe no good.

Land Hunger: the Promised Land

Two years earlier Joseph had thought the Labourers' Allotment Committee a waste of effort; it would be better, he had thought, to wait in the hope of new legislation which would enjoin upon local charities and perhaps upon vestries the duty of providing allotments when they were demanded. He had known also that the needs of weekly wage-earners were not the only ones. Thatchers, hauliers, carpenters were all trying, and of course failing, to get an acre or two, sometimes to grow wheat and animal feed, in some cases to pasture a horse, or for a cow and pigs. The times were discouraging and yet at Southam, not so many miles away, an Allotments Association had been successful in getting a good acreage. It was a larger and luckier village, the folk more varied. A doctor had grasped that starvation made for ill-health and allotments for good food, and had given help and support. Whatever the handicaps, Tysoe men must try again. So at Christmas 1886 a new start was made. Eighty-six signatures were obtained to a statement of the need for small parcels of land and a public meeting was held early in the next year, fifty men present. The Tysoe Allotments and Smallholdings Association was formed and soon had seventy-five members, an extraordinary number, representing a high proportion of the village, but perhaps some were young men living with their parents.

One may suppose my father's part in all this to have been a large one, possibly indispensable. It was the constant calls of members of the Association interrupting the kneading of her bread or causing her to drop the scissors at a crucial point in cutting out her children's clothes that made my patient mother agree that we needed more space. But Joseph was far from being the only effective member: the inclusion of tradesmen brought in a greater vigour and resilience and more 'know-how'. Then also, the Lower Townsmen joined, and in a tough fractious spirit. They were sometimes a roughish party, liking to stand apart a little from the other Towns. But now they had a story of frustration all their own, and brought power to the common effort.

Joseph became the first Secretary of the Association and held the office for many years—until all its main objects had been attained and its affairs reduced to routine. In these early days he urged his Committee to get influential support from outside the village; it might be possible to shame obstructors as they had been shamed in the matter of wages, fifteen years before. Get the local papers to regard their claim as news, get a well-known president, he urged. But to please the old Labourers' Association their President was adopted. Mr Daniel Fessey was a notable Tysonian—the only one I ever heard of who made a fortune. He was a member of a poor unfortunate family, one of whose members had been charged with manslaughter after the last crude boxing match. I remember him well; he decorated our early childhood. He had been the inventor of curious gadgets, for example a new stirrup which was adopted by cavalry regiments. With his small fortune he was undergoing a change into a dapper and mannered exquisite, reminding one of Shakespeare's Frenchmen. By the time I knew him his clothes were of the finest; his speech fantastically precise and his manner to man, woman and child elaborate—but as full of friendliness as of formality. Just as he was never ashamed of those disreputable ancestors so he sympathised with the poor and stood by their small movements.

The Committee thought it best to await the publication of the Government's Allotments Bill before moving far, so they drew up regulations for their non-existent holdings, visited the Southam Association and corresponded with the agent of the Compton estate, stating their needs and asking for a first refusal of land. When the Bill became law Tysoe's would-be cultivators gave it a sardonic attention. Under the Act, if no land were available after elaborate inquiries and other processes, the Sanitary Authority was given power to propose a special Act of Parliament to compel some owner or owners to sell land. What a strange body to choose! It neither could nor would use such powers, said the Tysoe Association. They were right: in all England only one of these Acts was ever proposed.

Meanwhile there was the Queen's jubilee. Why should men grudged by a government a scrap of land to dig celebrate the long reign of its head? Majuba and Khartoum and the new imperialism were sharpening the atmosphere. Many sensing future trouble looked back thankfully over fifty years of comparative peace. Fifty years on the throne, and a woman! —the Queen could be acclaimed. So the village was at one in a mild rejoicing. In May the village made ready—a committee was chosen to plan celebrations. The Managers of the School hung up a huge picture of the old Queen with her grey hair, her solemn face and wide blue Garter Ribbon; and on each side of her, smaller pictures of the neatly bearded Prince of Wales and of Princess Alexandra with a wall of tight yellow curls along her brow; another of the Queen was hung in the Reading Room, a full-length portrait with a profile of her face and of stout, gathered skirts sloping far back behind her, and yet another in the Peacock, flanked by Disraeli and Gladstone.

The great day was the twentieth of June. After the service in the church, an oak tree was planted on the green by the Vicar's wife, who was that rare thing, a woman of intellectual interests. Her speech stressed the hope for village unity. Two hundred and thirty years earlier had died, she said, a venerable Vicar of the Parish. After forty-nine years of service he had gone—said an entry in the Parish Register for 1654—'to enter on his eternal Jubilee'. In the seventeenth century England had known fifty years of doctrinal quarrels and civil war; clergymen had been turned from their cures, and churches irreverently used. But while in other parishes there had been bitter discord, John Stevenage and another Stevenage, his nephew, had quietly continued their duties in the old peaceful way. Let all take example by John Stevenage. Let all pray for peace—peace for the nation and within the nation, peace in Tysoe. Then the Vicar pointed to the trees, young and old, that had been planted on the green, witnessing to other occasions when the village had been at one—the

William and Mary elm, celebrating the coming of that man of peace, the Prince of Orange; the tree of constitutional liberty (the 'Franchise Tree'); and now this sapling, the tree of loyalty.

It was always the same; all Tysonians felt that the village ought to be at one. Those who opposed the Vicar were mischief-makers, disturbers of the peace; on the other hand he and his missus brought from inferior parishes notions that no self-respecting folk could put up with. The different patterns of community at the back of minds, the needs, the passions, the fantasies—these though doubtless understood in part were never made plain in the discussions.

The Jubilee interval was over. In October the Vicar invited the holders of the ten-pole allotments to a tea-party and made a speech to them on their duties. Allotments, he said, might be rightly cultivated by them, under certain conditions. They must have the necessary leisure to till them; they must apply manure; the produce must be consumed at home (which meant they were not free to sell it). A sixteenth of an acre was the right extent. Possibly if a man had no garden at all, it might not be wrong to have two sixteenths. They must on no account spend too much time and strength on the allotment to the neglect of what was due to their masters, not forgetting that their Heavenly Master required spiritual work of them on Sundays.

If it was natural to the Vicar to think of God as the men's Master, on the same side as the masters, nevertheless he had done his duty, as he saw it, in the matter of allotments. As long ago as 1856 he had, with his Churchwardens, taken twelve acres on Tysoe Hill to supply the Upper Town men, and later another small field for the Church Town. The men thought he charged an unreasonable rent and grumblingly asked each other where the money went. Perhaps they were wrong in their suspicions, but no account of profits and losses was ever given to them. Now, to satisfy the new Association, fifty more acres would be needed for a good start. A tall order that, especially in view of the Marquis's steward's answers to Joseph's letters: 'there is no land available for small holdings, nor likely to be'. The Committee of the Association had now in hand the question of a more convenient field for the Lower Town where the existing allotments were, at the best, over a mile distant. The small farms actually in the Town could not be asked to spare home meadows, but there was one landowner-farmer with an estate stretching from Sunrising to the Lower Town pound a mile away: he could certainly spare some ground. Sunrising House and estate had changed hands fairly recently and no one had much acquaintance with the owner, nor could they gain it: the President's letters to him went unanswered.

For its larger project the Association cherished a hope still. The Marquis was ill and Earl Compton was said to be in charge, over the steward, of the Compton and Tysoe estates. The Secretary breathed that it might be possible to by-pass the steward; he believed that Lord Compton's liberalism was of a practical sort. The men studied every farm in the parish, never mind whose it might be, and watched every change of ownership and tenancy, but nothing turned up. Despairing thoughts turned to the Town Lands again. There was dissatisfaction about the repair of the Feoffees' cottages and other parts of their administration, but before the Committee had brought itself into the frame of mind to try to struggle along that old dusty path there came a gleam of hope. The Marquis had one farm in the Church Town and the farmer was (someone chanced to know) ill of a fatal trouble, and he had no son to whom the farm must in justice be offered. There were difficulties, of course: the first three fields of the farm, as one entered from the Back Lane, were home grounds of the farm: you could not ask for those! But the three fields beyond could be reached from both Church and Lower Town. There was no road to them, but one could be made and would benefit the rest of the farm. If only the Association could get those fields and then presently another on the other side of the Middle Town! Well, then the Tysoe labourer could if he chose be both free and well-fed. The Committee had to keep mum about their faint hope; members would fall off if there were more disappointments.

About this time Earl Compton was living at Castle Ashby, and it so happened that Joseph was working a few miles from the mansion. How was he to get past servants and secretary and steward to talk with the Earl? There was only one way: Joseph stood in the road, waylaying his carriage. He met with recognition and welcome: an interview was arranged. It took place in the Castle Library with the gleaming gilt-and-calf book-backs all around and seeming to stretch to the dim distance. By now Earl Compton was a member of the London County Council and chairman of one of its committees. Both men were Liberals, late Gladstonian Liberals. There was nothing about their minds of the cold *laissez faire* which the books declare to be the ancestor of the Liberal creed. On the contrary both were eagerly working for the common good, and faith in God and in human nature made their work full of warm hope. However, Lord Compton made all the objections to Joseph's proposition that an enemy could have made. It had to be proved that no other solution could be found, that the Association was capable of managing land, that a road could be built and would not damage the property. What might dish the project was criticism, if only implied, of the great man's agent and other dependants. But dates, copies of letters, statements of wages, a labourer's weekly budget, and the Association's minutes were all-cogent and in the end a promise passed, that 'fifty acres of ground on the Marquis's estate in the most convenient spot possible would be made available to the Tysoe Allotments and Smallholdings Association as soon as occasion served'. But his lordship had no idea when that would be.

After the tough interview, a moment's relaxation. Compton guided Joseph out, past statues and footmen, to the head of the wide white steps before the mansion. At some little distance stood a man with his back to them in a frock-coat looking at a formal bed of flowers. 'You know', said the host, 'of Mr Bret Harte?' Joseph took in the frock-coat. It took time. 'Where's Frou-Frou?' asked he. 'Or the bowie-knife, eh?' said Compton. 'No wild west, now,' Joseph told Hannah, 'Bret Harte likes "mik mik" in palaces now.'

Thirty years had passed since the first Town Lands inquiry. Nothing had been gained then by the poor in their attack. The recipients of the Christmas doles (for doles they had become) had settled down to receiving goods instead of money; for the women, isolated for the most part in their homes, the insult had lost its warning bitter taste; they curtsied gratefully to the Vicar's wife and her sister who brought the flannel, as though it had come from the ladies' own stores. But the men, through their conversations in field and inn, kept their memories. The case against the Feoffees was built up again, now, on plaints both old and new. A petition was again drawn up, not by the Allotments Association, but by its members, in *ad hoc* meetings, complaining of the ruinous cottages, of money being spent on objects within the scope of local authorities and of lack of access to the accounts. All these defects of administration stemmed, so the petitioners said, from the unsatisfactory composition of the body of trustees. It was a closed, self-recruiting body, while in justice and for efficiency, it should be representative. A brief but more forceful document, this, than the earlier petition.

Only one of the present Trustees, the Vicar, remained from the group of 1859, but seven of the nine names were the same. Sons or brothers had been elected by remaining trustees to succeed those who died. The two men of new names made little difference; one was the landowner-farmer of Sunrising who answered no letters, and the other was also a farmer, and their ideas were identical with the Vicar's.

On the other side there was more change. The complaints no longer looked so anxiously to their own attitude, wanting to be 'fair and rationable'. Now they were all for exacting reason from the other side. Some at least of the besiegers could relate their case to nation-wide changes and movements (this very question of the administration of charities was being raised in scores of parishes), but the chief difference lay in the improvement in their techniques. The first step in the overt campaign showed this. A series of letters was published in the *Warwick Advertiser* and the *Banbury Guardian*, reviewing the history of the dispute, and raising all the questions. But the conduct of their case at the inquiry gave the men much anxiety. Lawyers had failed their side before. It was clear from the old reports that the Inspector, their own solicitor, and the Commissioners had all been on the side of the Feoffees. Mr Bolton King came to one of their meetings. 'No lawyers', he advised, 'but someone who cares, and who knows your case inside out and has some practice in speaking.' 'What of the writer of the letters?' he asked. He imagined, he said, that everyone knew who the writer was. He imagined that he was in the room. Yes, they said, naming no names, but that member must not lead; he must remain among them on the floor; they knew the way he had of putting in a word at all the right moments in a meeting. It is plain that Mr King thought Joseph would make a capital advocate, and perhaps a little jealousy refused him this more public and more difficult office, but if so what matter? Joseph himself then suggested Mr Fessey, the President of the Allotments Association. Yes! He would do! He would not be showy, but he would not fail, not in any way.

The Inquiry meeting was not so very different from the former one. There were roughly the same groups of people, though attendance was still larger. But there was only one labourer in a smock-frock, fewer women in aprons and caned print bonnets, fewer speakers used in full the old speech. The confidence gained by one party had perhaps been lost by the other. The indignation and self-defence of the Trustees' party worked itself out in their defence of the Vicar; he was an old man, they said, had seen thirty-five years in the parish; it was shameful ingratitude to trouble him.

The petitioners had been, it seems, well drilled in the tactics of their side. Their aim was to gain a more representative Board, and therefore any and every fault of the Feoffees, any advantage of the petitioners, must be pressed home; all fair and square of course, but no weakness. And so the inquiry covered many points—the cottages; work undertaken that should be done by the Waywarden and paid for from the rates; the inefficiency of the waterworks for the Church Town; the steady refusal for thirty years to use any part of the lands to provide allotments. The tough and rough Lower Townsmen spoke up here; they had waited long enough! But the Poors' Fuel Lands, said the Vicar, had been given them for allotments. The Inspector said that he had been taken to see these. Had he walked? asked Mr Fessey. No? That was a pity; a pair of legs was an excellent measuring instrument; the men had to walk. 'A mile and a half from my house', called out Cyrus Winter, and Hubert Soden, 'Two miles from mine, and carry your tools on your back too.' Was no other ground available? asked the Inspector. Oh yes! one of the Trustees had himself a very large farm with land in a convenient position; that was just it—the Trustees had no will to be useful to a large part and that the poorest, of the village.

All the old points had been dealt with and the Inspector was visibly impressed. But the process had taken all day, from ten in the morning till three in the afternoon. Now came the most important question, that of the composition of the Board of Trustees. It was late; the stockmen among the labourers, already troubled by the thought of their animals not fed or bedded, shuffled clumsily out. Others, in spite of coaching, had not grasped that this was the essential point and, tired by the long effort of attention, staggered uncertainly on tiptoe after the stockmen, but a good many remained.

Mr Fessey reminded the Inspector and all present that Sir John Swinburne had lately spoken in Parliament on the need for Trustees of important charities to be representative. Here we have, he said, not a charity as that word is usually understood, but a Town Estate, the village's own possession, once administered by the inhabitants. Apart from that basic right it had been amply shown that the interests of those with most at stake were not served by this close body. Two centuries had shown that a body constituted as this one was would always choose as recruits men like themselves. They interpreted the expression 'substantial men' as having nothing to do with ability, character, experience, knowledge, goodwill —only with the number of a man's acres or the size of his money-bags. Let the Inspector judge from the present meeting whether the men of greater weight were all on the platform. 'On the floor below us, gentlemen, are men of intelligence; they have no estates of their own, but they are responsible for the moneys of public institutions; many have proved their capacity in public offices and have long experience of the village. There are men among the Trustees without even the last qualification.' The principle of fair representation of interested persons had long since been adopted in larger matters. But the Town Lands were important for Tysoe.

It was the Inspector's turn. His chief hope was that the Trustees would consent to have additional members of their Board elected in the Vestry Meeting. No, said the Vicar, it would lead to political and religious strife. The Inspector brought up his heavy gun. Here, he said, was evidently a very representative meeting. Feeling was strong that representation was desirable. He believed the Trustees would be reasonably met. If the objectors to the closed body chose to proceed, undoubtedly a contentious case must be certified to the Attorney-General. Thereupon the entire income of the Trust would be absorbed in legal expenses, perhaps for many years to come. Surely an amicable agreement could be arrived at? The Trustees sat silent. The Inspector paraphrased his argument, a second and third time. But the Vicar said 'No'. The word seemed to express all his meaning.

Land Hunger: the Promised Land

Change, he said, would cause dissension. In the present state of the parish representation would be calamitous. The Trustees would be sacrificing their trust if they gave up their right to appoint each other. Six and a half hours of discussion had brought them all up against a wall of negation.

A few weeks later came the Commissioners' Report. It was skimmed through and put aside. No one wanted 'a contentious case', the fools' work of wasting an infinity of time and energy on the throwing away of the Town Lands' income. Well, every man had now a vote; let them fight on a wider field! No blood flowed in these village battles but from the wounds inflicted there ebbed away faith and patience; maybe Tysoe's life is still anaemic from the loss.

By now it was 1890, three years since the Jubilee, and more since the founding of the Allotments Association. After yet another two years of hope deferred Earl Compton was able to fulfil his promise to the Allotments and Smallholdings Association. The fields offered were the very ones the Association had seen to be the most likely to be freed. They were not so very convenient but would serve. From the Lower Town there was only a footpath to them: all manure and crops would have to go round by Church Town, a mile, sometimes nearly two. Still, this was a happy ending and beginning. The new allotments included old fields and old furlongs—Briars Meadow, Bishop's Close, Breach Furlong, Knitting Pin Leys, Sandy Furlong and the rest, but all these had long been prophetically subsumed under a single name— the Promised Land. The men reached it in 1893.

A road was triumphantly made, trees were cut down and drains laid and then the Association settled down to test its rules and its members. Not all the cultivators had the necessary health or industry. Thistles flourished here and there and in time one or two members were threatened with a summons to County Court for their rent. But after a sifting process the Association worked well until, after many years, a great change had taken place in village life.

The Vicar was right in supposing that a large allotment would involve the whole family of the holder in work. Primitive methods must be resorted to: for a long time many of the allotments were dug not ploughed, and the wheat was dibbled in by hand. Beans were planted by hand too, the father of a family dibbling with one hand, dropping in the bean with the other, and little son or daughter kicking in the soil. The women and children would often be weary from the reaping or potato picking, but good food more than compensated for that. Father might be ashamed to go to night-school and learn sums afresh, but his young son's attention to lessons would have a sharper quality because of seed-buying and the cost of tools. How different it was to glean corn on one's own land, and not by tolerance, and what joy for mothers and girls to carry hot dinner and steaming cans of tea for the meals among the stooks of corn, and to ride home on top of a small load of wheat that had been cut and carried by and for the family. Sights and sounds were all the more vivid for this sense of ownership. Mere anxious greedy grubbing was averted by comradeship within the family, between one allotment holder and another, and by the dignity of being responsible to and for an efficient Smallholdings and Allotments Association.

Joseph's part in this long work had been large and pervasive and remained so. The 'Promised Land' was far more to him than a mere economic field, and to his children. In the list of Daniels and Johns and Ezekiels requiring land in 1894 appears grandly the name 'A. W. Ashby'. Two years later occurs the minute of Committee, 'That a gratuity of two shillings be paid to A. W. Ashby for carrying round notices of all meetings, in the last two years'. This A.W.A. was Joseph's eldest son, eight years old at the first entry. Trudging round the three towns several times a year on behalf of the Smallholders was a suitable introduction to his life. When his hair was greying his advice on village agrarian institutions would be sought in countries on the other side of the world.

CHAPTER XI

VIGNETTES OF THE VILLAGE

M Y father's native gifts made for free expression but he never had, in writing, that conciseness that brings style! In conversation, a brief pause for a companion to see the inwardness of some incident, a smile inviting sympathy with a character in the story, comments from child or guest—all these helped to produce the effect he wanted: talk was his medium.

Nevertheless, he was a lifelong writer of one kind of thing and another. Some of his early essays (his early 'tries') are useful sources of a little knowledge of himself and his neighbours. In these his mind played as well as worked over village affairs. In his short 'vignettes' that were printed in journals now extinct—the *Land Magazine* and the *Land Agents' Record*—and sometimes in local newspapers, he showed with gaiety and pathos his view of Tysoe characters and incidents and groups. He liked to write as an onlooker, wide-minded and kindly, indulging, I think, in the fantasy of being at ease as to time and income. There were sometimes moments of the day, indeed, when he was so—that precious brief hour for him and Hannah of which their growing children would so soon rob them—in winter, when the babes were tucked in bed and they were together in the warm room, he with his paper and pen, she with her needle. My mother would refer to these times in her restrained way when even that little leisure had gone out of life, and a child felt her passion of regret for them.

Some of the writing cannot be recovered in full: there remain only printed fragments or faded manuscript sentences, but it is worth while to con them as if they were old photographs.

There are a few notes on Sabbath days as he knew and had

known them. In his small-boyhood, for example, he saw
cur-fighting matches on the green. A pair of bad-tempered,
half-starved old dogs were set upon each other by their
owners for five shillings a side. Their owners, he notes, so
far resembled their dogs as to make such a contest tolerable.
'But now', he writes in 1884, 'from the earliest dawn Sunday
is a quiet day. Even the cattlemen of the farms who must be
at their work at six in the morning walk up our broad,
straggled street with a leisurely air which is not possible on
other days. The church bells at evening ring out over a village
in which for hours all business, all loud voices, even the
children's play has been muted.'

By 1884 all the children had Sunday clothes. Who shall say
how much these added to the set-apart quality of the day?
Mothers were showing a degree of that divine, 'amazing
love' of which the hymns sang—laundering the little girls'
white bonnets of starched and goffered muslin, making
them Sunday frocks for summer out of old petticoats of
machine-made broderie anglaise, or winter ones from old
cloth garments rendered new by blue or scarlet braid. Even
the little boys had Sunday coats. It was more difficult to
retain a pair of breeches for Sunday, for the little boys felt now
that woman-made breeches, with their uncertain outlines, were
an indignity, and cried bitterly when their mothers made them.

Was it perhaps the Sunday Schools which now had had
over sixty years of existence, and one of them more, that had
made so holy the Sabbath? The children sat there in little
circular classes of six or ten and heard fascinating stories and
modern homely interpretations. There had been a great
change in fifteen years; they sang now of 'the lily of Siloam'
and 'Sharon's dewy rose' and hushed their voices to a whisper
to sing of little Samuel in the dark courts of the Temple.
Gentle confidence was being instilled, now, into their minds
instead of fear of death and punishment:

> I think when I read that sweet story of old
> When Jesus was here among men

How he called little children as lambs to his fold;
I should like to have been with them then.

Yet some disapproved of the changes. Old labouring
women might be seen eyeing the children and grown-ups on
their way to church and chapel so washed, shaven and starched.
To them this change was trivial. More pigs in the sty, more
food on the table, more independence to answer back to
farmer and Vicar—those were 'proper'. But the labouring
life as they had known it was of the earth earthy, and none
the worse for that. Gloves and starched bonnets and fringes
of whiskers involved a loss of dignity.

Sunday was curious from one point of view. Joseph noted
that if you stood on the green at about noon, or in the evening,
you might chance to hear the churchfolk, the Wesleyans and
the Primitives all singing the same hymn to celebrate 'the
birth of the same Babe, or the same sacrifice of the same
Saviour'. Why, then, not sing together a finer chorus?

Perhaps the distance between the singers was diminishing
but that brotherly mutual confidence had not yet been
achieved is shown by Joseph's record of a talk in which he
took part. (The Burial Act to which allusion is made was
passed in 1880: some of the names are invented.) Joseph
was on his way through the churchyard when he saw Jake
Wightman, an aged 'Primitive' labourer, now 'on his last
legs'. The old man stood in Joseph's path, leaning on his
stick, gazing around. As Joseph came up Jake spoke.
'I never took much account of the churchyard, Joseph, days
gone by, but now I likes to look at it. I be coming 'ere to
stop afoor long, now.' Joseph put off his errand to hear the
old man's mind. Though Jake had evidently a purpose he
would take time to come to his point. ''Tis a funny thing,
Joe,' he said, 'look you at all these stwuns. Never a man died
yet as 'ad any fault; ner nobody ever 'ated e'er a one on 'em.
'Tis different outside churchyard. But theers rich and poor
'ere all the saame. Look you; tons o' cold stwun to this side,
an' little uns or only graass t'other. Ever read old Blunt's

sentiments?' Jake pointed to a small low stone with faint outlines of a lozenge still showing on it, and crude eighteenth-
century cherubs smiling and gentle in each spandrel. The verse
was in another mood:

> This life is a city of crooked streets,
> Death is the market-place where all men meet.
> If life were merchandise that money could buy
> The rich would live and the poor would die.

' 1798,' said Joseph, 'that was the year the hedges were planted.
Perhaps the Blunts felt bad about that. Well, do you think
things have changed, Jake?' 'Parsons be chaanged,' Jake
affirmed, 'Duncombe 'ould'nt let Blunt say 'is say on a stwun.
That'll be George Blunt's grett-grandad. Queer folk they
Blunts was. Lawless they bin, cruel too. You know George's
little barn? You sin that piece o' horse skin nailed under
th'aaves? George's grandad 'ad 'is own back, 'e thought.
Marquis's aagent left 'is 'orse in the Paycock close an' Blunt
pricked 'im—'e were a saddler an' knacker saame as George
to this day—pricked 'im in a certain spot an' the poor craytur
bled to death. Blunt got the carcase o' coorse, an' somebody
else got the blaame. But Blunt told the taale when a noo
aagent come.'

After a pause for the horrid story to be realised the old
man resumed. 'Nobody wunt put no stwun o'er me an'
I dooant want 'em to. But I got a wish. I wants to be laad
wi' my old 'ooman. Us ought to waake up together. I know
what you ull say, Joe—as churchyards 'as precious little to
do wi' resurrection. I dooant know about that; but I thinks
of 'er lookin' for me, all in a confusion, bothered because
I ent theer. It's only a notion, but that's wheer I wants to be.'
Joseph said that, surely, there would be no difficulty? 'Well,
you says so, Joe, but I dooant know.' Jake went on: 'The
last yurr or two us chapel folks 'as our own minister to raad
the service, but since that begun the Reverent Duncombe,
'e ull 'ave us all buried together in yon corner, close th'
unbaptised babbies; an' my missus, 'er was buried bi 'im ten

yurr agoo, an' 'er lies o' this side. It can't be as parson 'as to
put us over theer. Gladstone ould never ha' let it be, as
I couldn't lie beside my missus. Joe! Joe! Duncombe 'ould
listen to you. I come 'ere five or six times now, o' purpose to
meet you an' ask you to goo to 'im.' The notes were written
before the story ended.

One of Joseph's 'vignettes' for this time records a scene in
the village street late one evening. It has the heading 'After
the Horse Show', but its true subject is an odd one—the
women against the men and the Porcupine, the name here
given to the public-house. There was less of drinking than in
Joseph's early youth, but still for the people's circumstances,
a tragic amount.

The evening was darkening and the Porcupine was already
spot-lighted by the oil-lamp over its door. A couple of
neighing stallions and some beribboned carthorses were tied
at the iron rings in the wall. Grooms and carters were inside,
slaking their thirst and discussing with the regular customers
the merits of the horses they were bringing back from the
Sheepford show. The warm look of the doorway and the
cheerful, rising sounds within were drawing in more men.
There was a group at the door chatting, waiting to move
forward. 'Then', wrote Joseph, 'a door at the further end of
the street was set ajar and the uncapped head of an elderly
female was seen. Some of the men turned towards the new
streak of light. Those who did not see it were startled by
the thin shrewish voice calling "John! John!" No John
answered and the voice called again. This time the heedless
John, who was or should have been the directing genius of
that household, called from a group of men standing on the
causeway on the same side of the street, "What do you want?"
"I want to tell you to keep away from that aal 'us, that's what
I wants." "You just keep that shiny yold yed o' yourn inside,
and mind your own business." The woman moved from
her own doorway and placed herself between John's group
and the door of the Porcupine, and quietly observed to her lord

and master, "You bean't agooin into that aal 'us tonight, so dooan't be thinking as you be."

'"Be you master, old 'ooman?" inquired one of John's companions. "I be so fur John's master as I be gooin wheer 'e goes this night, whether 'e likes it or whether you." By now other doors had opened and two or three other women were listening to the dialogue. "I thinks you wants a drop, old gel!" ejaculated a fresh speaker. "I dooan't want a drop, and our John bean't agooin' into the Porcupine this night, and you needn't think it." The other women drew a little nearer and their faces were serious as they watched old Jinny and the men. They said nothing but placed themselves so that Jinny could not be crowded. The men's sly and satirical smiles died on their faces and some of them slunk away. If they made fun, later, of old Jinny's shrewishness it would not be in their own homes.'

It is plain that Joseph was on Jinny's side, but he would certainly have frowned on even a 'silent unorganised league' of women except against the one enemy of drink.

One more choice I make from Joseph's sketches. These notes relate to the years 1892 and 1893—to the two Vestry Meetings of those years and the events between. There was much talk at that time of changes in local government. County Councils had been instituted and some day soon parishes, too, would have their elected councils to succeed the old moribund Vestry Meetings.

The first of the two meetings took place in the Old School on Easter Monday 1892 at eleven in the morning. The Vicar took the chair behind the old rickety table. In front of him on low scrubbed wooden benches sat five men, all in their farmers' second-best tweeds, two Suthertons, two Godwins and a Dannell (these must be invented names but later the names for places are the true ones). It was the traditional day and the traditional hour for the meeting. By this time all public meetings except Vestries were held in the evenings. Before the enclosure of the open fields and the growth of the village, when the customs of the Vestry Meetings grew up, labour must have been less pressing. In 1892 it would have been contrary to a deep set of mind for most small farmers, to say nothing of labourers, to wash and tog themselves suitably for a meeting in the middle of any morning except the Sabbath.

Just as the church clock struck eleven and the Vicar pulled the minute book out of his large pocket, Joseph Hardeman (the writer gives himself one of his family's names) entered the room and sat down two or three benches behind the little oligarchy. After a few minutes another man entered—old Ratnitt Hayward (men were 'old' by fifty or before). Ratnitt also was not quite of the inner circle and he took his seat by Joseph. Ratnitts and Haywards had been fifty-acre farmers in the village from time immemorial and Ratty still held one of the family farms. He maintained many old ways including, sometimes, attendance at the Easter Vestry.

The main part of the business did not take long. 'According to custom' was the ruling phrase in the minutes the Vicar read. A few looks of assent settled who should be, according to custom, nominated as overseers for the year, for final appointment by the magistrates; who were to be assessors and collectors of taxes, and who guardians of the poor. It was all a question of who, in the group attending, had recently held these offices; practically they were held in turn. There was just one more office to be filled—that of Waywarden. The Vicar looked at Ratty, 'Your turn, Ratty', he said. 'No,' said Ratty, 'it bean't my turn. I dooan't know nothing about roads. There be plenty of folk in the Towns better for the job nor me.' 'But they aren't here', said the Vicar. 'And for why?' asked Ratty, without staying for an answer. 'Folks have forgot the Vestry. Yurrs agoo—I've told you afoor— a fello' used to be sent round the Towns to remind the ratepayers. Now every householder can come and nobody dooan't.' The Vicar ignored these remarks, saying that the Highway Board did most of the work now—only occasional jobs fell to the Waywarden. He would enter the name 'Ratnitt Hayward'. 'I dooan't want to do it', said Ratnitt. All the occupants of the front benches turned with eyebrows high to look at Ratnitt and then at the Vicar. 'Put him down', they said, and then the meeting was over.

Meanwhile the writer, Joseph, had been like the ghost at the table, carefully ignored. Not even Ratty had made reference to him in any way, but now he and Ratty left the room together and walked, talking, down the street. What would Ratty say was the reason why the meetings were so very small now? Joseph asked. After all if Ratty and he could go, so could others. Was it because there was so little real business left? 'Plenty o' business to tidy the plaace up, if anybody wanted to,' said Ratty, 'but things be upset. You Methodis',' he said, 'you stopped gooin' to the Vestry afore my old grandad died in 1840; summat to do wi' objectin' to church raate an' election o' churchwardens, so my Dad said. You folk 'ouldn't goo, an' now the Vicar an' t'others dooan't want nobody.' As a good churchman and for Joseph's good, he summed up 'You blaames the Vicar an' 'e thinks you bin theer today to try an' upset 'em. 'Twas the Methodis' fault an' dooan't you forget it, Joe.' Joseph said he was no up-setter; he liked old ways, but there had to be change. 'Needn't be no chaange', said Ratty, 'except what be sense.'

In February, a few weeks before the Vestry Meeting, there had been the usual flooding of the Church Town brook; the New Pool, too, also fed by a streamlet from the hills, overflowed, and a swift brook ran down the street and made a large shallow pool in Saddlers' Lane. The school was between the two floods; some people could not reach the church. A few houses stood for a while in an inch or two of water. Every year these floods came, but this time they had been unusually severe. In November they came again. It was quite the usual thing to have a smaller flood at that time, but now they were considerable.

Vignettes of the Village

The Waywarden acted in a most surprising manner. He engaged men to clear out the Church Town brook and raise its banks. He found a mason to build higher the stone pillars under the footbridge by which the Lower Town children must cross to reach the school. In the course of a day or two every man and child and a good many women, too, as errands brought them near, took a look at the goings-on. Groups of men gathered at the edge of the mud and water and called out to Ratty and his men who were working in it. ' "Tyent no good, Ratty, if you dooan't draan all down from the New Pool as well.' 'Have to put them piles oop higher yet if the childer be to goo to school dryfut.' Ratty replied at last. 'You goo to school, an' study to tell me summat as I dooan't know.' Ratty's fellow Vestrymen came. Overseers and rates assessors naturally spoke about the rates, but only in a murmur lest the other school of critics should overhear. Ratty's crowd was growing, some on one side of the widened brook and some on the other. They called across, 'Oughto ha' been done yurrs agoo.' Mothers of schoolchildren had begun to arrive, rather timidly but with purpose in their eyes. 'Something like a Waywarden', was their word. They told Ratty, without requiring him to break his silence, how the boys had had to sit in school in wet feet, and how mothers had been cumbered all washing-day by the little children unable to reach school.

The local Highway Board has long since gone into oblivion, and we need not explain, though Joseph must, how its chairman's approval of the next stage in operations was almost secretly obtained.

Next, then, Ratty took his men up to the New Pool, nearly a quarter of a mile from the brook. There they broke up the road ready to lay drains. The water would have to be carried all the way to the brook, joining it at a point just below the bridge to Lower Town. That is, it must go down the street to the Porcupine's stables, along Saddlers' Lane, past the Curate's House, down the slinket that led to the school, and then beyond the school and through a corner of the playground. It would have to be laid deep along the street because of differences of level; after that there was plenty of fall. On one or two occasions taciturn strangers had come to look at the work, and gone away nodding satisfaction. This was the biggest job villagers had seen tackled by one of themselves for many a long day. What had happened to Ratty, asks Joseph? He had no reputation for audacity or self-assertion: nobody less the rebel or reformer. He was a pretty good farmer, but what did he know about draining? 'Plenty,' said the know-alls, 'can't farm Henleaze without.' The popular sense of humour had been stirred from the first. Ratty's continued refusal to talk of his intentions, the little mystery of his authority, the guessed-at disapproval of certain folk all increased the joke. And now it was sweetened by admiration for a big job tackled in the right way.

The little story ends at the next Vestry Meeting. According to custom the election of the Waywarden is left to last, but before that took place, there must be a report from the present active holder of the office. The Vicar waited. 'Well, Ratty?' he finally asked. 'Wun't be no floods down Saddlers' Laane for a bit, Muster Duncombe.' Someone must have quoted this adequate report, for it became a saying apt in thunderstorm and tempest, 'wun't be no floods down Saddlers' Laane'.

CHAPTER XII

SOCIOLOGIST INTO MISSIONARY

WHILE the road to the Promised Land was being made and the Waywarden was vanquishing floods, my father's own affairs must have been very pressing. He had to start his own large allotment of an acre, soon two acres, at 'The Promise'; he moved his family to a new home; he was writing articles not only for the Warwick and Leamington papers but also for the *English Labourer's Chronicle* and the *Land Magazine*. He must have found time to read books on history and rural affairs, or his own writings could not have achieved their quality. In some ways the years 1891, 1892, and 1893 saw the acme of his work as a young man: his fourth child, myself, was born in 1892 and from now on he would have to put first the work that would give his family a reliable background.

In his letters to the county papers before the second Town Lands Inquiry and in his articles on allotments and like topics Joseph had shown a power to set out facts clearly and to interpret them tellingly, bringing to light fresh implications. His friend Bolton King had renounced costly and risky experiments in rural betterment and now he had a different idea. His early efforts had been lashed by Joseph's critical whip: now let Joseph work and he would comment! The plan was for the two men to make a close study of a rural area so as to arrive at the facts about the condition of village labourers. Thus they would make ill-informed talk an anachronism. The *Economic Journal* was appearing quarterly and was eager for contributions; the editor had promised to print the report on a survey.

There was need for this job to be done. During Arch's campaign the condition of agricultural workers had come to be understood even in the House of Lords and in bishops' palaces, but in twenty years this hard-given knowledge had been lost. Optimism had won one of its easy victories: speakers in both Houses of Parliament were describing the happy state of the labourer—his wages raised, his cottage improved—while mourning the hardships of landlords and farmers in the prolonged depression of agriculture.

The depression was real enough. Farmers' fortunes had declined rapidly in the late seventies and early eighties. During the years just before Joseph and Bolton King started their work, weather and prices had been better. But anxiety remained. By now a ton of wheat could be sent from Chicago to Liverpool for twenty-five shillings! Enormous quantities were arriving. Argentine beef and Canterbury lamb had appeared at Sunday dinner-time on labourers' tables. They were decried as uneatable and the pervasive snobbery of the time put them beyond the social pale, but wise farmers quietly bought a joint and knew that they would climb the social ladder.

You could see in Tysoe and around that farmers had suffered. They no longer paid subscriptions to the Hunt or sent their daughters to Cheltenham College or the good Leamington school where a foreign princess had once spent a year, but to poor little establishments in Kineton and Banbury, with cheap teaching and much foolish lisping. But they kept their horses for riding and their larders still held game and poultry. The degree of adversity was sufficient to stir farmers' minds, and at last Mr Gardner of Burland and his like bought the self-binders and improved drills they had so often contemplated in the yard at the Britannia Works at Banbury. Soon they were calculating that machinery would allow them to market as much wheat from their reduced arable as they had done formerly from twice the acreage. The Marquis, owner of a number of London streets, had dropped their rents. Of course small farmers with poorer landlords and no bank balances were harder pressed.

Certainly the labourers were a little better off. A few men in Tysoe could now hold out for a wage of thirteen shillings.

Sociologist into Missionary

The price of toppings had come down with the price of wheat and the cottage pigs benefited, not only in diet: men built new red-brick pigsties that show up still against the old grey-brown garden walls. Sometimes after the old fashion of dating every house and every good piece of walling their builders studded the high back walls of the sties with blue bricks, shaping the figures for the year, 1881 and 1891.

But say what you might, the labourer's gains were small. To congratulate him and condole with landowner and farmer was to assume that he could live well on farthings while they starved on pounds, that his wife fed the family from a widow's cruse, and that he had the self-control of an Indian mystic in spending his money and his time. But in addition to that and worse was the view, still often quite consciously held, that it was right and proper for the labourer to have such conditions of life as fastened him to his native spot and drove his boys at the earliest moment on to the land, other people's land, and his girls into the kitchens of the better-off.

Joseph, of course, had no need to re-learn all this: indeed anyone who cared could see that over a large part of England the labourer was still half-starved. But Mr King's enthusiasm moved him. He could begin the proposed inquiry at once but at some point there would have to be an interval. Some of his articles had brought him an invitation it would have been hard to decline—to tour through three counties as a missioner in a Red Van. At that time fortunate English villages were brightened by visits from a rainbow series of missionary vans—yellow, blue, 'sunrise' and red. Their drivers taught lively lessons from pitches on the greens and roadsides. That the lessons were various and somewhat contradictory was perhaps the best lesson of all. One van taught the Disraelian outlook, one the Radical, and a third warned against the dangers of disestablishing the Church. No Irish Plunkett or Danish Grundtvig had arisen to lead the farmworker whither he wished to go, but many were anxious to take him by the hand to the ballot-box.

According to the Red Vans the disease of the countryside was 'landlordism'—and yet landlords were the rulers of England! The means of eliminating them was a tax on land, small at first but increasing as the years went by until there were no rent receivers. The vans did not offer the pure milk of the Single Tax: the Land Restoration League which sent them out saw no harm in land being owned by tillers of the soil. All the same the doctrine was perhaps a trifle narrow; a sound Liberal might have had more qualms about the mission had not the prospect pleased. To be peripatetic had always charmed Joseph. On the long slow journey he would be able to compare parts of Northamptonshire, Bedfordshire and Cambridgeshire with his own area. And the subsidiary aim of the vans, to recruit for the Agricultural Labourers Union, would give him scope he liked well.

In fact before the Van called for Joseph most of the work of the survey was done. The area selected lay about and between the homes of the two men—a substantial acreage of South Warwickshire. It contained fifty-six villages besides hamlets. The southern half of the district was ill-served by railways and remote from towns; in the northern section several towns were fairly easily reached. Some lime-burning and cement-making was carried on there—migration was easier and employment somewhat more varied. Villages varied in size and in being 'open' or 'closed'—that is, in some the land was owned by a small number (in a few cases, only one) of land-owners, and in others ownership was much divided. In short it demonstrated 'the immense variation of rural life'.

By local trains, on his old 'penny-farthing' and on foot Joseph visited every village, staying at the inn or in some cottage. There were some formal, easily tapped sources of information—registrars, secretaries of Friendly Societies and other associations, the County Constabulary, agents of Assurance Companies. Mr King paved the way for him to useful clergymen and magistrates; he had his own access to Methodists, and branches of the Union. But some of the facts

148

must be drawn from minds in which they had never been formulated. To go always to the fluent folk would be to miss much. But the slower-living folk had excellent memories. Walk over an allotment-holder's ground with him, bide his time, and presently every detail of time spent, the quality of crops and the use to which they would be put, and his few cash transactions, would be yours—if you were Joseph Ashby. Similarly, over tea with slices of bread and home-made lard and black pepper a woman who had never made a note of what she spent would tell him precisely what had become of her weekly ten shillings for several weeks back. As for information relating to a whole village—the rents of every farm, extent of each and every cottage garden, the agricultural machinery in use, how many and what sort of persons had left the village in the last ten years—he knew how to find the gathering places of the talkers—not always the public-house—where he would be provided with sound and full information, delivered by some, corroborated and modified by others. It was not that he was insinuating or familiar. Men and women felt it—as I saw often in my childhood—a pleasure and an opportunity to tell their experience in that large presence and to those blue eyes, darkening and twinkling at every turn of information.

He took first a general view of his district and was not cheered. There were quite a number of untenanted farms, especially in the northern section. Walking a sad mile from Southam station to the village, he saw pastures so rough that 'the sheep could have played at hide and seek'. Neglected ground must always produce gloom in a countryman and words from another native of the south of the county came to Joseph as he walked between the high hawthorn hedges: 'darnel, hemlock, and rough fumitory' were growing on the leas and 'hateful docks, rough thistles, keckses', on the 'even mead'. There were signs, too, as in Shakespeare's day, of folk 'grown to wildness'. Along the roads from town to town he met a great number of tramps in their flapping ragged top-coats and shuffling shoes, with great cuts to let out a toe or swollen joint. And in every lane off these highways were gipsies, sometimes a true Romany encampment with a fire and iron pots on it smelling of rabbit or hare, and an old woman beside it smoking a pipe (rather a shocking sight to a Victorian, to whom refinement in a woman was such a high virtue). There would be a pile of green willow sticks for making clothes-pegs, sheets of soldering iron and partly made tin bottles, and balls of string for netting game-bags and cooking-bags for cottagers' boiling-pots. Their horses were old and jaded; bread they had begged lay about in the mud. Other gipsies not 'of the true race' kept together in families with one poor horse and an old cart. But none of these was necessarily of any agricultural class; they were England's rather than Warwickshire's problem.

Whatever the state of farmers' fields, allotments and cottage gardens were well-tended everywhere. Gardens sometimes rose to heights in cults of this flower and that and told of something never revealed by field or allotment— of domestic harmony, attachment to home, and love of colour and scent. There were villages, however, where a score or thirty cottages had no gardens—hardly space to turn up the pails on. He instanced one—'a place of drunkenness and dirt'. It was near the railway line from Birmingham to Banbury, on the top of the northernmost spur of the Edge Hills. One could imagine it, with its keen air and glorious views of the Warwick and Oxford counties, becoming a small summer resort; it was missing its chances.

But Whatcote in the south of the county was even worse than Ratley. It 'would be difficult to imagine a village socially lower'. Though no further from towns than many others, it seemed 'half deserted and half lost'. Twenty-five years before, though the soil was heavy, the crops could hardly have been beaten for weight and quality: now the land had gone to the bad. On Sundays men and boys might be seen in their working clothes playing hop-scotch and leap-frog in front of the houses. A few cottages were rented at sixpence per week and were worth no more. Land was owned by the Earl of Macclesfield, who had certainly failed to lead or inspire, even in agriculture, but a Wesleyan chapel had recently been built there—and the reader gathers that there was now a glimmer of hope.

To contrast with Ratley and Whatcote no ideal village was found, but there was Southam with several well-filled places of worship, the largest Temperance organisation in the district, and its off-shoot, a fine brass band. It had also a co-operative society. In its gardens were seen its special cults, of carnations and chrysanthemums. It was a large village, though not the largest, and active in it was a certain resident doctor. It was he who had helped to get the land for allotments of three kinds—garden plots, large arable allotments, and a meadow or two for cow-keepers. Southam was large enough for varied social activities and had leadership unspoiled by domination.

Such general impressions as these Joseph recorded in his *Through Warwickshire Villages*, a long series of articles in the *Leamington Chronicle*. Then there were the final visits, the precise list of topics to be drawn up, and the record sheets to plan. Before all this was finished the Red Van had arrived at his door.

The Land Restoration League was a smallish but varied company. Subscriptions were paid by followers of Henry George; a number of young village clergymen, admirers of Charles Kingsley and touched by Christian Socialism, had joined the League and it was their journal, the *Church Reformer*, which printed the fullest reports of the Red Vans' tours.

Hannah had agreed that Joseph must go with the Van, though it meant a hard season for the mother of four, with animals and an arable holding in addition to care for. The beginning of the adventure was shared by all the household. An old horse drew the Red Van into the Back Lane and Joseph's elderly fellow missioner stepped out. Mr Murdoch, a good Scot, was vigorous, still red-headed, with a fine powerful voice both for singing and speaking. He had a fervent love of his doctrine and his explosive Scottish consonants lent themselves to a very downright exposition of it. But he did not talk of the single tax in Hannah's house; he had homelier doctrines to propound. The salvation of the cowkeeper was to be found in prickly comfrey! While her husband was away, Hannah must prepare to raise seed for the Tysoe folk (she did so, and had a 'beastly smothering mess' in her garden as the seeds ripened). Milk, it was another of his doctrines, was unfit to drink until it had turned sour. Hannah must find a can in which a quart of milk could safely swing under the van as the missioners went along. Still more entertaining and less exacting were Mr Murdoch's songs. He carried his kilt in the van, and the evening before Joseph and he set off he put it on. From the street and the lane men came in expecting talk about taxation, but what they heard, in a voice more powerful even than that of the strongest singer in the Primitive Chapel, were Scots ballads and merry songs. There was much talk at the time of miraculous electricity; to the little boy Arthur watching and hearing Mr Murdoch it was as if the elderly Scotsman was filled with the new power.

John Murdoch was quite a notable man. In his younger days he had fought hard against crofter clearance in his home country. He had been the rhymester of that crusade, 'Bard of the Braes', and now he was the hymn-writer of the Red Vans.

So John, Joseph, and Jonathan the old horse, started off for Banbury on their way into Northamptonshire. The van itself was a missioner. It shouted its own messages, announcing on its crimson sides the articles of the faith; on one side

FAIR RENTS

FAIR WAGES

THE LAND FOR ALL

and on the other:

JUSTICE TO LABOUR

ABOLITION OF LANDLORDISM

Sociologist into Missionary

In its big cupboard it carried a fuller exposition of the doctrine in books and pamphlets that were laid out for sale in each village—a few copies of Henry George's *Progress and Poverty*, a few of J. S. Mill's *On Liberty*, but chiefly scores of pamphlets, popular expositions of the Single Tax, of the Radical programme and speeches made at meetings of the Land Restoration League, and always a pile of the current *Church Reformer*.

The plan was for the van to stay two nights in large villages where they could be sure of audiences, and to make a point of visiting the most backward of the smaller ones, staying one night only. Early notice would have invited trouble in 'landlord-ridden' villages, so on arrival Joseph's first job was to give notice of the meeting to be held. He bought groceries in the shop, stamps in the post office, drank a glass of wine at the inn and bought milk at a farm, telling about the meeting everywhere. It was his hobby to get farmers to come—the distance between them and their labourers was absurd! And assuming that the tax on landlords was a good idea, they should be joining with their labourers to get it. The farmers were at least humorously attracted by the legend ABOLITION OF LANDLORDISM.

If a village had a green, there the van was pitched. The meetings always started with a song, easy of phrase, set to a familiar hymn-tune. The first time of singing, Murdoch read it out two lines at a time, then, sustained by his great voice, the crowd sang it easily. It might be

> We plough and sow, we are so very, very low
> That we delve in the dirty clay,
> Till we bless the plain with the golden grain
> And the vale with the fragrant hay.
>
> Our place we know, we are so very, very low:
> 'Tis down at the landlord's feet.
> We're not too low the grain to grow
> But too low the grain to eat.

Then Murdoch's speech followed—just such a one as the *Church Reformer* outlined in mere English. In Murdoch's brogue it seemed full of force and cogency.

'Are you satisfied with life here in *X*? Has life, and have your neighbours, made a fair bargain with you? I know the answer, No. And I will tell you what you complain of. Your hours are long, your work uncertain; you pay high rents for wretched cottages; your common lands and your roadside wastes have been stolen, your parish charities have disappeared. You ask for allotments and cannot get them or only at a rent three times as high as the farmer pays. Your squire won't let you grow what you like in your garden (or 'build a cottage' or 'put up a chapel', or 'hold meetings on the green'—whatever local circumstances called for). It may be the parson who gives the orders—the squire appoints him to preach contentment to you; or the farmer, who licks the boots with which the landlord tramples on him as well as on you. Have you water fit to drink? Dare the publican let you hold a radical meeting in his big room? Not if his house is "tied", either to a landlord or a brewery.

'When you are too old to work what is going to happen to you? You will be given a couple of loaves of bread a week or carted off to the workhouse by the hands of those you sweated for all your life.

'The fish in the river, the birds in the air, the wild creatures in the fields and in the woods, whose are they? If you fail to understand how a wild animal can be private property, your landlord sitting in the seat of justice will see to it that you have seven days leisure to think about the problem. The old English sports and gambling games have disappeared—so wicked they were. But it is all right to sell your citizen-rights at a Primrose tea for a few slices of cake and the sight of some juggling (political or otherwise). Education? Dear friends, you have the Reading Room, religiously closed on your one day of leisure, from which the Vicar's wife carefully excludes all the papers you want to read.

'Yet ye are many, they are few. Your labour is more necessary to them than their money is to you, for you have produced their wealth and can do the same again. Join the Union!...and better still support the Land Restoration League, and better again, get rid of landlords altogether.'

Then it was Joseph's turn. Murdoch left it to him to explain how the Land Tax would work, breaking up in time all the great estates, destroying the power of wealth and aristocracy, and freeing village life to go forward—or back, if you liked—to freedom. This dutifully done he was free to finish his homily in a more characteristic way. It seemed to him that the village labourer had lost sight of himself through oppression and depression and patronage. In the early seventies he had glanced in the mirror for a moment and seen in his own face some remnants of force and independence. Joseph would, so far as in him lay, hold up the mirror again. Fresh from his *Tour* and *Enquiry*, pictures and instances were in the forefront of his mind. He described villages where the labourers never changed into a decent coat, desecrated the Sabbath with leap-frog and tip-cat, where they consented to live in cottages for which they paid sixpence a week, and they not worth it! And others, how different, with small-holdings associations, temperance clubs, branches of the Union, gay and fruitful gardens. He would illustrate labourers' foolishness about their own affairs by stories of the shepherd he had come across who walked eight miles there and back to fodder a hundred sheep and then grind them a supply of turnips, for the reward of a shilling, or of the man who had paid into two of those risky institutions, village insurance societies, for fifty years, had seen them both go broke and then had nothing but his weekly bread from the parish. His emphasis was all on self-help, on thinking and understanding. But he could only talk that way where ears were already open. Often the simple propaganda and the songs were best.

When a meeting went well, a branch of the National Union might be formed. In one village the young rector offered to act as secretary for a year, till a labourer should be ready. In another a curate called at the van and explained that he would leave the meeting after the speeches—he knew the men suspected the clergy and wouldn't join the Union in his presence.

But sometimes the van pitched on the green of a village where tyranny was so extreme as to be decadent—where, to quote one case, the landlord retained the right to inspect a cottage at any time in daylight, and to survey the gardens and pig-sties, to order where flowers and where vegetables might be grown, so as to make a 'model village'! There were greater extremes than that but he would use no instance that was not typical. On a few occasions the van was without an audience; the men dared not attend. Once, when the missioners had established themselves on the village green, several labourers came along and pulled the van on to the road, mumbling the squire's abusive messages. Supposing he legally controlled the green, the mission moved on to a quiet road, but as soon as the meeting started two policemen turned up and dispersed it. In another village the missioners noticed an odd thing; when they appealed to the labourers to join the Union, the right arms of all the men were raised simultaneously. You could not tell who had given the sign. In another village the meeting was hampered in a novel way. The landlord's agents and larger farmers from two or three parishes stood grimly around the little group of farmworkers who had gathered to listen. Murdoch and Joseph went doggedly on with song and speeches before a totally silent and immobile audience. When it was nearly dark and the gentlemen had gone off at last to their dinner Murdoch declaimed yet two more verses in a hoarse, desperate voice and suddenly the group of labourers and their wives sang with pent-up energy:

> Ours are the voices which for ages were unheard,
> Ours are the voices of a future long deferred.
> Cry altogether; we shall speak the final word.
> Let the cause go marching on!

Sociologist into Missionary

OURS ARE THE VOTES that give us weapons we can wield,
Ours are the votes that make our proud opponents yield.
Vote altogether and our charge shall clear the field,
Let the CAUSE go marching on!

The final word? There were villages where the landlord
was reasonable and wise and the labourers phlegmatic and
stupid, unable it seemed, to take even simple points; or where
the Red Van men heard of vile cruelties to birds and animals
and could have longed for them to be better 'preserved' for
a decent death by gun or dog. And the sight of drunkards was
common enough.

It all raised one of the old questions: how is decent quality
in men produced? Religion, it was claimed, could be the
whole answer—but what a rare fellow was the young clergyman acting as Secretary of a Labourers' Union branch!
Wealth and poverty were both held to hinder goodness but
Joseph's friend King was the son of a landowner born to
possessions. His early friend, old Jasper, was poor indeed,
though King's equal in character. But King's qualities had
such a range—surely only the finest education could have
given him his powers, while Jasper's delicate, perceptive
'noticing' kindness had been nurtured in, if not by, his village.
Rearing of good folk was evidently a complex business but
the essentials of it could surely be worked out.

When Murdoch finally dropped Joseph at his door again,
he had to resume the systematic work of the survey. Chiefly
it remained to fill the record sheets from his notes, agree with
King the necessary deductions and inferences, and write the
articles. Mr King's part had been a double one, to bring
Hannah a golden sovereign for each week her husband spent
on the work and to discuss the questions to be asked and then
the answers. It is Joseph's style that runs through the articles
they published in the *Economic Journal* in 1893: the intimacy
of knowledge, the vocabulary and the conclusions all show his
mind. The work-sheets were all in his handwriting: they

remained in his home till the First World War and then were used, so it chanced, as the model of an investigation made by the Ministry of Agriculture.

If the two men favoured one section of their subject, it was the part played in the labourer's life by allotments. Surely they already believed that access to land for his own working was vital to his improvement and hoped to show that this was so. Perhaps it was this that drove them to see the topic from so many angles and to treat it in such detail. (Some years later Hasbach in his *History of the English Agricultural Labourer* wrote that their articles recorded the fullest study ever made of smallholdings in England).

Other matters investigated were wages of farm workers of all kinds; the size, condition and rent of cottages; changes in population; membership of thrift associations; pauperism; machinery and its effects on labour, with slighter reference to education and other subjects. The precise figures and conclusions arrived at are of little interest now, unless to some rare scholar, but the general picture is worth a closer look than we have taken.

Take wages: in 1892 the highest wage in the area was fifteen shillings and the lowest nine and sixpence. The full meaning of these figures can still be discerned from the labourers' budgets given to illustrate them—the insufficiency of food, the lack of money and many less familiar facts. The figures included the earnings of stockmen, shepherds and wagoners as well as the plain labourers (none should be called unskilled). In many villages the latter earned eleven shillings and the specialists twelve. It was clearly better for a man not to take on special responsibilities; he actually lowered his wage per hour by doing so. Stockmen worked some ten hours more on six weekdays as well as five hours on Sundays. For these extra fifteen hours they were paid one shilling. This odd state of affairs had come about through the view that a labourer should be paid not a penny more than the least he could subsist on; and because the extra shilling was an utter necessity for some households. But now that there were allotments the wise labourer refused extra responsibilities on his employer's farm and spent his evening hours in his own employ.

Sometimes such facts were new to the men themselves; when necessity drove what use to compute and compare? Another odd fact was the extent of local variation. In adjacent villages, wages would differ by two shillings a week, that is, by nearly twenty per cent, without any difference in demand or supply; in villages further apart though with similar circumstances there could be a difference of four or even five shillings—almost fifty per cent.

A refuge for consciences was the notion that the labourer received free milk and beer and other perquisites. Well, except for harvest beer there were practically none of these. On the other hand sometimes an employer would almost compel his workers to buy from him some of his products, and at current retail prices. Yet wages had not dropped quite back to the figures for 1872, and the prices of food were falling.

In cottages also there had been a slight improvement. The worst of them were always dying, collapsing; there were derelict ones in every village, from four to ten per cent. But now the depression in agriculture was preventing landowners from building new ones, so that in a number of villages there could only be improvement at the price of migration. The average labourer's cottage consisted of one room below with a small 'pantry' opening out of it, and two rooms above, one through the other, but in a few villages a considerable proportion had but one bedroom though families were large. In the purely agricultural villages the rent was from one to two shillings; in the largest, they ran up to six or seven pounds a year, and in five, where a high proportion of men were lime-workers, rents started at five pounds and ran up as high as eight. A rent even lower than the value of a poor cottage seemed to labourers one of those boons without which life could not be lived, and a sort of customary right, but in

Joseph's view such rents obscured the labourer's situation for himself as well as for others. They furnished an excuse for neglect. Henceforth he would always be advocating economic rents, but to little purpose. Labourers reasoned poorly, timidly, even about their own affairs: how they needed education and stimulus!

Overcrowding in villages was a topic of the day, since it had a bearing on morality: incest was not unknown. The Mothers' Unions (institutions to which perhaps the inquiry did not give an adequate place) were urging on the women care in separating the girls and boys for sleeping. Yet what could they do? There were several sorts of cottage-owning landlords, the chief being farmers, large landowners, and 'smock frock' men. In this district, though there were cottages on the farms built to house workers, they nearly always lived elsewhere. This was one of the points on which the men were almost immovable: any job rather than one involving a tied cottage, any cottage but the one on the master's farm. Landowners and 'smock frock' landlords might be contrasted: landowners' cottages were of fair size and in good repair, but the tenant had no liberty of mind; the fellow working man who had perhaps inherited a couple of cottages could neither repair his property nor wait for his rent. But he was chiefly to be met with in larger villages where one could hope to change one's cottage, and could call one's mind one's own.

The standard for a good cottage in the investigators' minds seems to have been two bedrooms and a 'landing', a large 'house' and a smaller kitchen below, a garden, clean water in a tap not too far from the door: they assumed children to fetch it.

Everyone interested in villages or in agriculture had to take note of migration—it had been going on for so long. While the population of England was increasing, there had been a reduction in the district of 3·7 per cent between 1881 and 1891. Railways were now a general influence, but did not

now tend to depopulate. Of late, men living near railway
stations left home less than others: they could travel a few
miles to work without leaving their homes. In 1892 the
causes of removal were unemployment, low wages and bad
cottages. The attraction of towns was a myth; men were not
so much drawn away as propelled out. There was an increased tendency for girls to leave the countryside for
'service'. Indeed what else could a labourer's daughter do?
There was no attractive life or work at all for a bright grown
girl. Once gone, she seldom came back. What then of the
next generation of village mothers?

The direction of migration varied. Few were at this time
going to the colonies. From one small area the migrants
flowed to Birmingham and its neighbourhood, from another
chiefly to Coventry and again to the railway works at Crewe
and the breweries of Burton-on-Trent. A certain number of
young men, encouraged by the clergy, were joining the
Metropolitan Police Force. A potent force against emigration was allotments of good ground.

Views were clear in the nineties on good and ill. Work and
thrift were twins high in the ranks of virtue. Friend and
patron pressed upon the labourer the duty of 'saving'. To
keep out of debt, to seize even the tiniest offer of good
fortune, he must have a reserve. There were a good many
institutions promoting self-help and savings—friendly
societies, savings banks, consumers' co-operative societies,
allotment associations, livestock insurance clubs and even
a building society. All these were managed by the labourers
themselves, or in association with small traders. A few
others—clothing and coal clubs—were managed on their
behalf by clergymen and their wives, and their funds were
subsidised by the well-to-do.

Of all these, Friendly Societies were the most widespread.
Forty-eight of the fifty-six villages had independent local
clubs or branches of national institutions, chiefly of the
Manchester and Nottingham Oddfellows and the Foresters.

In every family of tradesmen and wage-earners 1·25 persons were members of some Friendly Society. The branches of the national societies were prosperous. Some were finding difficulty in investing their funds; one Oddfellows lodge was lending money to members to buy their own homes. Some lodges were increasing sick-pay and others allowing sick-pay to slide into old-age pay.

Here, it seemed, were indications of a way forward. Better wages, smallholdings and Friendly Societies would enable labourers to improve their own lot. State pensions for old age were being advocated by some, but Joseph notes that many villagers expressed themselves as hostile to these: better conditions, even slightly better, and the folk could make their own provision.

To these admirable organisations for thrift a disquieting newcomer had arrived—the 'Insurance Company'. Young agents came to cottage doors and persuaded women to take out 'insurance policies'. Often they 'insured' the lives of their husbands or children. They did not know how their money was invested and received no training at all in its management. It occurred to Joseph that the 'Women had no part in the Friendly Societies unless as widows of members'. Thus it seems to occur to him that hearing no discussions, not exercising a citizen's functions might at least to some extent account for the lightness of women's minds.

In all but one of Joseph's villages there were allotments. The average size was far above the ten poles (one sixteenth of an acre) that some people had thought to be the harmless extent. Over the whole district the average acreage of allotment for each holder was over half an acre. There was one village where it was over two acres. In ten it was over an acre. At the other end of the scale were eight villages where it was less than a quarter. So allotments as an aid to life were being widely tried. Landlords were letting the land but not otherwise encouraging the movement. In many cases the rents charged for the working-men's plots were far above the rent charged for similar adjacent land, even when every allowance was made for occasional loss of rent. In only one case was land let at rent lower than its current value; not even the large estates were charitable. It was clear that labourers felt their allotments to be a supplementary source of food or money, but to look through the numerous allotment budgets given is surely to smile at the small profits made! If a man tilled an acre with his own hands, his wife baked bread from the corn he raised, and he fed his pig with the inferior vegetables, then he might make a profit of two shillings and ninepence per week. It was true enough that allotments worked entirely in spare time tended to overwork and ill-health, but after a season or two the men, in fact, employed some labour. There was always someone glad to dig a half-acre—old men past a full day's work, for example. As time went on farmers, finding that allotments tended to keep good men on the land and did no harm to their own interests, would hire out a plough team or even lend it to their own wagoner.

There was an investigation of the soils that paid best for allotments, with clay the winner. On clay cultivation was cleanest and the yield best. The acreage dug with the spade was compared with that ploughed; the average time taken to dig half an acre was worked out, and the amount of seed used in 'pegging'—that is, dropped into holes made with a dibber—was compared with that used by the drill. A detailed study of the relation of pig-keeping to allotments proved that the latter were seldom financially successful if the holder did not keep at least one pig. Another question was how much land could be successfully cultivated by men working under given conditions. By wagoners and stockmen, by artisans, by jobbing men? Were grass holdings successful? Only one village possessed these. Cow-keeping seemed to be more profitable than arable plots. But of course grass was no substitute for arable where gardens were small or non-existent. The produce of allotments per acre was compared with that of farm land and found to be twice as much; and the produce of the dug allotment with the ploughed. The destiny of the produce was studied; practically all the wheat was consumed at home; the flour from one acre of wheat would feed an ordinary family for a year. Numerous balance sheets were given to show what profit individual labourers made on their land. In each case the profit on a day's work was higher than a day's earnings, and in a few cases twice as much.

Profits to diet and pocket were valuable but there were others. 'No other cause could be assigned for the great improvement in the labourer's condition in the last ten years than allotments and their accompanying pigs.' 'A County Court process-server recently informed us that in two villages lately supplied with a large proportion of allotments he now served one summons [i.e. for debt] where before he had served twenty. Allotments have given stability and self-respect and a hope of advance which before was given only to those countrymen who migrated into towns. If popular opinion supported by statistics...is correct they have done much to reduce drunkenness....They have stimulated the labourer's observation and inventiveness; as an educating influence on boys they have excited a practical interest in agriculture more valuable than theoretic knowledge.' Of such great value might be a simple provision when it promoted freedom and responsibility, work and thrift.

Thus the inquiry showed that there were many points at which self-help and fellowship were being combined. But the initiative shown was diminutive—the labourer made his gains like a rat biting through wood. Not all his associations together amounted to an inspired movement. They were like his average self—poverty-stricken, unimaginative. Where was the leadership the higher classes advanced as their justification? It did not exist. In fifty-six villages there was one leader of social station markedly above that of the labourer, and he a doctor. The Church which should have held the lamp for the labourer's feet identified herself with the 'substantial men' and with their fears for their selfish interests.

Readers of the articles might draw the moral that one class of person must never, never, believe that other classes will guard their interests but, given an opportunity, will batten upon their lives. The researchers did not feel that: class, of all a man's relationships, was for them the most superficial. Temptations were universal and so were reason and fellow feeling: their work was an appeal to humanity, not ammunition for a fight.

Joseph's various activities in these years brought him a number of suggestions for gaining a livelihood outside Tysoe. The editor of the *Warwick Advertiser* invited him to join his staff; the Liberal Association of a nearby constituency urged him to take the post of agent, and a little later Earl Compton wrote offering to find a place for him on the Northampton Estates. Had his Lordship proffered a small farm and part of the necessary capital Joseph's life-story might have been different, but a wage or a salary would involve a more direct dependence than one can imagine he would care for. Again he made the choice to stay in Tysoe.

CHAPTER XIII

YOUNG PARENTS

I MAY be giving the impression that my father's family was something of a sideline of interest for him, but it is easy to see that it was primary—that village life, local government, political troubles were largely extensions of home, or threats or promises to it. A set of verses he sent to my mother before their marriage are a little curious as a young man's work. They concern the illness of a little child, parents despairing of their darling. His early childhood, we have seen, had given him knowledge of what a home might be, but not a home as he had wished it. The nature of their first-born, my brother Arthur, must have turned foresightful affection for children on my parents' part into deepest interest. He was a passionate, active babe, full of the vital essence that attracts and holds the love and imagination of nearly all whom they touch. His vivid attachment to them, his beauty, his quick responses, must have confirmed my father's assumption that children come fundamentally good 'from the hands of a glad creator', that if they could be guarded from bad conditions and influences they could grow almost infinitely good, and boys perhaps, infinitely sensible, if not wise as well.

I have now seen or experienced three generations of parents at work, each subject to special conditions. My parents and others of their time worked almost entirely in the dark. In the nineties you might search the pages of even the women's magazines and find hardly an allusion to the years under sixteen—only, just occasionally, pictures of highly idealised children. Stray gleams of light upon their job were almost as misleading as illuminating. The Bible itself was contradictory: Christ's command 'Let the little children come unto me' stood us, small children of the time, in good stead, as we well understood—we listened gratefully to the story of his blessing! but it only mitigated and did not abolish the effect of the Psalmist's bidding to 'train up a child in the way it should go' and of the proverb about spoiling the child by sparing the rod. Froebel had long ago understood children in an almost superhuman way, but unfortunately wrote in an untranslatable jargon, and though two or three of his toys and 'activities' had found their way into the infants' class of Tysoe school, his profound insights had not come with them.

That my father had intuitions of his own into children's minds some early memories show. An infant of two years or less put to sleep in a big bed alone woke in the middle of the night terrified, lost as on the Sahara. Her father heard her desperate cries and came. 'Big bed!', she howled, 'Big bed!' He took her up, straightened the appalling confusion of blankets, set her in each of the four corners of the bed in turn and left her with a sense that, after all, she knew her world. The first time Arthur saw telegraph poles and wires (the telegraph had just reached Tysoe) his hand was in his father's. Violent thrills went through his small body as if itself were galvanised. They stood together speechless for a while before my father spoke: he had learned then with what force novelty strikes a child and would watch afterwards for moments of new impressions. Once one of my brothers was dawdling behind his father on the road from the Far Fields and saw him come up with a group of three little girls, a comical trio, sitting in the wayside hedge under an oak tree, each with an empty acorn-cup on its stem held in her mouth like a pipe. Father sought among the grass for a similar bowl and stem, put it in his mouth. 'What a good pipe!' he said and walked on, his face as solemn as theirs. When a little daughter persistently took what was not hers, for no reason whatever so far as he could make out, he would not let my mother punish: 'We will leave ill alone when it is such a mystery.'

For my mother we were more difficult. She saw us morning,

noon and night, day in day out, and knew much about her children that she found no words to tell their father. They had strange naughtinesses she had never heard tell of, and could at moments hate and resent each other. Her mode of dealing with us was a speculative one: she gave herself utterly to our welfare, trusting that if she gave all, even if she made mistakes, all would be well. Thus like other mothers of the time, she gradually came to a degree of self-renunciation that is now, surely, extinct. With all our and our father's demands upon her, virtue became not so much easy as inescapable. To give all you have was a command to be obeyed as much as 'Thou shalt not covet'—or steal or commit adultery. But whether in the long run that was good for us, I doubt.

We children were constantly with our parents, walking hand in hand with my father in a hayfield when the moon-daisies brushing our eyelashes were as big as dishes to our sight; we stood by while he milked the cows, entranced by the sweet smell of the cows and the ringing of the milk against the zinc pail; my brothers carried his tools, longing to use them, always ready to attempt the impossible in his company. My sisters and I worked with my mother, getting 'under her feet' as she would say at last, fascinated by her brooms and irons, by the heat and smells of cooking and of washday.

But there had to be something more direct than sharing life with us; we had to be taught. It seemed to my parents that there were two straight roads to take; children must help with the work, learning to do so promptly, and they must have religious teaching. Boys fed poultry and pigs and soon were milking and cutting firewood. By eight years they could do much more than all that. Girls had to bath little brother and sister just a size smaller than themselves and stagger with pails of water from the tap fifty yards away when scarcely taller than the pails they carried between them. To 'help' was the price of contact with beloved and admired parents; even tiny ones understood that our parents 'could not manage' without us. So work in the early years was not

much minded. Lost in play or sunk in books, the thought of
mother or father in difficulties would work its way to
poignancy in a child's mind and the second or third call would
bring us flying. How effective children could be was shown by
Arthur when my father was away with the Red Van. He, at
the age of all but eight, was his mother's right hand. The
younger ones became 'his' children; he would take them off
'up the fields' out of his mother's way, or play long games
with them in the wash-house. But his 'famous' achievement
('famous' was one of the words of highest praise) took place
at the Promised Land. The grown men, Joseph's helpful
fellow-members of the Smallholders Association, declared
that the beans, that very dry summer, were too short to be
reaped: nothing could be done with them. But my mother
and Arthur pulled or broke the haulms one by one, a quarter
of an acre of them.

We saw my mother wonder why, if children could be so
often good, they were not always so. If a piece of work went
on too long or errands were too many, we would be filled at
last with a turmoil of rebellion. Arthur would earn the old
accolade 'You're a man!'—and then forget some monstrously
important message. His mother 'could not make it out', nor
could we children. 'Naughtiness' had nothing to do with
a child's self. It slipped magically into one's ways; one ought
to keep it out, but how defeat that wicked magic?

Religious teaching seemed to my parents relatively simple.
We were to learn of God, the greater Parent—all-seeing,
all-protecting, reigning all day, everywhere; and of Christ,
his Son, who interpreted the Father and taught us the way to
him. They had no religious extravagance except in this one
point, their anxiety to teach their children. Waking early, the
younger children would go into my mother's room, and sitting
on her bed spell out the illuminated psalms in four-cross
frames—'Thou wilt keep him in perfect peace whose mind is
stayed on Thee', and 'He will give his angels charge over
thee'. Their own love and labour were, they taught us, as

169

nothing to God's care. To be always 'good', to keep oneself fit to speak with God in grace before meat, in bedtime prayer, or in some inward talk—that was all too small a service for us to render. And thus it was that the evil we felt in ourselves seemed terrifyingly abnormal. As for any baseness we saw in the outer world—cruelty, or ugly sights at the back of the inn—that was an egregious mistake. It was many years I think, before any of us believed our eyes when we saw or heard evil unless it was somehow traceable to ourselves.

Over and over we heard and read (we were early readers) the story of Christ's birth, the healing miracles, his talk. His second coming was to be expected and we looked for it, so that when one of us opened the stairfoot door he might be coming down that way, standing majestic and gentle on the middle step. We were not afraid of that; he was a companion, as we often sang, 'a friend for little children'.

Sunday was the day on which the word-pictures drawn at home were heightened at Sunday School by magical details. Here were sacred vacant hours procured by Saturday's toil; the children wore their fresh, best beautiful clothes. By these and by the quiet that reigned over the village and the services in the chapel their minds were sensitised. It was the grown-ups' service that was divine, not the Sunday School, and on a special day the children might go in the evening as well. A service in the thin fine light of a sunny spring morning or in the fresh cold of a wet day was an ordinary rational experience compared with an evening service. The square chapel was filled with yellow light falling with literal warmth on faces and hands from the oil-lamps hung above the congregation. The six great windows (great to the children), three on each side, revealed in summer a world beyond of enchanting pale blue atmosphere, entirely suitable for angels to descend in and to carry to the children their silver trumpetings, and some day soon perhaps to the dead as well, to bid them rise. In the winter the windows were deeply blue, dark branches showed across them and rain beat on them, signifying all that world of

danger from which God and parents kept the children warm
and safe—the world in which the moon might turn to blood
or Satan appear unexpectedly when one had forgotten the
word that kept him back—'Get thee behind me, Satan'.

How many parents, themselves brought up in some less
responsible, more haphazard way, must at this time have laid
on children the burden of a too ideal and imaginary world
and, longing to give only what was encouraging, unconsciously
ensured a sense of failure!

And yet, for all that, in these early years our parents
illumined the world for their children. They lit candles as it
were for us and set oil-lamps about—lamps beautiful in
themselves, with translucent glass bowls and milky shades—
shedding warmth as well as light upon the children's surroundings. When several decades later the world for many
others came to be lit by the broad graceless light of mere
science, for them the 'house of thought' they had built would
still be warmed as well as lighted. We would complain a
little in due course that our parents had given us some rosy
illusions, but presently we would reflect that they had first
also shown that illusion can be turned into truth.

As they grew the children's home was extended to include
their grandmothers' houses. On weekdays we carried
messages and baskets full of vegetables and eggs; on Sundays
we went off to dinner or tea or sometimes both with our
grannies, leaving our parents in unwonted and precious
quietude. 'Church-Town Granny' or Granny Harriet at sixty
years was a little like old peasants you may see in Alsace or
Slovakia. She never read and had almost forgotten how to.
She wore always a linen apron with her knitting-pin holder
twisted into its waist-tapes, and, except on Sundays, a small
red cross-over shawl and goffered print bonnet. For all her
homeliness, her original home had been a farm, and a generation or two back the menfolk of her family had been in-
scribed 'gents' on their tombstones in Brailes churchyard.
Her peasanthood was her own self. Lively and affectionate

she was, but had no interest beyond things and persons, and the hours between sunrise and sunset. Her cottage was bright with polished furniture and with red and blue damask table-covers and woollen antimacassars. The fantastic day-dream pictures on her walls had been hung there by her un-married daughters. They showed ladies in trailing white gowns being helped across stepping-stones in a stream by gentlemen in equally immaculate clothes and with ringlets and steel buckles. There was a bookcase full of volumes of the *Girl's Own Paper* and *Good Words*. On the mantelpiece were china figures of old-fashioned policemen, pale blue and white, and small white lions with crinkled manes. On the wall above were hung long hollow glass 'walking sticks', twisted like barley sugar, one of them filled with tiny coloured balls like the confectioner's 'hundreds and thousands'. But her basic furniture was ancient—rough oak stools with splayed-out legs, for children to sit on, wheel-backed and ladder-backed chairs and a round tray carved out of a single piece of wood. Here the children had a perfect welcome. A good many years earlier some of Granny Harriet's qualities had maddened an intelligent and irascible husband, but these did not prevent her from being as kind and understanding to children as if she had stood for goodness in a fairy-tale. Eagerly the little children took their turns two at a time to go to her for dinner and tea on Sundays. There was always a little savoury roast and then· dripping cake for tea, and in between, hours of leisure. One did not even help to wash dishes. That was done in no time, and then Granny would sit down in her armchair, wearing her Sunday dress of black serge, looking like an even rounder, even more homely Queen Victoria—whose likeness to Granny in the school portrait was such a comfort on week-days. One of us would read to her till she slept, but that was soon, and then we could settle in utter comfort to our books.

Upper-Town Granny, the ageing Elizabeth, and her house were kind but frigid; there was no comfort. Yet we went often to her and sat, patiently extracting what interest we

could from her brief speech and her faded pictures. There
was a stone floor almost bare; the big ugly-shaped Bible,
like a leather-covered box, lay by the window on the little
pillar-and-tripod table that one had to be so careful not to
overturn. Her other books also were large and shabby, and
incomprehensible. Both grannies were a little hard of hearing:
one said 'You should speak more distinctly, child', but the
other drew you to her side and said 'Say it again, my duck.
Your old Granny is deaf.'

There was one other house to be frequently visited besides
the grandmothers'. Aunt Rouvray's was well known to the
older children. Just as with Joseph years before, she received
the children with a little formality, serving them with wine
and biscuits. Her house was a little heaven of the senses, with
shining rich wood everywhere, and coloured, enchanting
pictures, bright china and embroideries; in the language of
later years, a complete tiny Regency house. There was one
marked change in Aunt Rouvray: she had taken to talking of
her husband. His father—the children thought it was himself
—had brought from Paris her brooch containing the painted
picture of a tiny boy, naked except for the basket of flowers
in his hand and the wreath on his head. The picture was only
half an inch across, but every time the children asked to look
at it, Aunt Rouvray said solemnly that it was 'by Booshay'
(i.e. Boucher). He had brought also the china vase that was
exhibited tragically in pieces, but some of the shards were
whole tiny flower-buds. 'M'soo doo Rouvray' had lived, it
seemed, in a strange place, the King's Bedchamber, until he
had been chased away by the terrible mobs in Paris.

Presently Aunt Rouvray had provided the children with a
stranger experience. After a long illness, during which
Hannah had to work two houses, she was brought to Joseph's
house to die. Such a strange unrelated thing was this death.
It changed the grown-ups and a new awe came into life,
unlike anything else. But soon the feel of the time was
softened for little girls by new black dresses, ruffled and

gathered along the yokes and at the wrists—their other dresses had hardly ever been new throughout. It was to the children's mother that Hannah Rouvray left her worldly goods—such a right expression that, for the gay things. There was talk the children did not understand about a little money in Railways (what a strange place for money!) or in the Funds.

As a consequence, perhaps, of the Money in the Railways we moved in 1895 to Church Cottage. It was a small old house but it had been brought up to date by a porch and a bay window and by enclosing a passage off the rooms so that it had a modern privacy. To complete its frontward gentility it had, of all suburban features, a little front garden with a selection of the Victorians' favourite decorative trees— a variegated maple, a mountain ash, a 'mock orange' and a deutzia, with a rockery at their feet. It was as if a small piece of the curate's garden opposite had thought the other side of the pavement sunnier and had slipped across: but at the back the house was old-fashioned and practical enough. There was a small room used later as a dairy and a fair-sized yard with sheds.

The scarlet rowan and the fairy maple, so freshly green and white, were great gains, and a greater was the spare sitting-room from which children could be excluded, and to which again, they had admittance. Here tea was laid when guests came and here Father's committees met. Its bay gave a full view of the path to school and the other window surveyed the church gate by which funeral processions went in and 'weddings' came out.

The little sitting-room was furnished with Aunt Rouvray's things; the Wedgwood jugs with swelling stomachs, rope handles and narrow necks, the rough brown jugs with metal rims and their bodies encrusted with trees, dogs and a deer, the patchwork cloth covering an octagonal inlaid table that so entranced and inveigled young eyes! The centre of the cloth was made of tiny octagons of broadcloth, scarlet and black

174

and green. Around these were squares, always tiny, of the same cloth, and then again octagons filled with more mosaic, and every tiny patch braided with gold. The patience and the craft of it might have built a cathedral; and the children's eyes explored its intricacies and gloried in its colour. There was the picture of the Bay of Naples and the piece of painted velvet with fantastic passion-flowers of ivory and red, large corn-flowerlike blossoms of deep blue, and brown roses whose pink no doubt had fled. Aunt Rouvray's tea-chest was as good, of brilliantly polished dark wood, inlaid with thin lines of apricot colour and on each end, lions' heads with delicate rings of the apricot-coloured wood hanging from their mouths, which small hands could turn round and round. On such things did little girls feed within doors while the boys roamed the world.

Aunt Rouvray's legacy must have been very timely. Beside a larger home it provided a horse and gig, the latter elegant though old, with two high lancewood wheels. Perhaps a gig was a luxury, but how like Joseph to go for something that would enlarge his own life and his children's. Now he could reach more distant villages to preach, to speak at Liberal meetings; now there would be drives at ease through sunny keen spring scenes and autumn colours. But the gig must pay its way and more! Joseph, and Arthur too, quite soon, would drive to Kineton station to fetch and take visitors for half a crown. Six miles there and six back—it does not seem dear, but Arthur sometimes got twopence and once a three-penny piece, in addition. The horse would also fetch and carry from the five acres at 'The Promise' and gather in Joseph's share of hay from the glebe fields.

More practical was the acquisition of two cows. It seems that the railway money would not quite stretch to cover their cost. Each of the children had a Post Office Savings Bank book and these had to be stripped down to the one shilling which let you retain the book. But Arthur bade the little ones not mind; they should have rides on the cows and cream

on their blackberries! It was Arthur himself who chose the
first cow—Jersey Beauty. Joseph had gone to preach at
Radway, four miles away, one Sunday, and had taken Arthur
with him for company. (His Methodist hosts came to know
that they must always lay two places at the table when
Mr Ashby came to preach.) On this occasion the host was
Mr Ridley Brown, a substantial man, almost a gentleman
farmer, with a fine rich burr in his voice, a bachelor come
south from Northumberland to a more comfortable climate.
Mr Brown had fifteen cows (large herds were not so common
then) in a square brick-paved yard. Miss Brown, his sister,
was delighted with her quiet but passionate-looking small
guest and listened to his talk about the gig and the cows that
were to come. When the two men and the small boy walked
round the farm in the afternoon Mr Brown said that he and
his sister had decided that Joseph and Arthur should have
any cow they chose from the Jersey herd for a certain
generously small sum. Joseph's knowledge of cows was not
sufficient for him to make a reasoned choice among such well-
bred animals, so here was a chance of pleasing a child!
Arthur chose a beautifully marked small cow—so soft her
colours, so gentle her ways, such a fabulous milker she proved,
among the heterogeneous small herds of Tysoe! For years
Beauty figured in the children's lives; other cows came and
went but they continued to milk and ride Beauty and take her
out to feed by the roadside in springtime. The second cow
Joseph bought from a friend near Rugby, driving her all the
way home, nearly thirty miles, sleeping in a roadside shed
on the way.

After the arrival of horses and cows the children's work
changed. Lady London the pony, if she were to be useful,
must be often at home in the stable, so Arthur and Richard
had to mow grass on the roadside and bring it to the yard.
Presently Father rented old Lucy Bower's orchard half a mile
away, and a little later three small fields more than twice as
far from home. Once a day before or after school Arthur

had to walk to let out or shut up the fowl there. If he went after school and could not have Lady London to ride, dusk would be falling. He would cross the first field singing and shouting, so that if a tramp were dossing on the hay in the manger, he might be alarmed and make his getaway! On Saturdays when school was closed, he would sometimes work in these Far Fields with his father. As assistant, it was for him to gather sticks for a fire and to cut a thin green wand from the hedge to push through a slice of raw bacon to be frizzled on it. On one great occasion he took a moorhen's egg from the pond and cooked it in his tin mug. This bright rustic urchin had in his pocket a great source of pride. His great-aunt Rouvray had signified that her small double-case hunting watch was to be his. It was far too precious not to be carried with him everywhere, but then later it was too precious to be carried at all, and as commendation for good work in the hay season his father gave him a 'five-bob, gun-metal self-winder'.

This wonderful engine ticking loudly in his pocket (he could hear it when he stood still) had great significance. Father had given it to him and yet he had earned it. But the price stuck in his mind and the fact that there was no small key to be for ever lost and sought for. Such a price opened the door to a golden day and not for himself alone—the men, the labourers, were buying such watches. Dreams were to be fulfilled; plenty was on the way. But the door had only opened by a crack and it was ill-hung, had a way of slamming to, over and over again.

CHAPTER XIV

NATIONAL POLITICS AND
PARISH PUMPS

AFTER the enfranchisement of the farm worker in 1884 both the main political parties began to work in villages as never before. Political clubs were formed in the larger ones, branches of the Conservative Primrose League, and member clubs of the National Liberal Federation. Here and there a remote or once-remote village still has a shuttered, weed-sheltering building with a carved stone label over the door: BEACONSFIELD HALL. Political meetings, hitherto unknown in many villages, became the most popular part of every winter's entertainment and stimulus. Nearly all the men attended and a small, growing number of women.

Naturally this was a moment for the Tysoe Radicals. Joseph was the most adaptable speaker among them and he had begun long since to speak and organise in the locality.

The most prominent Conservative in the neighbourhood was the Honourable Richard Greville Verney, son and heir of Lord Willoughby de Broke. He and my father were neighbours all their active lives. In material ways their lives were poles apart; they were on opposite sides in all social and political campaigns that affected both; but whether they ever felt it so or not, they certainly had something in common. Both knew the South Warwickshire fields intimately and affectionately, both loved and partly lived in the works of Dickens; both had charm and kindness in their homes and friendliness in their larger circles. Both also were ready writers. Verney's, or rather Lord Willoughby's, memoirs *The Passing Years*, written towards the end of his life, is a fluent and delightful book. One might feel perhaps a brief bitterness that my father could never have leisure to let his imagination fly higher than in his Vignettes and Tours, that he should have to write penny-a-line articles instead of dwelling on his experiences till they flowered in a fine book, like his neighbour's.

Something like seven miles lay between the two when the Hon. Richard Greville was born and Joseph was a small boy. From 1906 to 1915 they would sit beside each other on a certain Bench. (Joseph's elevation to the magistracy might seem to bring them nearer together, but political events would drive them mentally further apart.)

It was a few years after Joseph's mother had put his meat ration in jeopardy by rejecting a pair of pheasants probably poached from that favourite hunting ground, Verney woods, that young Richard Verney 'watched the sirloin hanging by a chain, turning slowly round and round, and being basted by the stout kitchen wench' before a huge open fire on which a ton of coal was burnt each day, in the kitchen of his home, Compton Verney House. Richard was heir to an estate of some thousands of acres, 'just enough to live on', to live, that is, in the eighteenth-century mansion, with decorations by Adam and wide grounds grandly planned by that busiest of fellows, Capability Brown. Both Ashby and Verney families had been affected by Arch's campaign. Since the early seventies the Verney magistrates had earned their reputation for leniency to delinquents of the labouring class and for a more genial attitude to the world beneath them.

The Verneys belonged to a decorative and useful order. It is usual to underline the fact that great landlords provided agricultural capital, which after all can be obtained from other sources. But who else has shown so well the heights to which the simpler pleasures can be carried? Such wealthy squires had no message for the high minds of saint or poet, but they could teach the ordinary man the arts of his life. They showed the dog-lover how great an interest breeding could be; taught the angler to seek his pleasure in Canada and Norway

as well as at home. The Verneys were steeplechase riders,
played cricket, excelled at tennis (not lawn tennis, of course,
but the tennis of kings); they were Masters of the Warwickshire Hunt. It was not an easy life that men of this type lived.
Excellence in each of their chosen activities was the result of
exacting practice and much thought. So deeply had their skills
organised their physical being that they could practise them
far into old age and long continue to extend their range.
Their life had its responsibilities: it cost the Willoughbys
de Broke a long if empirical study of heredity and a hard life
of hunting every winter to build up the pack of hounds for the
Hunt—a pack of great beauty 'on the flags' and immense
endurance in the field. Photographs and drawings show the
developing type—the air and attitude growing more tense,
the feet more ball-like, limbs cleaner, heads broader. Estate
management could be left to others, but not a responsibility
such as that.

There were other responsibilities—the training of the
Yeomanry was as important as sport; in the late eighties some
thought it their duty to sit on the new County Councils—even
though they might be, as Lord Willoughby the nineteenth
Baron thought, new-fangled and unnecessary. It must be
added that they went to the country's wars, when possible on
fine mounts from the home stable.

Some also like Lord Willoughby wrote lively memoirs,
travel books and books on sport—highly readable books, full
of the verve of wilful personalities and bearing the mark of
the freedom wealth confers, and having an especial style. In
the whole volume of *The Passing Years* there is not one
metaphor which is not drawn from sport or game or weather
or the table. The writer's opponent 'lies down in the saw-
dust'; he hears a 'torrential downpour of invective'; a perora-
tion 'tasted of Burgundy', someone used 'a polished rapier'
of parliamentary fence; a politician held 'a royal flush'.
Descriptions of great folk, estate servants and fellow
politicians are genial and beguiling: the whole book is

written under a pink-shaded lamp of genial fantasy made possible by wealth.

It was when they came to politics that the wealthy squires were wont to show a certain levity. They held many seats in the House of Lords; they made it 'the assembly which did not assemble'; their duty, as stated sometimes by themselves, was to turn up to prevent changes, except any guaranteed harmless to their own order. To them democracy was a vision of idleness indulged in by the working classes—as though they themselves did not daily show how charming and satisfying and even attainable a life of 'idleness' might be.

The Rugby constituency had three times returned a Liberal member, once in 1885 and twice in 1886. Lord Willoughby describes H. P. Cobb as 'an excellent man, a well-informed barrister, not at all hampered by his learning, a hard hitter'. His blows at privilege, for example, reached home; they had 'a very unpleasant sting for members of the higher orders'. Mr Cobb was indeed the faithful representative of Warwickshire labourers, voicing their demands for improved wages, their doubts about Empire and heart-searchings about education and their demand for better local government. But to what purpose? Gladstone had lost votes over Khartoum, the Lords had thrown out the Home Rule Bill, Parnell prevented debates on home affairs from being carried to conclusions. Village Liberals worked hard and gained votes, but the Bills they were interested in never became Acts.

In 1893 Joseph had undertaken a voluntary 'agency' for the Liberal party in the southern section of the Rugby Parliamentary Division. His 'circuit', to borrow the Methodist expression, included fourteen villages, with Tysoe on its southern edge and Kineton and Gaydon both containing much Verney property and influence roughly in the centre. The more distant villages were as much as ten miles away and means of access very poor. The agent's work was to visit and arrange a meeting in each every winter and where possible to

start a Liberal club—and then of course when elections came
to intensify effort.

The two campaigners, Joseph and the Hon. Richard, both
worked hard in the election of 1892. They spoke at meetings
in the same villages, often on consecutive evenings. Both felt
the absence of railways but met the difficulty in different ways.
'One had to get about by carriage and pair' notes Verney.
Joseph had more varied vehicles—his penny-farthing, a tricycle, and Shanks's pony, as they said then (this was some
three years before he bought his gig). In the Kineton
Wesleyan circuit Joseph had been known for a number of
years as a preacher of thoughtful, slow style, but his friends
found him different on the political platform. That was the
place for Old Testament ways and virtues, in so far as the
New did not entirely rule them out! It was the place for
sharp attack with facts and figures, for presenting in high—
and true—colours the contrasts of life. But his audiences did
not laugh and clap like the Hon. Richard's. Mr Verney would
arrive fresh from his· drive, from his sandwiches and wine,
with a gay friend or two. He had his aristocratic charm and
yet a demagogic manner of exploiting it. His plan was to
distract his audience from his own programme by making fun
of his opponent's and by telling them anecdotes of that fine
fellow, his candidate. But the Radical Mr Cobb was elected.

The next year there was another general election, and this
time the Conservative candidate was Verney himself. Now
he could not quite ignore his party's programme to support
and develop the Empire, and to maintain the union with
Ireland. The Liberal programme still included Home Rule for
Ireland, the Disestablishment of the Welsh and Irish churches,
local option on the licensing of public houses, and the
abolition of plural voting. But there were also certain new
projects: compensation for injured workmen and the reform
of local government so as especially to give villages modern
representational councils. Mr Gladstone again gained a
majority in the country and H. P. Cobb in the Rugby Division.

Presently the Employers' Liability Bill was passed by the Commons, but so drastically amended by the House of Lords that Mr Gladstone dropped it. As for the Local Government Bill, its apparently innocent purposes, to rationalise outworn institutions and to give all villagers a chance of faithfulness in their own community's affairs and to become thereby better fitted for their national responsibilities, greatly alarmed the squires. The Bill would promote a village leadership which was not that of the landowner or of the incumbent whom he could influence, so some of the larger duties of the proposed Parish Councils were cut out. Villagers had looked forward to their Councils as promising a new interest as well as new duties, but Lord Salisbury, forgetting perhaps that rustics might overhear him, opined that 'for amusement a circus would be better'.

The half-loaf left by the Lords was not this time rejected, but now it was that Mr Gladstone saw his famous vision of the future. 'The differences of conviction, differences of pre-possession, differences of fundamental tendency between the House of Lords and the House of Commons' were such that some day there must be a trial of strength and one House give way.

In the summer of 1895, the Hon. Richard Verney was again Conservative candidate for Rugby. His opponent now was Mr Corrie Grant, another successful barrister, but of a different type from Mr Cobb, 'philosophical' as Lord Willoughby, his rival, says, 'and courteous'. But though less aggressive than Mr Cobb his qualifications were good. He had prepared to woo his rural constituency by mastering the legalities of land tenure and by becoming his party's authority on the Smallholdings Acts. Another witness says of him that 'he could maintain the interest of a village audience while presenting many facts and a long argument'. Corrie Grant was indeed a natural teacher; he loved to stimulate and help young Arthur and Richard Ashby to read and care for books, and in the same way he wanted to coach the rural

Liberals. How well that attitude suited Joseph and how happily he and others worked beside and under this candidate! His meetings were spirited, but with always some careful exposition of proposed legislation on smallholdings, safeguards for workers and temperance measures. One subject moved Mr Grant to denunciation—the House of Lords. They had lost the American colonies, would lose Ireland, had stood against every reasonable reform till the last moment and beyond. Nor would that leopard change his spots.

The Hon. Richard had, however, his Committee thought, a special advantage over the Liberal candidate. He, the heir of the Verney estates and of the barony of Willoughby de Broke, chanced to have fixed his wedding for a day shortly before the election. He did not put it off, but took his bride straight into the contest. The newly wed couple, handsome and full of affability and liveliness, drove their carriage and pair about the constituency. It was a simple programme the Hon. Richard laid before the electors. Having found the world around him so satisfactory he had determined, very honestly, not to promise any changes in it. All change, of course, must be for the worse. Those who wanted change were 'cranks, faddists, prigs and doctrinaires', 'trying to make the world come into line with some abstract principle of their own creation instead of taking the world as they find it'. Speeches against Home Rule and the 'local veto' raised no difficult questions, but when a visiting supporter, a follower of Joseph Chamberlain, adumbrated Unionist Bills providing workmen's compensation and old-age pensions he was told that the local Primrose League had plenty of speakers, and he went his way. An economic millennium could not improve the estate in life of the Willoughbys de Broke, but the prospect of a half-crown rise in wages or a five-shilling pension at seventy years was 'romantic nonsense'. There was no harm, however, in his humbler neighbours sharing the romance of Verney's own dazzling rank and his lovely bride.

The Hon. Richard tells himself of his visit to Tysoe, where

his shadowy programme was a good deal derided. For him it was a famous village, unlike those around which his estate lay—a free village, active-minded, and therefore, for his lordship, comical. The Tysoe folk, he says, were 'ardent Radicals' and yet—a line or two later—'always behind the times'. They had planted their William and Mary elm a day late; when Royalist met Parliamentarian at Edgehill they 'heard nothing of the gathering armies till the guns began to go off'. But they had 'unerring noses for threats of food taxes'; were dead keen on allotments; and 'expected the millennium in a very short while'.

But the men knew that these gibes—he voiced them often long before he wrote the book—were due to the uncomfortable time they had given His Lordship and other speakers of his party in more than one election and did not grudge him the laughs his stories drew. Meanwhile Grant and his agents and speakers, though not perhaps promising the millennium, were certainly advocating a little self-help by means of votes.

However, the Hon. Richard certainly had the laugh, this time, of the Tysoe folk; he was elected by a small majority. Had romance paid in the villages? Or had Rugby town for its own reasons swung somewhat to the right?

Naturally the new member was a little apprehensive when he first took his seat in the Commons, but on looking round, his selective eye saw 'countless Etonians', members of the I Zingari Club and other clubs only less famous, Masters of Hounds and younger sons—and these on both sides of the alley. Looking along the other side's Front Bench, he saw Mr Asquith and John Morley, both with the broad brain-pans and deep chests he had learned to associate with ability, alike in the estate's higher servants and in the Warwickshire pack of fox-hounds. Parliamentary duties did not weigh upon the Member. Mr Balfour 'could do what he liked except re-enact the Corn Laws'—no need to worry. Keenly the Member objected to the cutting down of Private Members' time, for that was when one could go off with the best conscience to join the Hunt. Had someone dreamed that this genial, flippant, fox-hunting squire would be a leader in the struggle Mr Gladstone had foreseen he would surely have waked himself by laughing in his sleep—only to find it, somewhat later, true.

In 1895 Tysoe elected its first Parish Council and also its first two representatives on the new Brailes Rural District Council. If one turns over the pages of Tysoe records for any period between 1895 and 1914 one sees Joseph's signature over and over again. Among smooth, workaday ex-copy-book hands, his stands out unique, its nervous, speedy angularity revealing a live, imaginative mind. Was the work of these minor local bodies worth the while of such a man? The House of Lords had shorn the locks of the proposed Parish Councils; the Rural District Councils, though a great improvement on those *ad hoc* bodies, the Sanitary and Highway Boards, had but meagre functions. County Councils had been set up in 1888, but had for long no intimate or general influence on village life. Villages and counties are the old units, and it was a pity, Joseph Ashby thought, that the old relationship was not revitalised and the old local feeling raised to a new power, county leaders inspiring villagers to a new ideal of village life. The new District Councils might make themselves useful, but who would ever know their boundaries except the men who served on them? And where was the interesting nucleus, such as the county town, to serve as a focus for feeling?

However, the men of Tysoe felt that it was policy and their duty to use to the utmost such powers as had been allotted to their new Parish Council. The sound discharge of its functions would provide an argument another day for larger responsibilities. Meanwhile every trade and grade of man might serve. They thought, with Joseph, that half the usefulness of public office is the civic training it gives. Men should not be greedy of office; it should be shared as widely as might be so that in time every family might have its sense of

participation in affairs and its insight into them. The first
Parish Council election in Tysoe was as lively an affair as a
parliamentary one. The day of village Radicals had come at
last! The Allotments Association was determined that the
full powers of a Council to control charities and provide
allotments should be used. They would take no chances and
that meant demanding a ballot. Perhaps they were right;
certainly they had it all their own way, only one Tory being
elected. But then at once their hearts melted; they remembered the duty to make for village unity and chose the
lonely Tory as their vice-chairman. From the first meeting
to this day the minutes are full and precise. They are entirely
superior to those of the old oligarchy, the School Managers,
the Vestry and the Feoffees! That was perfectly natural; the
new Council contained tradesmen more accustomed to
writing and figures than were farmers, and drew also upon
the experience of officers of Friendly Societies and the Allotments Association. Besides that, the Council was able to get
free advice on its business from an eminent barrister soon
to be a Q.C., and other outsiders.

Almost the first work of the Council was to bring to a close
the old difference about the Town Lands. It put forward
a new scheme to the Charity Commissioners (a great change
had come over this body) by which the Council would elect
a majority of the Trustees to serve for a limited period, to
which the Commissioners added the provision that this
majority should choose a small number of Life Trustees. The
old close corporation gave itself an ungracious end. Having
held sway for centuries and having had forty years' notice of
a popular wish for change, its members now resigned in
dudgeon, refusing one and all to have any more to do with
the Estate. The village wished to give them thanks, for they
had never failed in honesty, nor failed to spend the income in
ways of some use. Practical men knew that this was much,
realising that the frame within which the Feoffees had worked
had not encouraged more. But their leader, the Vicar,

refused all graciousness and now resigned not only his
Feoffee's seat but also his living. The village was sad: he
had been an active vicar, and most folk have a liking for an
energetic, colourful personality. Little stories began to be told
about him in the Peacock. He had said to his old gardener,
'Made a good job of that, John; which part ha' ye done?'
When two small boys stole apples, he had put his irascible
terrier under the tree and told him to keep them up in the
branches, and then he forgot both urchins and dog till there
was a hue and cry. Joseph smiled about him at his table,
saying that the old Vicar had specialised in the stern Father-
hood of God to the exclusion of the Brotherhood of Man, and
recited with a laugh the texts of the three last sermons he had
heard the Vicar preach: 'And when the wicked perish thou
shalt see it'; 'Cursed shalt thou be in the city and in the
field. . .'; 'And a great fear came upon all them that heard it'.
And, after all, Mr Francis did not depart unrung. Until a few
years ago the church bells still pealed out on his birthday,
and maybe do so to this day, the ringers wondering perhaps
the reason for joy, and some archaeologist peering for an
explanation into a past far dimmer even than the nineties.

Joseph was, of course, one of the new men. With the single
exception of the County Council he served on all the bodies,
new and old, of local government. He held in turn every
office in the Parish Council, became a Life Trustee of the
Utility Estate, and was for many years a member of the Rural
District Council. Sometimes also he was a beneficiary of the
new local government.

A second story that came to an end now was that of the
search for allotments. Would the new Vicar want the glebe
land? Mr Francis was the last parson for miles around to
farm his glebe. Was not this a chance for the Council to
obtain grassland for those who wanted it? Someone suggested
'Act at once!' 'Yes', came support, 'Not even by telegraph!
Send two men to see the new Vicar.' There was no need to
add 'before he can be prejudiced against us'. Joseph ascer-

tained the number of men wanting land and was one of the deputation to receive the new Vicar's promise. Eleven men wanting from three to six acres each could not share the twenty acres of glebe, but by good luck a small farm was shortly offered field by field. Thus was the demand for small allotments fulfilled. There were still men longing for mixed family holdings—miniature farms—and no prospect of those. But things were moving; the new County Councils had powers. (In fact the county did nothing in the Tysoe area till the nineteen-twenties.)

In the drawing of lots for the glebe land Joseph had been lucky. It was there that Jersey Beauty grazed; there that his older children waded in the brook and cut whistles from elder stems.

Another occasion on which he profited by the new Council came later when his large area of thatched roofing was saved by the Fire Brigade. The Brigade was a comely offshoot of the Parish Council. Its personnel was different from that of other groups (Joseph, for example, had nothing to do with it after its earliest days): a special prowess was needed in its spirited and ingenious practices. The little engine was not capable of putting out a raging fire, but the brigade was better than its machinery: the members learned to strip off thatch with speed, to organise bystanders for water-passing, to know in which outhouses were the longest and lightest ladders. Recruitment was never difficult: too many small boys longed to wear the brass helmets and blow the bugles, and growing lads to show the older folk how to be truly skilled and valiant. And now the Fire Brigade is part of the National Fire Service.

There were many routine duties for the new Council—the improvement of footpaths and greens; the care of bridges; the constant stimulation of other authorities to attend to roads and sanitary defects; and now and then some small special job. For example, some seven years after the founding of the Council a young Tysonian had come back to his village and—to the general astonishment and admiration—had built and

189

opened a new shop for drapery and ready-made clothes. His next idea was to obtain an 'off licence' to sell beer. Persuasively he wrote to the Council for support before the magistrates. But, instead, it sent two men, one of them Joseph, to oppose the application at Petty Sessions. 'There is no public need', said these, 'for an increase in licensed premises for the sale of spirituous liquors of any description.' Thus appeared the old anxiety about drink, the old feeling about sanctities. 'Such an increase would lead to deplorably more of drunkenness, immorality and profane and indecent language.' To this day the Peacock has it all its own way in the sale of 'spirituous liquors'.

Joseph's membership of the Rural District Council continued for sixteen years, until his available time was required for another office. On alternate Saturday mornings he went to Shipston on Stour where the meetings were held. Once a month there would be two meetings, the Council sitting in the afternoon in its second capacity as the Board of Guardians of the Poor. Though most of the work of the new R.D.C. was concerned with pedestrian matters of sanitation and minor licensing and registration, there must have been something enjoyable about the early meetings. The sedate and meagre minutes reveal the low official standards, but conditions frequently fell far below them. There must have been a sense that stables were being cleansed; the Inspector of Nuisances was very active; wells had to be cleaned out; pigsties were removed from contact with dwellings; landlords were ordered to 'whitewash and cleanse' cottages, or to 'provide six privies' for cottages which shared them. There were problems of water supply. Some Charity Trustees were neglecting their duty to maintain a 'fountain', that is, a public water-tap. One village's problem was 'solved' by the payment of four shillings annually to the host of the inn to allow his well to be used by the public. The Council's work grew, but only in petty kinds, the Tysoe rate remaining for long at about twopence-halfpenny in the pound.

Why did this unexciting, expensive attendance on such small works fail to exhaust Joseph's patience? Perhaps because few men of his particular status and experience could free themselves for it on, of all days, Saturday. (When at length Joseph resigned his place it was taken by a local small landowner, a good man, but no villager.) Perhaps also he liked his drive through six miles of charming country, differing only in quarter-tones from his home vale, but for him so distinctly; and certainly he liked the company of one of his elder children, asking questions about wild flowers and cloud-names, and clambering down from the gig to open the seventeen gates on the shorter road to Shipston.

But also when the Council became the Board of Guardians he liked the work for its own sake. He had long been a self-constituted guardian of some of the poor; now he had status in the work. His greater interest in it was shown by his references to it in talk. He was amazed, he said, by the change that came over some farmer Councillors when they took their seats as Guardians. Men who saw black ruin ahead if wages rose by sixpence a week, and who sent their men home the moment that rain made profit-making work difficult, would deal 'downright tenderly' with applications from the old and sick. The word 'Guardian' seemed to release in them Christian and paternal sentiments, or perhaps they eased their consciences. But occasionally Joseph thought their leniency was uncritical and even harmful.

An article in the *Land Magazine* for 1898 'by a Rural Guardian' is his by every sign of style. The writer is critical: he is trying to work out, for himself and others, a set of principles so that relief shall do only good. Mere charitableness and leniency may do some harm. The Friendly Societies are finding that they are called upon to continue sick payments longer than seems at all necessary to experienced officers. This is what is happening: a man in ill-health receives ten shillings from his Friendly Society. He applies to the Guardians for 'bread for the children', and this is granted.

In such a case the Guardians are disposed to help him on the ground that they are helping one who helps himself. But there are other reflections to be made. The applicant's usual wage is eleven shillings; now his income is twelve and sixpence and will go down when he returns to work. He has accepted relief and lost his vote. As in the days of the 'Speenhamland Act', relief is too easily gained and wages are too low. Also, applications are being made to the Guardians for 'medical relief' and 'midwifery orders', but only by families who never try to make any provision for the future. Sometimes, he writes, subtlety and shamelessness are practised upon the Guardians by applicants whose neighbours know perfectly well that they have concealed means of support. He has noted in the Parish Overseers' account books for the eighteenth century that payments are made to the unfortunate, 'the neighbours agreeing'. Guardians should be 'neighbours'! They should have intimate knowledge of the villages they serve. In another connection Joseph records about this time his view that old-age pensions should not be provided by the State. Poor Law Relief could come to the rescue in hard cases, but for the most part men should insure with their Friendly Societies for an income in old age: thus a man's pension would be his own; he would have the assurance of his rest having been earned. No man should earn such wages that he cannot insure. The agricultural industry cannot indeed afford to pay starvation wages. It has lived on the labourer's moral quality for a long time, but at last it is beginning to get the poor work it pays for. Wherever urban industry is its serious competitor for labour a higher wage is paid—and the farmer is better off.

Joseph's view seems strict and perhaps unduly individualistic. But then we have for the present lost his estimate of the importance of character. For him it is an injury to an unfortunate man to take his responsibility from him, and therewith his respect for himself. He thought also of the importance of a man's understanding his own affairs. Friendly Society schemes are made clear to members and at need modified by them. A simple person using his own powers of insight and criticism, retaining something more than mere economic freedom, is helped to reach his full natural stature. The worst theft, however carelessly or accidentally made, is this of responsibility for himself and his children. The family is the chief social unit and after that the small civic division.

In this view of his on pensions Joseph may have been right, but he was now out of step. Both Conservative and Liberal parties were studying the question of old-age pensions, and both would come to the conclusion that they must be provided. And Joseph, becoming like all the world more of a party man, would modify his views.

Something of a new era had begun in Tysoe. The new institutions were being worked with a will and were far more efficient than the old ones. The Fire Brigade had had some great successes and was famous for miles round. More than that, the new Vicar, after a mistake or two, was showing a desire for unity. He became a member of Court Greenwood Tree as well as of the Provident Club. He also asked for general support for the Brotherhood of the White Cross (or some such title) which he had started. It met in the church on Sunday afternoons, when the Vicar talked to the men on matters close to home. Families were too large! No one denied it, but the men would not go to hear such things. What did the Vicar know about their home life? Nevertheless, it was clear that under the Vicar's strange haughty manner and within that divided mind was a heart of courage. If there was not a reign of Peace in Tysoe between 1895 and 1899, efforts were made to enthrone her. It was now that the Plymouth Brethren built their 'tin chapel' on Joseph's one-time garden in the Back Lane. Methodists and Churchmen discussed the tenets of the Brothers in all friendliness, and a few even sampled their services. Fred Woodfield told Joseph that he would rather have his hand cut off than make a cross on a ballot paper with it. As Joseph told Hannah about this incident he laughed at the doctrinaire view. But Fred had shown the chasms of thought that lay between the Brethren and all other Tysonians—Tory, Radical, Socialist, conformist and non-conformist. The Brethren postponed Heaven to another world; the rest all now believed that Tysoe ought itself to be, for everyone in it, one of God's many mansions, and even that its transformation was beginning.

But this brief period came to an end in the autumn of 1899 with the opening of the Boer War, a conflict that would come closer to Tysoe than other wars had done. George Paxton, a retired soldier on the 'Return' list was called up early. The possibility of war had caused thoughts to turn to physical training even in Tysoe. Ex-Sergeant Paxton had been engaged in drilling youths and boys in the evening and day schools. A question had arisen as to whether his evening classes were or were not 'Technical training' and whether, therefore, they could be paid for out of the famous 'whisky money'. The difficulty was solved: Paxton was shortly 'shut up in Kimberley', and no one was available to 'teach drill'. The war was a painful idea. Gold and diamond mines in South Africa seemed as useless as the rubies in the crowns of Indian princes. Kruger was not altogether a strange figure to the grown-ups, being a farmer, a reader of the Bible, a homely man who dug his heels in. But gradually they succumbed to the urban notion of him as fantastically old-fashioned and obstinate, a figure of fun.

Less than three months after the war began came the New Century. For the children there was tremendous magic about it. Centuries came rushing in like mighty winds, sweeping away one state of the world and depositing another. The new Twentieth Century was to have been a lovely golden time; in fact they found it toned and coloured with evil. At the concert given in January 1900 by the children and teachers of the school strange and moving songs were sung about 'the red, the white and the blue'. On this occasion was first heard 'The Ten Little Nigger Boys', with its terrible conclusion, 'And then there were none', which became linked with the thought of the Tysoe boys who had enlisted. Would none of them come back?

A few men were strongly against the war, among them melancholy John Price and choleric Tom Gardner. Joseph was one of them also, though his expressions were not as strong as John's or Tom's. On the other hand, the Vicar, with his army connections, was devoted to the families of all the lads who volunteered. Some felt that he was all but recruiting, for the drum and fife band of the Church Lads' Brigade so often seared the air at twilight. It was felt that he should not have consented to give Christian babies the names 'Kimberley' and 'Paardeburg', those grotesque keepsakes of the times.

Of course the 'Pro-Boers' held meetings on the greensward between the blacksmith's shop and the Peacock, when the length of days permitted. Joseph is recalled with his arm outstretched towards the Franchise Tree. The case the government made was hypocritical, he said. The Boers had been provoked: there were hidden factors in the war. 'They say Kruger refuses votes to the Outlanders. Look at our Franchise Tree: it has never borne an acorn yet.' (The stripling of eighteen years was visible against the western light.) 'An Outlander can hardly vote till he is forty years old. If you had been a hundred years old in 1883, you would still have been voiceless, not in a foreign country but in the home of your ancestors. And if you had threatened violence to get your vote, the British Army would have been used to suppress and not to support you.'

Meanwhile British arms fared badly. There was anxiety for the men besieged at Kimberley, Ladysmith and Mafeking. Then the outbreak of enteric fever among our soldiers added to the violence of emotion. The three leading Pro-Boers of Tysoe were all Methodists: they found that even their Church was against them. 'We are fighting', said the *Methodist*

Times, 'for the most sacred rights of millions of human beings who have more claim to Africa than either Boers or Englishmen...the British Empire has no diviner call than to stand between the slave and his oppressor.' More important still, the *Daily News* took for a while the view that the Boers deserved the war. More influential than the paper's opinion were its vivid reports and lively maps: these tended strongly to carry sympathy to our men. Then, too, the casualty lists, given in detail, made refusal of support seem callous. '2nd Lieut. Smith, both thighs, severe: Capt. Brown, abdomen, dangerous.' People became bitter towards the 'Pro-Boers', though always less so in the country than in the towns.

Kimberley was relieved in February and Ladysmith, a bigger job, a while later. When at last the Boers fell back from it there was excitement everywhere. In Tysoe the drum and fife band was out. Tom Gardner, in a speech on the green, objected to this mode of teaching patriotism. It had the wrong effect on the children's minds; it was militarism. The meetings became frequent again, Tom and Joseph speaking on alternate evenings. By 18 May, 'Mafeking night', feeling was high in the village, as everywhere in the country. Arthur Ashby was thirteen and remembered it well as long as he lived. The Boys' band was out again (the Wesleyan Temperance Band was silent throughout the war). Tom Middleton at Church Farm sent his men to cut gorse on his hill fields, and his brother's men built the bonfire by the Church Town Brook. It was a fine evening and a great crowd waited for the lighting of it. When Mr Middleton went forward with his torch the sons and younger workmen of the Pro-Boers rushed upon the heap of faggots and scattered it wide. One seized the band's drum and beat it. (The sober ideas of elders are not soberly reflected in the minds of their young.) Still, the boys and youths could suspend prejudice; the next evening they all joined to rebuild the bonfire and rejoice in the wonderful beauty of a great fire. Arthur remembered watching golden translucent branches of gorse sail into the turquoise light of the sky, like souls floating heavenwards, leaving weighty bodies.

The 'firebrand of politics', as the Vicar called it, was still in the village. But it was 'douted' at last. There was a day, nearly a year after Mafeking night, when Daisy Ashby was washing up breakfast things and Father came in asking 'Where is your mother?' 'Mother', he called, as Hannah hurried towards him, 'Mother, Charlie Botterill is dead. His father has just heard. Died of enteric fever.... Harrismith.' The two gazed at each other for minutes, it seemed to their onlooking daughter. Charlie was very young and one of those persons born to be loved. Everywhere you went that day, there was only one topic of news—Charlie was dead. It was not long before the news came that Frank Freeman, a promising fellow, 'Despatch rider to Colonel Forbes', had also died of enteric fever, at Heilbron. Looking back it is difficult to believe that a village could be so at one in grief as for these lads, but now our emotions are so worn down by world wars and by catastrophes reported hourly from every quarter.

The old Queen died in the next January and men could express their trouble round the symbol of her funeral. Roberts's blockhouses had not yet been built, but the end of the war was coming. All the newspapers, Tory and Radical, conformist and nonconformist and sporting, were writing of the terms of peace, all advocating generosity and a new start. Jingoism was dead. In Tysoe it had never had vigour.

CHAPTER XV

YOUNG VILLAGERS

As his children grew Joseph remembered how much he had learned through talking with and watching his elders, and wished to do for us earlier and more fully what his friends had done for him. So when the children had gone up to bed in their goodnight cleanliness, soothed into sweetness of spirit by Mother's attentions, Father would follow and tell them about his day. He might perhaps have seen some clever work—Mr Groves of Hardwick Farm breaking in a vicious young horse spoiled by other horse-breakers, using no whip, having no fear, no hurry. Or he had seen the quarrymen cutting through vast stones and moving them with levers. But also sometimes his mind was on some sketch of an amusing experience he meant to write for the *Warwick Advertiser*, or a story he was writing for the *Land Magazine*, and he would try out a first version on the children. Most of the stories he told have gone beyond recall, but one was remembered by its tragic occasion. Father had come home one evening from 'The Promise' to hear heartbroken sobs from the little girls' bedroom. They had taken tea to him at his work and on the way back through the three fields had stopped to watch boys flinging wet clay balls against a willow tree. While they gazed, the tea-can lid had fallen off, and could not be found. The day before they had broken a china cup that had cost sevenpence. A second loss was too much: their mother in terrible severity had sent them to bed. But heartbreak is too much even on account of sevenpence. Father soothed Mother—'They didn't mean to, they won't again'—and launched into the story.

Before the very last hunt of last season there had been a meet in front of the big house at Upton that looks so new, with its long bright windows and white stone, but is really centuries old. There were the huntsmen in their pink coats and black helmets, on shining horses; ladies sitting side-saddle with wide skirts spread over their boots, wearing little hard hats with round crowns. And of course there was the pack of hounds. They were like Mother's rolled herrings, all their tails up and their heads hidden. Among the mounted gentlemen was the new owner of Upton House. He made beer in London—beer that smelt so good and tasted so nasty—and his house was full of money-bags. His mount was a wonderful great chestnut, a fifteen-hander. Though the children did not know what 'fifteen-hander' meant, the word made the horse vast and powerful, their Sleipnir or Bucephalus. On the edge of the crowd of greater folk and beyond the hounds, there was old Farmer Greggins, on his Grumpy, an old horse with sides like giant hay-rakes. There was a boy on a donkey, too, determined to see the hunt. In an outside circle were men and boys ready to follow the hunt on foot, and among these was Miller Mosthorpe from a little village just under the hills. (The boys were listening at our door, and at the miller's name they laughed and came inside; they had seen him and could guess there would be a funny tale.) The moment had come: the first of all the pinkcoats gave the sign. The hounds rustled, the horn called. The women and children left behind on the green heard the hunt more and more faintly as they went off across the fields towards Ricewell Covert. The big brewer on Fifteen-hander was not very used to riding, he was so often busy in London, but he rode bravely, following the others. The reason he lagged behind was that he tried to make Fifteen-hander do what he wanted, but the big horse knew better about jumping hedges and brooks, and so they did not get on very well. When they came to quite a little brook and a low fence most of the huntsmen lolloped over like children on rocking-horses, but the Upton gentleman pulled at his horse's reins just at the wrong moment and splash! Fifteen-hander had him in the brook! Meanwhile Miller Mosthorpe knew the way well that the hounds had chosen and took short cuts on foot where horses could not go, and was not so far behind. But he had to go as hard as he could: his breath was coming in great pants, his face was red and his legs getting heavier and heavier. If he could only keep going a little longer he would see the hounds head the fox out of Ricewell Covert. Suddenly he heard a shout. 'Here you, fellow! I am hurt!' called the master of Upton House, 'Fetch the doctor!' But the doctor was far away in front riding on a swift light horse—the miller had seen him. 'Get on my horse, then', the brewer shouted, and called the miller 'a great lout'. He had a terrible pain in his shoulder, that was why he shouted so. 'I can't mount him, Sir! I can't ride his like!', the miller shouted back, and then the poor gentleman groaned and groaned. So, as Miller Mosthorpe was a merciful man, and as Fifteen-hander stood munching grass, so large and quiet, the miller led him to the railings by the brook and contrived to fling a fat leg over him. All went swimmingly; the hand-some Fifteen-hander went on with a slow dignity and the miller sat up grandly in the saddle. But the huntsman's horn sounded and the horse quickened his pace. Soon he was going Smack! Smack! in a smart trot, and the miller jerked up and up like a boy on a bare-backed pony, without ever coming quite down to the saddle. Every moment the hounds and the horn were heard more clearly. Suddenly the miller got a frightful bump on the saddle. Fifteen-hander tossed and snorted, and then, with his head stretched out, nostrils blowing, and heels up, he went full tilt towards the hounds. To hold on, the miller had to slip his arm through the reins and grip the saddle so tight that as he swayed, he looked like a dummy stitched to the seat. His coat-tails flapped, his spring-fastened leggings came undone and the steels in them hit the horse little stinging blows.

Fifteen-hander felt now that he had a mystery on his back and he completely forgot the hunt. Now the miller could hear nothing but the terrific thuds of his gallop. Horse and rider tore out of the fields and into Sugarswell Lane. That, the children knew, was miles long and ended in Ratley village. In the Ratley street the children at play caught sight of the miller and laughed to see his clothes blowing wide and his hat go flying into their low muddy pond. The miller still held on by the saddle though he felt his fingers would break, and bowed low along the horse's neck.

At last even Fifteen-hander was tired, a little, and began to think that after all there was not much harm in the miller, so he dropped from his gallop to an amble. The poor miller undid his aching fingers gradually and slid down the horse's flank. Limping like a poor old man he led Fifteen-hander all the way back to his grand stable behind Upton House.

After the little story there was a long pause while the little girls stopped their laughing to sorrow for the miller, and the boys went on thinking of the great horse. Then some child asked 'Daddy, is there a moral?' and 'Of course, my beauty', he said, 'Millers must learn to say "No"!'

Instead of stories, there might be chats about someone the children had seen. There was the woman who came to the door now and then with a tray full of cottons, Torchon lace and buttons of linen and pearl—a foreign-looking woman with a weather-reddened face and neat dark hair in a thousand tiny plaits. Part of her fascination was her pedlar's manner, treating even the children as important folk and her own wares as treasures. There were other little shops that came to the door—Mr Harrison arrived once a fortnight from Northend with his heavily laden van. He brought the paraffin oil for the lamps and sold cups and saucers and brushes. He had none of the air of a pedlar, but appeared quietly at the door and spoke so low you could scarcely hear him. There were the gipsies—short folk, with shining black hair and dark faces. They wore rich decorations—gold ear-rings and little bright shawls. What they brought were clothes-pegs, but these, in a careful household, have long lives, so the children smiled and said 'no', but the gipsies wheedled and the more they said that Mother had no need the more the gipsies pressed, with an arm on the door lest a child should shut it. There were fewer pedlars than there used to be, Father said, but they would never die out. As one kind ceased another came. There was now the welcome Friday fish-man: fish was a wonderful change from bacon! There was the bearded melancholy Mr Fisher the draper, with his rolls of cheap stuff and packs of black woollen stockings. But in days gone by the pedlars had brought more varied trays. It was they who used to bring the silver 'Mizpah' brooches, velvet ribbons, and embroidery patterns. Shakespeare had a pedlar who brought songs and music for pipes, but that was before the Puritan time; he and his kind had been succeeded, so Father had heard say, by Bible-and-pamphlet men. It was only a few years since a man came with brass-bound Bibles that the people paid for by a few pence a week. He brought pictures too; one could see them hanging in the cottages—*Moses Overlooking the Promised Land* (not the allotments, mind, but the Bible 'Promised') and a companion picture of Abraham half-way up the hill with Isaac the sacrifice. 'And did he bring the *Rocky Path to Heaven* and the *Broad Highway to Hell*?' asked the biggest child, who had seen those exciting pictures in a playmate's home. 'Yes,' said Joseph, 'more's the pity, he brought those too.' So today's pedlars joined a procession out of centuries before, into ages to come.

We were of course making contact in our persons with the village. To church we went with our grandmothers: to the 'Primitive' chapel on its high days, and to the 'Camp Meeting' when services were conducted from bough-decked wagons, we were sent by our parents, to show their friendly interest. As schoolchildren we went to tea at Compton Wynyates, with the Marchioness presiding. The Flower Show was the most scented day of all the summer and the blaring music from the merry-go-round organ blew over vast distances, echoing and mixing with wind sounds: the family triumphs in the show added something to the quality of the day, not that they had much ability as gardeners, but sometimes they would beat those who had, as when Father sent a perfect triplet of little marrows, all exactly alike, and took the prize against elephantine specimens.

The boys of course knew the fields somewhat as their father had done. From his leaving school Arthur accompanied his father on all his errands to measure crops and ricks, holding the roller-tape or the chain. Soon this work was child's play to him and he would be sent to do the job himself. But he never went without brother or sister; some of my own early memories are of my pride in carrying the tape even while the pools of water in the huge cabbage leaves were poured into my boots as I walked.

Though brothers were better acquainted with the hills and neighbouring villages, sisters knew more interiors. It was we who delivered eggs or butter and who took round Mother's bills and Father's political pamphlets. Thus we came to know all the farmyards and the insides of a good many houses. Nearly always there was Apollyon to be passed in the yards— a terrifying dog, or a collective Apollyon, a flock of geese, each with neck and beak in a straight line for bare legs. Full of our mission we clung together, but still with our faces to the farm kitchen door, so brave that presently we would be cowards for ever at bark or cackle, and maybe in larger matters. But there was a difference even in these early days in the quality of our acquaintance with our native village and my father's in his early days. We knew it less thoroughly, perhaps also with less of imagination, but our minds were more affected by the imagination of others; our own background was more complex and the village filled at this time less room in our minds.

Of course many things had changed in the village since Joseph's early boyhood, while keeping the same names, but school was not one of these. There was still the same schoolmaster and the same Vicar. School for the children was another world from home, one within which you were ignorant

and helpless. Pupils awaited instruction; they were seldom
called upon to proffer any capacity except memory. Out-of-
school merits and abilities and knowledge were completely
out-of-sight. But school was accepted as all in the proper
order of things, for parents spoke as if school were good and
teachers always right and just. Because of this attitude, no
Ashby child would have dreamed of commenting on matters
that nevertheless left acute impressions—the Babel noise, and
then such an artificial silence that you could hear creakings in
the church clock: or the strange horrible smell in the boys'
cloakroom, stirring to young nostrils. But work was a little
less uninteresting than in Father's day. The snippets in the
reading books were still more oddly varied. They caused the
children to build extraordinary pictures of the world. Of
other countries, one was all compound of pigtails and gorgeous
palaces, another was full of baleful prodigies—birds like
animals and trees like mountains, and cherries with the stones
around the flesh! 'Object lessons', except for the first two
standards, had gone, and geography had come. It was called
a 'class subject', but in fact promontories and isthmuses and
gulfs were treated much as the cow had been in Father's time;
definitions of island and archipelago were learnt and so were
lists of the headlands and capes all round Britain. The 'class
subject' was always in danger; their distant Lordships who
paid for it 'could not' the Inspectors said 'regard the
children's answers as bright'. They only paid the grant 'in
hope'. But map-making came at last, and then the children
began to remember. There was a poetry lesson once a week
and then also the memorised lines were chanted to fill up
vacant minutes. How very often:

> The deep-mouthed blood-hounds' heavy bay
> Resounded up the rocky way!

Still, poetry is the toughest substance of all. Not all the
sing-song could remove the pathos from

> O that those lips had language! Life has passed
> With me but roughly since I saw thee last.

Perpetual repression kept the energies of the children in a cave of Aeolus, where the strong winds whirled around rags and gauds of imagination. Any escape was often better than the noise and nagging—even a visit to the stinking closets, seats arow. If you could get there alone, your mind was free to scale the nine-foot wall and see trivial fairies over there; but if you had all the luck in the world you might see the clear-cut vase of a convolvulus flower looking wondering over. Sometimes, too, in the emptiness there would be a peculiar deep stirring of the imagination, so that formless, unconnected, indescribable, moods and thoughts pressed into the vacuum. The poverty of school-life ground especially upon the children who had no gift for day-dreaming. They had to play truant physically or, when they could not do so, to play loutishly and get themselves caned. Nor was it only the children who suffered, as they discovered once, by the way the Master changed when half the school was away in some epidemic. School was quiet, 'discipline' unnecessary and the Master suddenly smiling, fresh in his teaching and talk, rushing out into the girls' cloakroom to get a flower-trimmed hat to explain the word 'artificial', or even laughing with a class about some incident.

School was never, and never seemed to be, a community. The seal of patronage was on it, of having been provided by some persons for others, but not for their sake, by one class for another, without emphasis on shared humanity or culture. It was a little better for children of the church than for those of the chapel. They might have a relative among the pupil-teachers and friendly instead of inimical patronage from the Vicar. 'Do not let these Dissenters beat you', the old Vicar would say, in a Scripture test.

It was when Arthur was nine that the new Vicar arrived. One day he came into school shortly before midday and talked to the children on the subject of manners. He spoke of his father, the General, and the order of ranks in the army. The children were omitting to curtsy to his wife and daughters

and their governess. Girls should not say 'Good morning';
they should silently curtsy. Boys should not raise their caps
but should touch them only. God divinely appointed us to
our places in society and we should learn the appropriate
manners. Arthur enlivened his family dinner table with a
spirited account of this talk, and was surprised to see his father
rise in terrible anger and go off there and then to the Vicarage.
He would not have his children taught ridiculous manners!
The Vicar must confine himself to Scripture periods, and he
and his friends would withdraw their children from those,
under the Cowper-Temple clause!

The Vicar had an aristocratic view of society and yet
he was an evangelical Christian! He visibly alternated
between stress on his own and his family's social claims and
his wish to be a simple follower of Christ, between an ardent
wish to bring about all possible unity in his complex parish
and the sense that it ill became him as Vicar ever to accept
any place but the first. Joseph soon began to understand that
divided mind, but not so his children. They would never,
never forgive his haughty manner to their mother, as he stood
at her door—no smile, no lifted hat: there was no other person
but rendered homage.

When Arthur and his hereditary friend Wilby Wells were
nearly eleven years old, they entered the Master's top class.
Once for a whole month the pupil-teachers were away with
scarlet fever and the Master busy with other classes. Then the
two boys raced through arithmetical textbooks and even went
on to a little algebra. They could work at a single subject for
a whole afternoon, reading or mapping their fill. At the end
of the year Wilby, being the son of a farmer, was to go to
Chipping Campden Grammar School, but Arthur was needed
at home: they both left school just before their twelfth
birthdays.

Both boys had decided to be scientists. It was some time
before this that Arthur had made his magic lantern—for himself an experiment, for 'his' children its name expressed its

nature. The dark room was Mother's wash-house; the screen
was a clean tea-cloth hung over a clothes-horse. With
children's extraordinary patience the audience peered through
the vagueness and blurring of the pictures as they shook up
and down in the manipulator's hand, till they discovered in all
amazement a donkey or a wagon of hay. The marvel was the
greater because the children saw the experimenter's difficulties—his oil-lamp smoking and the cloth falling. Arthur
was patient, explaining over and over though vehemently,
why the picture had to go in upside down before the light.

Wilby was learning chemistry in a proper laboratory:
Arthur tested soils in vessels on the kitchen windowsill and
made coal-gas in the sitting-room grate. One day, two of
Father's visitors, his old friend King and a new friend, the
Liberal candidate for the Rugby Division, Mr Corrie Grant,
saw the curious-looking, messy compound Arthur had made for
his mother, to 'save the expense of soap', and heard of the
gushing blue flames of coal-gas. A fortnight or so after this,
two great packing-cases arrived at Kineton railway station.
Arthur fetched them with the pony and gig. One was addressed
to himself; the whole family stood round to see it opened and
the strangest objects emerged—glass tubes, bottles of
coloured powder, retorts, spirit lamps; in short, equipment
for a miniature chemical laboratory. Out came text-books,
also—the *Chemistry of the Garden*, and others. There was no
attic, no spare outhouse, the children's bedrooms were
crowded with children, but still the experiments in the books
were performed—on the kitchen table, on the hearth, wherever
space could be cleared. Wilby Wells came home for his
Christmas holiday expecting Arthur to make humble gleanings from his descriptions of doings in the school laboratory,
and was astonished to see what a princely and exotic gift had
come Arthur's way. He came to tea, and in his own later
words 'to regain his prestige, proposed to conduct an experiment Arthur had not yet ventured on'. Should they make
crystals of copper sulphate (interesting, because this was the

same as vitriol that Wilby's father dressed his wheat with)? No; digesting a penny took a long time. Besides, honour and the expectant company of children called for something spectacular. There were the oxidising properties of potassium chlorate—that was the thing! He mixed some potassium chlorate with sugar on a watch-glass, and dropped a little acid on to the mixture. There was a startling flash, faces felt scorched, the lamp slid off the table, the big milk-white globe smashing to pieces, smoke and oil-smell filling the room. But Father and Mother rushed in and all ended well except for three great burns on Aunt Rouvray's Spanish-mahogany table.

The second of the great boxes was full of books. Mr Corrie Grant, lawyer, parliamentary candidate, author busy on a great volume on electoral law, had spared time to ransack his library for hungry country children.

Beloved volumes from the chest were two of weird violent American atmosphere, Frederic's *The Copperhead* and Bret Harte's *Bell Ringer of Angel's*—wild men, wild women, wild horses and a wild boy, all fine images for a child's oft-frustrated self. There were (a rare thing), some books especially for little girls. How many good things get swilled down time's sink: lost are those books except for dim traces in one memory. There were full instructions for a doll's washing day, rhymes about roasting and baking, drawings of bed-making and sweeping. My sister and I wished we might, like railways and laundry-maids in our conundrum book, 'iron all England' and make every pudding under the sun. When we heard someone quote 'Who sweeps a room as for thy laws' we thought it odd that the poet should choose sweeping to exemplify dull work.

Hans Andersen's tales were the only children's classic, not counting *Pilgrim's Progress*, in the house, but probably they did not come in the box for they were in tiny print, blotty, on soft yellowish paper, unreadable except by very young eyes. They took you into a sorrowful world, to learn of a sister sewing stinging-nettle shirts for brothers, sad saucer-eyed cats and dead grandmothers, those who killed them so oddly unreproached! For Arthur there was Gibbins's *Industrial History of England*, one of the first books he ever 'really read'; it and later books turned his mind from chemistry. The boxes were worth years and years of school.

The large world was coming nearer to us, to the whole village. A cyclist, ignorant of the district, trusting to the flimsy brakes of his new Safety Model, crashed to his death down Sunrising Hill, the first to do that but not the last. The first motor-car to visit the village stopped outside Church Cottage. There was trouble in the Balkans and Father must have a daily newspaper, the *Westminster Gazette*; even a village politician could not live without daily information about distant scenes.

A happy impingement were the visitors from the bigger world. When they were expected the house smelt rich and sweet of cakes and buttermilk scones and hot jams! They did not all send treasure-chests, but how they all—to our intense absorption—talked! The political visitors were our favourites: their talk was more vigorous and their laughter merrier than that of the preachers on Sundays. Of them all Mr Grant was the bright star. He and his companions came on errands of the parliamentary constituency, but the talk over the table would be about books, notable folk he knew, and old and new discoveries. He would draw in the boys and girls, challenging them to read this, or explore that before he came again. And back in London, he would remember them and send a post-card with some bit of information, or a book, and the latter would have a special look in the bookcase because of this brilliant friend's kindness.

The family group was growing; it grew till there were eight children, Arthur the eldest fourteen years older than Janet Rouvray the youngest—late Victorian children, with on the whole late Victorian names. Family names from the eighteenth century, Mestor and Robert and Dinah seemed associated with a mean, marred past that was to be left behind, and were set aside in favour of Elsie and Wilfred and Daisy. But towards 1900 older names came back, William and Sybil. So the group had, as the nineteen-fifties say, texture. There was scope within it for protector and protected, tease and teased, for many attitudes and activities. Experience changed too. While the older ones were children of puzzled young parents, anxious and struggling, Janet Rouvray's father was a farmer and respected magistrate. She herself was the protected darling, where Arthur had been a second father.

CHAPTER XVI

SATURDAYS AND SUNDAYS

It was in the second September of the new century that my father and mother removed their family to their fourth home, a little farmstead in the Lower Town. My father would now round off his knowledge of his home village by seeing life from the most detached of the three towns. For him and my mother the removal to The Orchards was an essential step in gaining a living for their children. There were home closes beside stables and sties and implement sheds. Now Joseph would be a farmer, if of a miniature farm. His forty acres, growing towards fifty, were still made up of an odd assortment of small fields and allotments, scattered wide, like a farm of strips in the open fields.

But also Joseph and Hannah understood that space and interest in their home would be a vital gift to their children. Their youngest, eighth child Janet Rouvray had been born in 1900. If the house at The Orchards was none too large for such a brood there was ample space outside. By this time their eldest son, Arthur, was fifteen years old, happy enough, but passionately exploring his environment to find scope for himself. Working, reading and discussion were not enough: he tried fantastic ways to add to his few shillings of capital, responding to advertisements, buying, for example, strange trinkets to sell again.

But with the move to The Orchards these little enterprises ceased: temporarily there was scope enough. For all the children the 'new' house was perfect. For the middle-sized ones it was as if the ideal homestead laid up in heaven had descended and taken its seat on earth. In the centre was a long thatched house running from east to west and attached at right angles to it ran a series of outhouses, whose roofs were as high as that of the small farmhouse, in all, as their father said, 'a quarter of an acre of thatch'. To the south was garden ground, and on the east a combined animal yard and rick yard, and north-west again, two ancient picturesque cottages, all these embowered in orchards. Village houses had at that date usually no names of their own, but the Ashbys' new homestead had to be christened lest Joseph's letters should go to an old relative; and being named, The Orchards became in the course of time a friend and a beloved, all its details noted and adored with passion.

From the beginning the children had, in a measure, to earn their home. They took many journeys from Church Cottage to Lower Town, carrying a basket of frail objects, large glass shades of oil-lamps, or Mother's best china—journeys taken while thoughts of the Boer War still threaded their experience through with its poignant and macabre quality. But these strands faded as the children explored the rich autumnal paradise of The Orchards.

Through the north orchard flowed a brook where water-cress grew, beyond which stood the Ribston pippin tree and the pear tree bearing two kinds of pears. On the hither side of the brook stood a single tree, the 'queenings' apple, whose rosy, striped, and ridgy fruit dropped into the long grass while other apples were still hard and unattainable. The ridges were 'quoins', Father said, and the apples descendants of the 'quoinings' that grew in Queen Elizabeth's gardens. This information the children rejected, for they thought queenings a better name for apples so lovely, though as a rule of course, Father's comments made the children's eyes rest observantly on many things.

In the south orchard, below the house, the grass grew deeper, and under the two great walnut trees in the centre the children trod off the soft hoods of the nuts and snuffed up the huge scent of them, their feet deep in the misted grass. That pleasure was matched by the first morning taste of the big round Burgundy pears. Here were also apples of many sorts—those quaint ones, four or five small elongated fruits grouped together, not valued for flavour but good for their quaintness and their name, Ladies' Fingers. Autumn joys lasted till October frosts, when the children gathered the golden-ruddy bullaces, suddenly changed from hard green marbles to russet sweet-sour fruit.

But it was in the spring that the south orchard was not earth at all, but heaven. Beyond the brook at the bottom, in the tiny paddock, a great perry-pear tree, huge as a forest giant, was a snowy pyramidal mountain of blossom. Around every apple tree grew sweet violets, white or pink or blue. Whiteness in violets was like Sundayness in a frock; it made them sacred, saintly.

A greater fact than the riches of the orchards was their space—space for the ten-year-olds to form their rebellious little clubs, for older children to read memorable books and walk with exciting folk, for girls to give parties for smaller children, for which they had made ginger-snaps, burning their faces in front of the hot fire, as they 'creamed' the butter. Here, later on, the younger ones would re-enact the great Warwick pageant, becoming Druids and Crusaders.

The house itself was built on a most ancient pattern. A single long roof covered stables, barn and house; at the east end were Lady London's and Captain's loose-boxes, then came the 'Gatehouse', lately used as a wheelwright's shop. The kitchen came next, a compromise between house and barn, the dark thatch high above, and groundwards a tiled floor that glowed rosy-red after washing, a shell of a room, with no contents but a heavy table, some washtubs, the churn and a furnace: but soon it was to be adorned by the beautiful Alfa-Laval separator. Next came the 'house', the central living room, with the cooking stove occupying the great space originally intended for the burning of small tree-trunks. This central room had many doors—to the kitchen, to the stairs, to the dairy and the study, and then also the main door to the outside world: and yet it was never cold there and though it was not large, the children were not cramped as they ate and played and read, except when the black dog of sulks was troubling them. And yet it was well, of course, that there were rooms beyond the 'house', where quiet fell on one—the cool dimly lighted room that served as larder and dairy, where for a while Hannah would set shallow tin bowls of new milk and take off the cream with the curved skimmer, and where she laid bacon in the great stone trough for curing; and then, last, the little study. There was always a fire here on Sundays and on those days of the week when Father wrote his articles for the *Warwick Advertiser* and the *Land Agents' Record*. When he had finished the children could do here their own reading and writing, and the quiet they made for Father they kept for themselves. Above were only three bedrooms, but up more stairs were the attics, one for apple storage, and one for boys to sleep in. Aloft here, there might have been space for the old toy laboratory to come into use again but it was rifled of its lamps and its useless powders packed up—space, now, but no time.

In the gatehouse, with the two barn-doors thrown wide, there was room for many occupations. Here bicycles were mended, and Mother's chairs and sofas were upholstered, and fruit was packed in wicker 'pots'. Brother Dick ranged along the old shelves and hung on rows of hooks his large collection of tools, he being the only member of the family the current of whose life flowed smoothly from hand to brain and from brain to hand. Here it was that once the boys brought back clapnets from a nocturnal raid on the winter hedges, but next morning their sisters cried to see the little greenfinches entangled in the string.

Teasing and sulks and tears there were among the children at times, but as rarely as might be. For by now the family was woven together in an elaborate pattern, on the whole richly harmonious, composed of the loves and admirations between brothers and sisters. Infantile exclusions had been lost in the thrills of common activities.

Saturdays and Sundays

The children's photographic visual memories of this time show their father as happily contemplating his family. He would stand tall in a doorway gazing on the ring of young heads, bent over books under the warm lamps, and listen over the tea-table to their accounts of all their experiences with a face full of pleasure. He never feared to admire and praise. It is evident in these memories that he was satisfied that even his fast-growing older children could flourish here.

But there was one condition on which the family might be happy; one and all they must help constantly to gain the wherewithal to live. It was not only the growing of the corn for physical life. There were Hannah's domestic standards; there was entertaining (no guest from distant parts must miss his comforts at Joseph's table); there were books and papers to buy; beautiful best clothes to make.

Life was divided into two qualities; the Saturday quality, the effort and strain and triumph of getting through the work, and the Sabbath leisure, and unworldly atmosphere. Saturday's arduous preparations for Sunday and the week to come involved such intensity that the girls could at any time in later life re-live its every hour.

For a year after the removal they helped their mother with the beloved first job of the day—the weekly baking in the bread-oven in the wall: the girls made and fed the fire, while mother kneaded the dough. When the loaves were in and the big oak block pushed against the oven's mouth, they fetched and carried for their mother while she shredded the white lard, marjoram-scented, into dough for lard-cakes. Men and boys came in, to enjoy the orgy of heat, scent and promise, offering help early in breaking the faggots and later, wielding the long wooden peel to take out the loaves from the cavern. But this old method disorganised the house and the day and made so much litter that mother bought a small modern range, and baked more often.

Afterwards, Saturday's routine began for the girls with washing-up and sweeping. Then they would go on to bed-

215

making. Kathleen and Daisy would work together one on each side of the beds. Rhythmic and monotonous movements allowed of talk and even song. Once, in imitation of chants they heard in church when they accompanied their grandmother thither, they composed a chant for the illuminated psalm hanging in Mother's bedroom, 'Thou wilt keep him in perfect peace, whose mind is stayed on Thee'. At least the chant expressed the peace of their partnership which lasted day-long.

Then one girl washed the stone floor of the house, and the other scrubbed the table—the latter a favourite job because it was ticklish, not a drop of soapy water must drop on the stones, and because of the charming result in the white spotless surface, showing, like the ragstone flags, its vigorous graining. Then, while Mother cooked the day's dinner in the house they washed the 'milk things' in the kitchen. The Alfa-Laval separator had been installed, a beloved instrument. Both boys and girls loved to strain the warm milk into it, to start turning the handle slowly, slowly, with a hard, weighty pull, increasing the pace to a rapid speed and rhythm, with the machine's own song rising from a thin air to a deafening organ roar. But the greatest charm lay in the two streams, the thick small one of cream and the larger gush of skimmed milk, which the little machine had so magically made from the single descending column. Of course, the boys and girls understood their separator's workings, having carefully considered all its parts, but while its monotonous ringing song filled the dark roof of the kitchen and gatehouse they forgot the centrifugal motions and the differing weights of milk and cream, and were absorbed in the magic.

Once while the girls were 'separating' the milk, their father and Corrie Grant stood by watching them. In the intervals of the various noises of their work, they heard snatches of a conversation about their own life. Joseph had said something of the children's zest in what they did, and the two agreed that it was never interesting work that hurt the young. It would be valuable later to have worked as well as played. The girls could never call in question the opinions of these elders and betters, but dimly they wondered where the play came in.

One of the biggest jobs of all was the cleaning of everybody's better pair of shoes. In theory these were kept, after they had been worn, in long rows at the back of the heavy rough table against one wall of the kitchen, next to the sacks of corn for the hens, but by Saturday they were usually in a great confused heap. You needed your courage for the shoes; there were so many of them, and some would be covered with mud after a long wild walk seeking kingcups or mushrooms, or after two or three times of wearing. The big heavy things fell off a girl's thin left hand and the wide polishing brush made her right one ache; the bars of sticky blacking had a smell that hurt. But the row of bright shoes promised Sunday leisure and there was the fun of counting; twelve pairs to do, now only eight, only four! By the time there were only two, the danger of tears was past, and even of that terrible sin of 'being cross'.

The two girls could tackle job after job through the morning and still proceed after dinner to wash up, to clean knives with bath-brick on leather and then—something pleasant to finish with—to clean Aunt Rouvray's silver spoons with the long narrow bowls, so that Sunday's dinner-table might shine. But everything must be finished by three o'clock or joy went out and ill-temper came in. There must be time to heat a copperful of water, to bath, and to rejoice awhile in the clean 'house', with the deal table in its afternoon dress of embroidered green serge, and its bowl of daffodils or field flowers. This precious small island of afternoon ended soon in preparations for tea, and after tea there was always the evening dairy work.

Beyond the routine labours, every new comfort in the house was the result of some special *tour de force*. Hannah and the girls papered the rooms, they baked and cut feathers to make new beds and pillows. When the boys had dug and fenced it, they planted a new small garden on the north side of the house to be given up to lawn and flower-beds, to aid the snatching of brief half-hours from the constant purposefulness of life. From June onwards, in fine weather, they lifted the big table outside and laid all meals here. The family lived the whole long summer days on the paving before the front door— a gipsyish proceeding in a Victorian village.

Sometimes the girls would feel that fate did not deal even-handedly between the sexes. Father and brothers when dark fell or the weather was stormy could sit reading newspapers and books, but if Mother sat, it was to darn or patch. And they themselves, in the worst times, spent evenings making next day's pudding, chopping suet in the cold kitchen or stoning raisins on the hearth.

But the time came when the sisters lost this envy. By the time he was seventeen Arthur had decided that farming would never support the family; something in addition must be tried. He worked on his reluctant father to let him start a coal business. Hitherto customers had trundled their wheel-barrows to the dealers or hired a horse and cart to fetch coal from Banbury; but Arthur would deliver to their doors and charge them fourteen instead of fifteen pence the hundred-weight! The boys liked the driving to and fro that the business involved, but there was also much heavy lifting, from the railway truck to the cart at Kineton, from the cart to the stock at home. Then it was sacked, weighed and lifted to the trolley again, all by two boys. The girls wondered to see the tough strength of the fifteen-year-old Dick, lifting the sacks of coal. But the boys' work grew slack when the fires died down in summer and there was a new problem; the horses they had bought could not 'eat off their heads in idleness'. The brothers' next idea was to haul stones for road-making. A Dutch auction for carrying stone for various lengths of road in the district was to be held at Brailes. Father was very loth for the boys to make bids for work so heavy but his sons overrode him. He was himself a member of the Rural District Council and thus precluded from acting for them. The older hauliers were accustomed to divide the work among them, arranging prices beforehand, and were annoyed at the youngsters' irruption. In the end, the boys took one section of the road at a price which meant that a horse, 'man', and cart earned one shilling and threepence per day. Joseph was too disturbed to be angry. 'You boys', he said, 'must be foolish.' He was darkened and grieved for days on end, knowing the toiling in prospect, helping the horses down the hilly fields from Sunrising and then the long haul. However, the boys had learned one lesson and their fellow hauliers another. Next year they were invited into the little ring.

Money came in too painfully and slowly ever to be a joy. But the partnership with parents was too close for the lack of it to be resented till the pressures of adolescence grew very great. Kathleen, for example, from her thirteenth to her fifteenth year, kept account for her mother of money spent on food and small household matters. The total each week was in the region of three pounds—several times the total of a workman's wage. One day she heard bells ringing for the wedding of a girl of her acquaintance to a labourer and chanted to herself under her breath in the speech of labourers, to the rhythm of the bells, 'Twelve shillin' a wik! Twelve shillin' a wik!' Her mother caught the sardonic words and chid her daughter.

Father was the only person who could spend money happily. Perhaps he regarded the fruit from the orchards as unearned, a God-send. At all events when he had taken a load of apples or plums on the 'trap' to Stratford he would bring back perhaps a map of England to hang on the house wall so that the children might learn from it, or an armful of Scott's novels from a second-hand shop. Once Providence rained down silver and it lay in circles, many circles, in the middle one of the Far Fields—always a magic spot. Then Father and Mother went happily together to sell the mushrooms in the wholesale market and came back with a tremendous purchase—a box of croquet mallets and balls, for Joseph realised that there was a lack of lightness (such a lack as he had never felt for himself) about the children's lives.

But Hannah was anxious and even critical about Father's purchases and then the children's thrilling delight in the new book or extra reading-lamp would be shot through with anguish. So young Bill wrote many years later, 'When I was between eight and ten I often went to Stratford market with Father, behind the old mare Lady London, and those days were great ones, both the long drive and our companionship and small-talk. One day Father bought me a Compendium of Games—draughts and halma and a horse-racing dice game —the immense cost of it, five shillings, being to me the greatest wonder then and ever since. On the way back he felt foolish to have spent so much, felt insecure about his impulse, imagining Mother considering the cost in her silent way, or even saying, "Oh Joe!" So the joy was gone from the homeward journey but I hugged the thought of having had Father to talk with all the way out.'

It was relatively little that parents could do about this Saturday life of their children. It was shot through by their influence, but that was itself complicated by the stress between material needs and the imperative standards of their desires and ideals. Sunday was different. Faces were turned from work and minds cleared of tension. Time was made in which there could be communion. But leisure hours had an unrestful preliminary. Everyone who could must dress in Sunday clothes on rising. Hence those cries, 'I can't find my clean socks', 'Oh, isn't my new shirt finished yet?' Toilets complete, essential jobs were done with speed, girls protesting 'Mother, you go to chapel; we can cook the dinner'. By ten o'clock, as many as could be spared set off for the morning service, and then leisure fell, and minds were opened.

The hymns of the new Wesleyan Hymn Book pleased the young, with their new tunes and their modern verse, but it was the sermons that most exercised them. In their close attention to these they were with their father, taking from him no doubt, his attitude of appreciative selection. Every Sunday came a different preacher; there followed each other farmers, blacksmiths, saddlers, grocers, drapers and, when the children visited the 'Primitive' chapel, often labourers. The preachers' minds were filled with experiences of weather and natural scenes, of family, of daily business and skills. They had the impulse to relate life's aspects to one another and here in the pulpit was the opportunity to give vital expression to the result. The poetry of their own particular spheres was what the keen ear heard from many of the speakers. Each preached salvation in a way a little coloured by his temperament, as every truthful mind must, but since each preached but a few times in the year, his reflections on a notable experience or his interpretation of some passage in the Bible could be subjected to the further experience of many days and in some cases of much reading.

Of course some of the preachers had few verbal techniques; they were confused between their dialect and conventional English, dropping their aitches and fumbling about grammar, or were maddeningly slow. A preacher's clumsy struggle to make plain his homely novel figure of speech might distract a listener from its aptness. But not all lacked facility. There was Mr Ridley Brown, for example, the northern gentleman farmer who had sold Jersey Beauty to Joseph. He had a rich voice that rolled and echoed in the chapels with the fine periods of his fluency. His sermons were interpretations of the more dramatic Old Testament stories—Naaman and Gehazi, or Joseph's dreams, or part of King Saul's life-story. There was Richard Lean, one of Joseph's best-liked companions, product of a Methodist public school, who ran a model farm on Lord Willoughby's estate, a fanatic for hygiene and machinery. His motto might have been 'Thorough'; he had the temperament of a revolutionary. Admiring God's Providence in ordaining a Sabbath, he refused to eat Hannah's delicious hot meal when after his sermon he dined with the Ashbys, and she was obliged to add to her Sabbath labours by providing cold dishes for him. It was hard for this ardent spirit to avoid politics, and once when he expounded the message of Amos old Mr Styles rose and left the chapel in silent disapproval.

One sermon so much impressed Kathleen that her father bade her write it out—old Job's sermon on grass. Job was one of the few labouring members of the Wesleyan community, a great-grandson of one of the founders of the chapel. He was a shepherd and no appearance could have been more suitable than his for his office. He was of the long type— tall, with long face, long hands. His old clothes hung loosely about him. His face had the look of one who sympathises and weighs, and the quickly shifting expression of almost excessive sensitiveness. Among the spruce tradesmen and well-clad young farmers his looks had become remarkable.

' It is harvest time, but I won't talk to you about harvest. . . . I'm going to talk about grass. Here's my text: just "The grass of the field." You know how the full text goes. God cared for grass so as to clothe it wi' beauty and adorn it wi' flowers.

' The pity of it is that the Bible wasn't written in a beautiful grassy country, not as I gather. Perhaps it wouldn't ha' done for Christ to walk too often up our hills in Spring. He'd not perhaps ha' thought we needed his salvation and we'd have had maybe only a Nature worship, and that for such as us is not enough. But it does me good to think of Him looking down on our ground. Beauty he loved, an' I don't doubt it lightened his suffering. There's no daisies, nor yet celandines in the Bible, not even in the Psalms. And yet it's a sight most freshening to the mind in Spring to look down the fields in this and Oxhill parish and see the daisies on the crowns of the old broad plough ridges and the celandines in the hollows between 'em. They wouldn't be there if we was to drain better, but out of ruinous farming comes the shining gold of celandines. But that's going back to the Spring of the year, which with Autumn on us, I shouldn't. Only I love to compare the seasons. The softness of this September mixes well in the mind with the blustering winds of March. And the smell of the walnut hoods challenges a body, can he remember the smell of the may and the lilac? But I am forgetting. I'm talking o' grass. Of all the natural gifts of God I thought of grass to talk about. Grass is always with us. It never fails us, even in the farming sense. It clothes the whole world as with a cloak. It feeds the beasts and they feed us. Permanent grass is a rest for the thoughts. "I lay me down in green pastures." The green colour o' grass rests the eye, the never-failingness of it rests the anxious mind; and the feel of it is rest for the body in summer season.

'The Bible says of the Spring grass "The tender grass showeth itself." Tender—that is the word. Tender green to the eye, tender to the jaws of the young calves just turned out. The tender grass. There's one text that dooant seem to spake well o' grass. "The grass withereth." If everything withered as sweet as grass, 'twould be a good world. The grass that withers standing makes a fine music in the wind, though it takes a fine ear to hear it. And have y'ever sin the red sunset reflected on a million shinin' dry bents in autumn? It's a sight I can't talk about: but you may look for it in August when the sun's rays come level wi' the ground, out of a red sunset. I mind I see it every night o' that week when my bwoy came back from the war, back home to die. A man's eyes and ears be sharp when his blessings be slipping away.

'Ay, but that reminds me, grass robs death of its terrors, for who but feels soothed at the thought of the green grass waving over a body that is weary and hurt, and laden with hard and painful memories? When I was young my thoughts would be too much for me and I'd long to be beneath the daisies; not up in heaven. For that you want newness of spirit. But God in his mercy lets us throw off our weariness and leave it kindly buried beneath the grinsw'd.

'What I really want to say is—look around you at the common mercies of the Lord. There's trees; there's bread: and I'm saving up a sermon for you about little childer—all things that be around us now and always.

> Count your blessings,
> Name them one by one,
> And it will surprise you
> What the Lord hath done.'

Certainly there were sometimes cruder subjects. At the 'Primitive' chapel young William once heard a sermon in which wine-bibbers, scented ladies, horse racing and betting were denounced in fiery fashion, like Isaiah dealing with the daughters of Zion, their stretched-forth necks and their mincing walk. But it was only in the summer holidays that a Tysoe labourer could sniff up perfume in the wake of a rare visitor, and in this time of singular moderation and rectitude it was becoming rare even to see a man the worse for drink. Still it was fortunate for 'Old Deutero' as William called him, that he thought so well of the simple life!

Father laughed at William's story: after all, had he heard the sermon he too would have been amused. But there were pitfalls for youngsters, in amusement. One of the most notable preachers for the young Ashbys was John Price, the blacksmith. A man like him might well be listened to on Sundays. William reported a certain Saturday speech of his, at the smithy to a carter who had brought a horse to be shod. 'Ought to be ashamed, farmer and carter both, of old Nobby! Ent fit to be shod, ought to be turned out to grass, and if you bring him here again in the like condition you'll take him away again.'

But on Sundays John's note was different. In his sermons he found a voice for melancholy, for a tragic view. John's mind had resisted the Victorian optimism that Joseph Ashby perhaps shared: he had looked on life and found it largely evil.

There was a discussion over the dinner-table at The Orchards, after a sermon of John's. 'It was all sewn with black pearls', said a girl, and Arthur, 'John sees nothing in a hedge but the nightshade.' 'Black pearls, nightshade?' asked their mother, not much given to metaphor. 'I beheld the earth and lo it was dark and void', quoted a girl and Will followed with 'They tread their wine presses and suffer thirst'. 'Terrors are turned upon me; they chase mine honour as the wind.' (Kathleen had underscored these passages as John quoted them.)

Was not John's view darkly extravagant? William indicated this question as he said in imitation of John's mournful tones: 'I will take from them the voice of mirth and the voice of gladness, the sound of the millstones and the light of the candle.' But the children were going too far. Father ended the sardonic comment, as he pushed back his chair and rose. 'It is not everybody', he said, 'that has the ability to suffer.' But he need not, perhaps, have frowned. The children had felt that John was reckoning with something real: it might yet enter their own lives.

Father's influence on this Sunday life was indirect. His children sometimes heard his own sermons, but he would never have been, I think, one of their favourite preachers. Censorious clever sons found his delivery slow and his distinctions too many and 'too fine for his audiences', but all the same it was a happy way of combining Divine Service with lay leisure, to go with Father on one of his preaching errands, to drive through a rich autumn gloaming to an evening service, and on the way back through darkness and storm, with the gig lamps lighting up rich patches of hedge-maple leaves among the bare purple and slate-coloured hawthorn branches. Invitations to dinner and tea between services naturally came from homes with the larger and more laden tables. So there were days spent sharing the dignified old-fashioned life of large peaceful farmhouses, with rich cakes and dishes of greengages on long mahogany tables and walks through rickyards with golden stacks of corn. And Father's sermons, it could not be denied, always gave one something to think about. He would choose some large topic; for example, with some verses of Romans as his text, he would argue how little Christians need fear the name of Darwin; see here that Paul was an evolutionist; in their Bibles his hearers would see evolution proceeding—the changing idea of God; refining of sentiments in family love, and in that first friendship of David and Jonathan; the growing beauty of biblical literature. He tried, it seems, to bring large comfort to simple hearers, and doubtless to himself. He talked on the conscientious unbeliever. Parents must have faith in the power of Christ to bring clever young people to himself and remember that the honest critic and sceptic is essential if faith is to be enlarged and kept reasonable. Though his children did not distinguish any of their father's sermons by recording them, he was not without honour in the circuit. He was quite frequently asked to preach at Harvest Festivals and Sunday School Anniversaries—a proof of the maturity of some of his hearers.

So Joseph's boys and girls had a certain introduction to the more important aspects of life; they had a not infertile background. But he and Hannah were not always happy about them: time came when they seemed often tense and hungry. Arthur their eldest had shown a passionate love of mother and home, but now sometimes his energy overflowed in an excessive fit of anger. The occasional bitterness of William's wit could only come of frustration. If these boys' opportunities should never match their force, might there not be tragedy? Getting a living, marrying, might 'settle' them and the other children—but life is more than settlement. Hannah said that not all the children were a problem, and indicated the two youngest, as gay and loving as girls could be. Happy together, and basking in the love of their eight elders, one must imagine them creating peace and contentment in the future. If only there might be openings for education and training of all these young energies, explosive or serene!

CHAPTER XVII

VILLAGE AND EDUCATION

For several years after the turn of the century the young Ashbys still attended the village school. It had not greatly changed, even now, and perhaps the younger children were less patient than the older ones had been. After a day of it William was at his most irascible and sometimes the little girls would cry when they were despatched thither in the morning.

But there was something new and valuable for those who had left school—the evening 'whisky money' classes in technical subjects. The odd description alluded to the source of finance: County Councils had been allotted the proceeds of a tax on spirits to provide technical education. Only keen pupils attended the evening classes and the special local committee could be asked to provide teaching in any 'technical' subject.

Arthur had asked for a class in mathematics and the old schoolmaster, whose highest attainment was some knowledge of algebra, taught a small class. The teacher was hesitant and the pupils puzzled and anxious but two or three of them felt the joy and power of using symbols. There were the carpentry classes that Richard liked. Two craftsmen taught joinery in the admirable stable at the curate's house. Mr Styles was 'the craftsman par excellence', while Job Jarvis claimed to teach 'how to do a good job quick'. You chose your teacher according to your temperament: and to this day, sixty years later, there are men who feel that in those classes something real was given them. There were even lectures on architecture and astronomy, with lantern slides, and on the wonders of experimental science, but those stirred no more than a little passing wonder, as far as I ever heard. For a while there was an extraordinary passion for shorthand, perhaps as a key to the modern world, but after a short course of it, the claims of the daily rural life seemed stronger.

There seemed no chance that the 'National' School at Tysoe would become for the present more satisfying for its pupils, but meanwhile schools had become one of the national topics. On the very day that the war in South Africa ended in the Peace of Vereeniging, on 31 May 1902, there began the debate on the Government's Education Bill. The nation's education was a chaos of poor expedients. The Church of England could not maintain, let alone improve, her many schools nor the nonconformists their few. In the towns some of the rate-supported Board Schools were excellent and the Church's schools falling behind. In the country some schools were being run by almost illiterate Boards while in many villages, as in Tysoe, the Church School was resented as having a bias, rather social and political than religious.

Instead of a new start in a new spirit some felt the Education Bill was to give eternal life to 'that great draughty barn and all that it stood for'. There was to be no village school belonging equally to all, but in a village where at least half the folk were nonconformists the Church was strengthened. 'By money you pay, and I pay' said Tom Gardner to his fellow Methodists.

Controversy raged in the street. The Vicar and Tom Gardner addressed meetings from the old wagonette. At one meeting both sides expressed themselves; the Vicar made the speech, and a group of Methodists expressed their view by question and comment. Church people, said the Vicar, had worked their fingers to the bone, to build schools in a majority of villages. Ratepayers would henceforth have representatives among the Managers; it would be possible to accept selected nonconformist boys and girls as pupil-teachers. Children could be withdrawn for religious instruction. Then came questions as to 'working' to start the schools; did the Vicar know just how the Tysoe school had been built? Joseph

Ashby would tell him; the Marquis had subscribed four hundred pounds and provided the site; the Trustees of the Utility Estate had given sums; there had been a Government grant, and a few well-off folk had subscribed a pound apiece. For a pound, you became a Manager! Popular subscriptions were neither asked nor wished for. Take any local village the Vicar chose, and he would find the school was financed in much the same way. 'Where is the justice', asked John Price, 'of our paying rates for a school that must always have a member of the Church of England for headmaster—worth as much as two curates to the Church?' Then someone asked 'Would the Vicar admit that Methodists were Christians?' 'Surely, surely!' said the Vicar. 'Then if we drop our local opposition will you urge the Managers to meet some Methodists and discuss the religious teaching to be given?' The problem might be difficult in towns: here surely Christian co-operation could solve it. The idea may have appealed to the Vicar, though he gave no reply. And then, John Price, less slow and mournful than usual, asked why there could not be a village school. 'We had one for 'underds o' years.' Twice there had been Bills of Parliament proposing schools to be managed by the villages' elected vestries. Wouldn't the Parish Councils be a better Board than the Managers?

Though Joseph asked his questions, he took no more active part in this controversy. It would not prevent the children's time being wasted. And then, too, Bolton King believed in the Bill. There were to be secondary schools to serve all parts of the country, administered by County Councils. These would appoint professional administrators of schools, bringing knowledge of education to bear. King meant to be one of them. He believed he had at last found his life-work. It was a Tory measure, said he, but Joseph would see the schools improve.

So Joseph did not refuse to pay his education rate. Only two or three Methodists pledged themselves to do so. It was so small; the refusal seemed a little absurd. Tom Gardner kept his pledge a long while. Auctioneers would come now and then and hold up one or two of his silver spoons for sale. And sometimes—and that enraged him—an enemy would call at the District Council Office and pay the rate on his behalf. Nevertheless, exasperated parents withdrew their children from the school's lessons in religion. Having no bell to warn and scold, they were sometimes late, sometimes a little disorderly, always a disturbance, and Mr Dodge sometimes lost his temper about them. 'Tell your fathers', he cried one day, 'it is for pennies, not for conscience that you are kept away!' Certainly the children had done many a useful job at home in their hour's respite.

So school was a contentious institution: it did not exist primarily for the children and it despised and rejected their parents. Daisy Ashby once witnessed a dramatic scene. A parent, a shrill and dirty mother, arrived to complain that her boy was being 'kept in' day after day. (Not finding the school worth his while he had been following the hounds.) A pupil-teacher, laughing and contemptuous, ran to fetch a large piece of soap and insultingly offered it. Daisy was standing by Sally, the protesting woman's small daughter, and shrank and was miserable as if someone had been rude to her own mother. And yet she a little admired that merry, insensitive insolence!

Once again it happened that just when some of the Tysonians felt that dominant parties and classes were taking a mean advantage of them and their children, they were called upon to celebrate national unity and concord. The coronation of Edward VII had been fixed for 26 June. The children looked forward to the day as if all the stately processions and the great ceremonial and the feasts were to take place in their own village, and when telegrams came to say the King was ill, life was brought down to unbearable flatness. But by the second week in August when the coronation in fact took place grown-ups and children too were ready for a quiet day of pleasure. I recall the long talks in a tent, and the latter end of a fine meal—plum pudding and speeches. Of what was actually said I recall only my father's part. He had found a parable for England's continuity in the long history of the Middleton family. That is why I remember: I knew vaguely that in tugs of war Middletons were always on the opposite side from my father's, and yet here he was, talking admiringly of them, of how one of them in Elizabeth's reign rode regularly to face the Quarter Sessions at Warwick and pay his fine, because he, a Catholic, would not attend Elizabeth's Church; of the length of time they had held this farm and that; of the folk tales about them—and never mentioned how one of them had foreclosed the mortgage on his own ancestor's farm. After grace, two or three Middletons came up to Joseph and asked how he knew so much about their family. They hadn't known! The speech was a little bouquet of flowers laid on the altar of unity.

The old regime in Tysoe school came to an end dramatically, if in many respects only temporarily, in 1905. The schoolmaster was now sixty-five years old and about to retire. Ever since he was twenty-six Mr Dodge had run the school with his wife teaching sewing and coming to the rescue whenever an epidemic of colds or influenza laid low the pupil-teachers. At the thought of their leaving the school there had come over the mind of the village an understanding of what they had done. For thirty-nine years Mr Dodge had faced and controlled the school's two hundred children, and also he had instructed them. Without the Dodges it could never have been said that every child could read and figure and every girl could mend.

The farewell gathering was held in the old tithe-barn of Upper Town where the Club's annual procession formed, in which the poor had threshed their corn with their stick-n-a-halfs. It was no church-like edifice, but roughly built and thatched like the nearby houses and as liable to decay. Since schools and chapels had been built it was losing its function of meeting-place and this was in fact its last great hour.

In the early afternoon the barn had looked fine, and had smelled like a harvest festival. On trestle tables covered with white sheets and brilliant with dahlias—a new-come flower—and yellow autumn daisies in stone-ware jam jars the tea-feast was laid.

The old pair—indeed they were worn—walked up and down during tea to greet everyone in this vast crowd of two hundred and fifty who had met to eat and drink in happiness together because of them. They could hardly talk, for the brass band burst now and then into triumphant paeans. While the great quantities of bread and cakes were consumed a new crowd was gathering at all three doors of the barn. It was a marvel, how speedily the children carried cups to clothes-baskets, girls removed the flowers, women gathered up the food plates and boys and men clapped together table-tops and stored them outside under the sheltered south wall. People streamed in, from very old to very young. Old Mrs Winchcombe from Brixfield had not been in the village for ten years. Both the Gees were there! They must have locked up the Peacock—positively against the law!

Mr Dodge's favourite subject had always been arithmetic; his excitement expressed itself in a rapid calculation of numbers—seven hundred persons! With a bird's quick turn of the head he looked repeatedly at his Henrietta, but she no more than he 'could make it out', for not even popularity—a quality that had never been theirs—could draw a crowd like this.

The Vicar began his speech. He went back to the days before the Dodges had entered on their life-work. He had been reading their letter of application to the Managers of the School. Mr Dodge had said that he would spend all his time and energy in any work the Managers laid upon him and in fulfilling this undertaking he would be aided by his wife. They had, you see, said the Vicar, promised their lives and they had given them. Mr Dodge had lived through all events and with all men as a humble God-fearing simple man. He had never made an enemy. Even in the stormy days when the firebrand of politics was in the village he had steered his course so as not to arouse opposition. He was a true Christian. Once the Vicar had heard him tell the children in the school that they must believe the Bible from cover to cover; the Bible had been his own guide and authority.

Just because the main dissensions of the village had related to the Education Act, and thus been in a measure religious, a nonconformist, Joseph, had been asked to make the first of the speeches by old pupils. Within the framework that they had been given, he said, their old schoolmaster and schoolmistress had done a splendid as well as a long day's work. Agreement on the management of the school might not have been achieved but the whole village was united in gratitude for faithful and devoted work. The Master's and the Mistress's Christian characters had been their first and greatest lesson.

But of chief interest was what, after many had spoken, Mr Dodge himself had to say. He had 'never in his life made a proper speech before'. (He had been humble indeed!) He would fail in words: his motto had had to be deeds. He was not blessed with an eloquent tongue but God had given him enthusiasm. It would please God, he trusted, to take his and his wife's earnestness to prove thankfulness. The honours done them were such as few people could have had.

He reviewed the years. Two thousand scholars had passed through his hands. Of two hundred and fourteen children now in school, two hundred were the offspring of men and women he had taught: in the infant school were five grandchildren of his early pupils. In all parts of the world his pupils might be found. Many had had far more remarkable experiences than himself.

God had given him enthusiasm but the government had given him red tape and but little else. He had been thinking and that was his conclusion. Under the old rules, made by men who had never in their lives stepped inside a National school, the attempts to teach children had been like trying to

make a triangle with a pair of compasses.... Now at last
things were different. A master was encouraged to make
schemes in part for himself, to suit his district. A head-
teacher was allowed, now, to take children out of doors and
show them something practical. He had taken the top classes
to see the stone-cutting at Hornton and he had had one of the
surprises of his life to find what sensible questions the children
asked, and on the way they had talked to him like friends!
Not a thought of the cane had crossed his mind or theirs. But
schemes! He had found he could not make his own; it was too
late to begin to choose for himself. The County Council had
said it was time for him to go; and they were right.

This simple speech amazed Joseph. That their distant
Lordships who administered the schools could have put out
their cold hands and so frozen the life of them! It was worth
all effort to get change. But also the speech had released and
enlarged his sympathies. Perhaps many of those he disagreed
with were working in a wrong framework. As he walked
thoughtfully home the Vicar caught him up. 'What a beautiful
meeting!' said he. 'In all reverence I think Christ was in
our midst.'

That was the end of the old regime in the school, for the
time being at any rate. Spittle, rags, broken slates, dirty
books vanished at once. The pit closets were gutted and pails
installed, enamelled bowls and roller towels appeared in the
cloakrooms. The children became so ready to go to school
that one week every child was present during all the sessions.
The agent of this rapid revolution was the newly appointed
schoolmaster, a small, quiet, youngish man, who came from
a large seaside resort. His grandfather, grandmother, father
and uncles were all teachers, heads of schools in towns or overseas. His father had a university degree and was a Fellow of
the Royal Geographical Society. Why had Mr Ullyett come to
this remote village? Certainly for no very unhappy reason:
the serious small man had an unusual serenity.

But before he had the school in order his temper broke

down once. Patient for many days, but at last suddenly flushed and angry, he caned the children for their inveterate chatter and slovenliness. The blows were never forgotten but the Master was soon forgiven. Noise and mess having been eliminated, rich lessons could be heard and exercises set upon them could be understood. Interests began to grow in young under-furnished minds. How good the listening and looking lessons could be! For example, that one on volcanoes and earthquakes, just after Vesuvius's eruption and the catastrophe of San Francisco, in which the Master made a miniature volcano and showed it 'in action', or the lessons on Canada in which, though there was no eloquence, the detail was built up till you felt you had walked on the prairie farms and sailed on a great lake. And yet those lessons were not the best of school. That, for some at least, was the long quiet times when a child could work in peace. A whole hour would be given to write a 'composition' or to illustrate your notes with a map. If you liked writing, the Master would contrive to let you go on with one essay or story day after day.

It was not only the Master's 'top classes' that flourished but the younger children too. All classes were furnished with schemes of work suited to the teacher and the pupil. As children and teachers tasted success, smiles were exchanged between them. A new relationship was born. One day an angry parent, behind the times in school news, came to rescue her child from a detention and found that he had begged with tears to stay in and write afresh an untidy exercise.

In September 1905 Tom Gardner was still keeping his children at home till Scripture lessons were over, and was taken aback when the Master sent him a message to say that this was illegal; the children must be inside school. But it was Mr Gardner who, after a month or two, lent the school a playing field. For a while the Methodist children might, if they wished, have other work during religious instruction, but soon any distinction in school between 'Church' and 'Dissent' had become almost unthinkable; the catechism lessons were given in church by the Vicar while the Master stayed with the others. All contention, indeed, fell away. And yet the Master was a good churchman, reading the lessons and training the Lads' Brigade.

The Master spoke with parents about their children, commenting on their willing work, or on what they did well, or asking them to encourage a boy or girl to practise some bit of technique. Fathers began to knock at the schoolhouse door to ask what a boy was good for, and could the Master suggest what he should do when he left school?

After a few months the school football team was playing schools miles away and had the reputation for being the most 'gentlemanly' team in the district. 'Gentlemanly'—the word is important. It indicates the nature of the social change that had come over the school. Time was when to have a pleasant manner was to 'ape your betters'. Now the school was bent day by day, half hour by half hour, on helping the children to be and do all that was in them. At last the school was for the children—for the children, not in isolation, but as having parents, a family. It would not have been far to go to recognise their village also.

And yet the Master was no educational genius. Nothing he did was other than simple and age-old. But then, his father was a real geographer; he knew the look on the face of one absorbed in learning and waited for it to come on his children's faces. He had a sound conception of his work, and an hereditary faith in his own capacity to teach. This last quality enabled him to make good use of that gathering cloud of superior persons who, after the County Councils took over the administration of the schools, had begun to be a nuisance to the old Master—Attendance Officer, lecturer on hygiene, Infants' Inspector. He had for his use few or none of the charming ideas for pleasing and stimulating children that ingenious teachers have now made so abundant, no help from the science of psychology; yet with his modest equipment he made a Golden Age. It lasted however only two years.

After that time he was invited to take charge of one of the largest schools in the county—and left desolation behind him.

After Mr Ullyett left you might visit the school and find it in a high or a low phase. The old artificiality of school ways comes back: it is like ground elder in the garden: so long as a particle remains uneradicated it grows afresh. What could sweep it clean away? Half a century later, the way an artist works or a scientist explores and the motives that lead to interest in hobbies or success in construction are still often set aside.

CHAPTER XVIII

FAMILY, VILLAGE AND NATION

FROM the dying down of disputes on the Education Act of 1902 there was peace in the Tysoe street for some three years. The only meeting on the green of which I recollect hearing concerned Chinese indentured labour for South African mines. But then came the great eagerness of Radicals for the General Election of 1906. One may guess that even some Conservatives felt that the political lane was due to take a turning to the left for a while. The election being quietly taken in his own village, Joseph took up his unpaid Liberal agency for the south of the Division. Arthur, now twenty years of age, earned money as party agent for the villages north of Kineton. First, he was trained for a whole week in Leamington by the constituency agent; next he scrubbed and whitewashed a room in an old cottage for an office. Electioneering was strenuous work, but a fight well and willingly fought is always good for health, and this junior agent was active from early morn when he cycled to Kineton till he returned home towards midnight. He writes of how at that hour he explored his mother's dairy and pantry for food and would eat a whole family milk pudding and bowl of fruit. He knew his mother would be listening lest he go to sleep unrestfully in a chair, so he dragged himself to the attic to fall on his bed. Many evenings he had three meetings in his charge, in villages a few miles apart. Mr Corrie Grant changed from a distinguished and kind friend into an over-conscientious candidate who would insist on staying after each speech to answer questions, so that his agent must rush substitute speakers to keep waiting audiences interested. It was quite difficult to find local Liberals or Radicals not too prone to turn a speech into a sermon, and not too exclusively interested in schools or licensing. It was better if their topic was the House of Lords or Free Trade.

As he went about his work, Arthur received just such lessons in village society as his father thirty years before, when he drove the stone-carts from the quarries. Some audiences liked a little vituperation, others became cold at a suspicion of it. The Hornton quarrymen were 'nowhere'! They would not have the leadership of social superiors and developed none from their own ranks. At Pillerton the men slunk about; there would be no one in the schoolroom till after the opening time of the meeting and then suddenly a whole crowd would come in, holding close together like a settling swarm. Kineton itself, Lord Willoughby's little town, was assumed to vote Conservative, but in fact Liberal meetings there were large. Oxhill was under the thumb of a group of hidebound old Tory farmers; hardly anybody would turn up to a meeting there, and yet Oxhill was 'all right'.

The old days had left a mark, but except that he was refused the use of one village schoolroom, the only nefarious deeds that Arthur discovered were perpetrated on his own side! Riding his 'bike' past outhouses and gate-posts he noticed that a high proportion of the posters they displayed were flapping in the wind. He would dismount in vexation—but find the damaged posters almost always Tory ones. Paste had been smeared on them so freely that they had not dried before the evening damp came on, and in the night they peeled off. Both of Kineton's billstickers showed the same depravity.

The main job of other members of the family was to set the two 'men' free. But even the youngest did some electioneering, Sybil and Janet tramping round with Mr Corrie Grant's picture and Liberal pamphlets, including the old account of Owda Freeman's triumph in the matter of his bread bill. (Some years before this, Freeman had challenged a Conservative candidate, Mr Steel-Maitland, to pay his baker if a certain small import duty on corn brought an increase

in the price of bread.) Almost every day they had to make
a fresh flour-and-water paste to put up a fresh poster on
the back of the brick barn by the road—the big and little
loaves of Free Trade and Tariff Reform, and the line of huts
behind a group of pig-tailed Chinamen.

The Liberals having hopes of this election and Tories no
great fears because of their powerful second line, the House
of Lords, it was at first as happy an affair as it was in the
nature of General Elections to be. Some toys for children
symbolised this quality. From a school party Sybil and Janet
brought innocent pieces of pale-coloured paper. You applied
a match to a small spot of print and a spark ran quickly along
an invisible but predestined path drawing with impartial
magic a schematic portrait of Chamberlain or Campbell-
Bannerman, Balfour or Asquith. The children were astonished
and protesting when Father took down his early, only
remaining painting in oils, the donkey and cart wending its
way to a little stable as mysterious as the Dark Tower, in
favour of one of these odd portraits. The frail paper, carefully
pinned, survived for months, and Campbell-Bannerman
received his daily glances of respect and admiration. Had he
not been the soberest and best leader of the Pro-Boers? Was
he not the halting speaker come to fluency because he cared?
The rich man who had passed through the eye of the needle?

As results began to come in, feeling at The Orchards
changed from simple optimism to mingled anxiety and joy.
Winning would not be enough: only a great majority could
open the way to Liberal Bills, especially for any that would
disturb old patterns of village life. But it began to seem that
C.-B. would have an irresistible majority. Day after day
young Radicals drew on deep fountains of enthusiasm to
welcome successes, but emotion failed at last, and results were
marked mechanically on the *Daily News* map of constituencies.
In the Liberal majority might be counted the Irish members,
and a large group of Labour members—the last a parliamentary novelty. In his 'Villager' column of the *Warwick*

Advertiser Joseph welcomed this group without qualms. He had not yet made the acquaintance of the young doctrinaires of Ruskin College or his comments might have been a little different. He assumed that the new group were men like village Radicals—a trade union version of local preachers, and as to most of them he was right.

The great battle having been fought and won, the rhythm of life at The Orchards was resumed. Back to work (not that it had ever ceased) and back to books. Arthur, especially, had by this time good guidance in his reading. Mr Grant would throw out 'There's a new idea for you!—out of Jeremy Bentham'—or Malthus or Mill. He would bring him books such as Eden's *State of the Poor*. The *Daily News's Realms of Gold* gave a weekly quotation from a notable writer, with the dates of the author and details of a good edition of his works. Mr King brought the prospectus of the Ruskin College correspondence courses that proved so useful and the catalogue of a 'remainder' bookshop where interesting editions were sometimes cheap. *Realms of Gold* naturally included Utopias—Bellamy's *Looking Backward* and Morris's *News from Nowhere*. The best of elder brothers thought these might be an introduction to high political thoughts for his juniors, and dutifully they read them. He urged them also to modern novelists—past Dickens and Thackeray, Henry and Charles Kingsley, to Hardy and Meredith and Mark Rutherford; on, further, to modern poetry, Browning and Arnold and especially Meredith.

There were other realms, less golden, and yet making higher claims. For the younger ones the Sunday School prize books were apt to pitch moral standards distressingly out of reach and to be unduly optimistic as to the rewards of virtue. 'Doe no Yll' was the motto of the family in the *Children of Uplands Farm*, and in *Matthew Mellowdew* there were ringing sentences: 'Truth shall win the crown of the causeway, though all the world plot to keep it in the gutter'; 'Harry Hardwick! Tell me how he fares?' 'As those who keep a good conscience

241

always do fare in the long run.' And that was, of course, very well indeed. From the Methodist Book Van, pitched once or twice on the green, came books at once wildly romantic and pious, with backgrounds of Canadian cold and immensity.

There was that strange periodical the *Boy's Own Paper*, supplied by an aunt. Why was it that when it arrived boys, and girls too, usually reasonable, became hungry wolves, greedy, each for himself? It would come late on Saturday, Father bringing it from Shipston after the District Council meeting. On Sunday the first boy or girl home from chapel or from some work about the farm buildings would have the *B.O.P.* till he had read an instalment of a story, and then must yield it up. Once a boy hid it in a table drawer and his character bore a stain for some time. Perhaps the long voyages of the boys in the stories, over mountains or in sailing boats, and the wonderful expeditions to collect tropical birds and plants compensated the children for their own continually interrupted adventures and the severe usefulness of their errands. To the more easily fatigued of the children such mingled pap and spice was perhaps harmful; they lingered in the dream world. But those who drew on deeper vats rested briefly and then went eagerly back to life.

Young William, who never read the Sunday School prizes, and who was the least interested in goodness of all the children, lost himself in Wesley's sermons. His sisters did not connect his cutting directness of thought, too sharp for family comfort, his satire, and his hypersensitivity to their lapses of intelligence, with this interest in sermons. But in fact theology was his way to the open, where he could think unencumbered. A small event was the arrival of Hasbach's *History of the English Agricultural Labourer*, containing praise of Father's old researches. So Father at any rate had his own touch and even hold on the great world and its tradition. Today, with many rural voices carried on the air it is easy for a village child to feel such links, but early in the century it was difficult indeed.

Rustic children's eyes opened unusually wide when they fell on chapters that held up the mirror to villages and fields. They stumbled awkwardly through an old book on Linnaeus, hoping to learn more about such strange plants as cuckoo pints. George Eliot was truly familiar; her tone of voice was so like Father's. John Clare's intensest vision never came their way, nor Crabbe's deep unprejudiced sympathy. But Housman came, and made them recall every tragedy and failure and final departure that they had ever heard of in their village—till, as one of them said, they saw a shadow across every threshold. Thomas Hardy's effect was greater; it amounted to shock. The loveliness of the descriptions in *Tess* raised the life of the fields to a new poetic height, a happiness dear bought. In their own village life religion, politics and their father's outlook were all concerned with the joint work, under the Almighty, of man and Nature, with emphasis on man's will and responsibility. But Hardy showed Nature as breaking in upon and ruining the patterns of man and of God.

Novels could be read while you expected the next urgent call but sometimes the children started big, tough books or tried to learn French or geometry from printed lessons and then, always, an interruption would come, too soon for an argument to be mastered (except by a very strong mind) or for rule or usage to be securely learnt. And yet perhaps there was a gain; what they heard and read was brought so immediately into contact with events and with work: perhaps that accounted for a faculty they came to have for discerning unsuspected aspects of a topic and expounding them in terms of their own.

There might have been for the children a dearth of all but the literary arts, but for a certain fashion in advertisement. Advertisements had become pictorial: Colman's starch boxes contained pictures of British cathedrals and later of castles and great houses. Some other commodity brought with it pictures of beautiful young women with deep naked bosoms, which somewhat puzzled the younger children. They knew that landscapes and cathedrals could be admired and collected, and these joined the hemstitched handkerchiefs and lace for the collars of Sunday dresses, in small top drawers. But must they also admire these ladies of bountiful bare flesh? There was no doubt about the lovely pictures in *Bibby's Annual* and *Bibby's Calendar*. No mere advertisement these, even though they came from the firm who supplied cow-cake. Only true enthusiasm could have had the faith that farmhouses would welcome Constable's *Haywain*, Maris's *Ducks*, Hogarth's *Shrimp Girl* and fine cartoons of ploughing and planting and animals. You would see a chosen picture pinned up in many a farmhouse. Joseph framed his favourite ones and hung them beside Aunt Rouvray's old coloured prints of the Bay of Naples and Chinese junks. The latter were the more vivid and forceful, but you could gaze at the new prints longer, pore over them as over a book.

Always the children firmly believed themselves to live in an area of remarkable natural beauty. To them the Edge Hills were high, though not too high for one to stand often on their top and look out over the world. It was a girl who first tried to describe Tysoe. A Methodist newspaper had offered a prize for an essay entitled 'Description of my Village'. Kathleen's essay was never sent to the newspaper, for one had to declare that it was one's own unaided work, and in this house how could you escape from comment and suggestion? So the essay was stuffed into the back of a drawer. 'We no longer', she had written, starting with the great arm of hills that protected the village, 'see our country as did the old painters, the distance dark and threatening, the great elms near at hand admired for strength, their leaves individually drawn as each a sign of life and power.... Looking from the top of Sunrising our landscape is friendly to its bounds; we interpret its light and shade with the great Constable's help to mean corn and plough and meadow.

'From below our hills are high; "Man lifts up his eyes to the hills." In the vale is a man's home; the market and the milkpail. The poetry of these may be more profound than that of the heights but it is not easy to feel it so. On the hills is exhilarating wind. There in June the harebells and thyme "waft prayers and adoration to the azure"; the firs on Old Lodge toss their boughs in a rarer, quicker, air. Here a few romantic young folk load the wind with shouted poetry. Many through the nineteenth century have thrilled to feel their minds expand with the wide view. "Yonder see the Coventry spire", they say, or "as far as the Severn", but what they mean is that here the soul is large and free. These long-sighted folk are mostly men taking a Sabbath walk. On Sundays village women are busy dressing each member of the family in Sunday best, and then afterwards cooking the finest, largest meal of the week, but here they come on summer weekdays gathering mushrooms or blackberries. It is difficult for them to shed the numerous and pressing cares of the household, but gradually in the keen air sight and smell become heightened, hands fall idle and the gatherers note the tiny flowers and the cloudlets in the sky. It is animal life that attracts the little children; they like to frighten the clumsy sheep—so often it is they themselves who have been afraid. They fly with the birds that are freer even than their holiday selves. The bigger children remember that they came here in February, when the wind was at its keenest, to chop boughs and pick up chips from the trees that had been felled. The pale sunlight and the pale primroses asserting themselves against the cold had promised summer and now the promise was fulfilled. Very soon the visitors to the hills return to their life of custom and work in their homes below, but they will come again when time and labour permit, to look outwards and heavenwards.' So these young simpletons still thought that to look at Nature was to look towards heaven.

The use of the pen came pretty naturally to the children, reporting meetings for the local journals, writing papers on exciting authors for a club of young Methodists or on the Tysoe Church for some magazine. Usually their father's influence was more pervasive than direct, but he taught them to write as far as anyone can, laughing at a neat turn, looking dark at a silliness, standing between them and crude criticism.

What peaceful hours reading and writing brought!—but outside these, harmony had more actively to be attained. There were such fierce arguments as the boys mended tackle in the gatehouse, over how and when work should be done. 'Do not quarrel so, children', their mother would beg and they reply, 'We are not quarrelling, only thinking.' It was a clumsy technique of controversy, disturbing to little girls learning from their mother to pursue peace and family harmony at all costs short of wickedness. Another mode of learning, very ungracious, was criticism of elders, chiefly of Father. Father was beaten in every deal, said William, who was developing a good eye for animals and for the chance of a bargain. 'Our father and mother', was another word of his, 'have ruined us. They have taught us always to trust our fellow men. We shall always be cheated'; and 'Father doesn't get to essentials for all his definitions'. Once the boys spoke of their life as too hard. 'The harder we work', they said, 'the more there is to do, and no money for it.' But the tone of voice broke Mother's heart and that at least was never said again.

Almost all the criticism came from boys but the girls' hearts could be sore. Their mother would teach them, always by action and sometimes in words, that girls and women find it best to submit to husbands and brothers, and of course to fathers. Their duty was to feed them well, to run their errands and to bear for them all burdens save physical ones. The boys' teasing would 'rub in' the inferiority of the female sex, and Mother's pleading 'Children!' when mischief was afoot was always addressed first and foremost to her girls. Yet they had no technique to protest except brusquely, and that meant a bad conscience. Of course the main source of the doctrine on women was Father's head! Independence or 'separate action' for women 'would be false, foolish, destructive of woman's best and holiest qualities'. It was not a mean point of view: he thought that fathers ought to provide for their daughters and to give a better schooling to girls than to boys. At this time there were people claiming the franchise for women, and Joseph had the Liberal party's great fear that women, being politically foolish, would vote Conservative, and that his girls found annoying; but just as for these children, with orchards all round them, orchards did not exist between the last gathering of bullaces and the first of violets, so these moments of tension dropped out of time. When the tea hour arrived with Mother at the head of the table and Father safe back from some long drive communion was perfect.

Alongside these adolescent occupations and developments ran reactions to public events. The Liberal Government's first work was to give unity and self-government to South Africa, which could be done without legislation. The Lords threw out the Plural Voting Bill, but after all plural votes were no very great matter. Then their Lordships allowed some minor reforming bills to go through, not because a majority approved of them, but because so many Peers did not come to town to vote. Among these Acts, in 1906, was the Justices of the Peace Act. For all country folk magistrates were prominent, and, as one might say, morally picturesque figures. They represented the Sovereign; and when crime had been committed the Bench was the bottom rung of the awful stairs of justice—for long of injustice, indeed, but since 1872 they had mended their reputation and now the letters 'J.P.' were a high distinction, and respected. Still, it was said in the Radical newspapers that the magistrates were all Tories. Joseph in his Saturday column pooh-poohed the idea that 'the County Magistracy has been wittingly crammed with men of one political faith', but the next week he quoted figures from the new Liberal paper, *The Tribune*; ten thousand three hundred and more Conservative Justices to between two and three thousand Liberal. Well, soon it would occasionally happen that the burden of the Kineton Bench was one peer of the realm, and two Methodist lay preachers and Radicals. And of these one was Joseph.

The first consequence of his elevation to the Bench was that the postman brought advertisements of wine and cigars and fine tailoring, so many of them that as they arrived Hannah shoved them into the big baking oven till they fairly pushed off the oak slab that closed its mouth. The younger children had a vision of old-style magistrates as vain fellows and tipplers, but someone pointed out that after all Father liked his cigarettes and fine sleek cloth for his coats.

However, the passing of the Justices Act was a great exception. The House of Lords threw out the Education Bill; other bills they amended beyond recognition. If nothing could pass this great barrier, what was the franchise for? Or the House of Commons? Liberals felt frustrated but there was nothing for the Government to do but plough on. 'Plough' was a suitable word; the Agricultural Holdings Bill was being prepared. It was to make farmers' tenure more secure and give local authorities power to provide and manage estates of smallholdings. To do this they must have the power to acquire land when necessary from unwilling owners. Late in April 1907, Joseph Ashby and Arthur heard their admired Campbell-Bannerman forecast the Bill. They were sitting at a table in a vast London restaurant within a few feet of the Prime Minister. A twenty-year-old on his first visit to London filled with 'first' experiences could hardly remember a great deal of a mere speech, but he recalled that C.-B. had said 'Somehow it must be made possible to obtain land for vital purposes', and that next day the newspapers were full of the word 'Confiscation'. Father and son had been invited to stay with their Member and his family for that period new to them, a 'weekend'. The Member took his young visitor to the Houses of Parliament and Arthur, old enough to listen to Prime Ministers and act as election agent, was young enough to dash excitedly to sit for a moment in the Speaker's chair. There is an insoluble problem about this visit; an elderly professor, writing a few sheets of reminiscences many years later, would be rapt back into the past wondering frustratedly 'Who *could* have milked the cows while we were away?'

Although several months later the Agricultural Holdings Bill was passed by the Upper House, it was after drastic dilution of its provisions. There was enough left, however, to stir Lord Willoughby de Broke to an especially long speech at his rent audit. It was iniquitous, his Lordship said, to interfere with the rights of property, especially with landed estates. As for smallholders, they would never have the capital to equip land. Usually his Lordship was the only speaker at the audit but for some reason on this occasion a tenant, as it happened a Radical, had been asked to propose his health. It gave him pleasure, he said. They all found his Lordship a good landlord, and they all enjoyed a chat with him. But you didn't have to agree with a man to enjoy his company. 'Your Lordship can't bear compulsory purchase, but it isn't compulsion you mind! You are perfectly ready to force children into schools which their parents object to, men into the army, and man, woman and child into the doctor's surgery to be vaccinated!' Before his Lordship had much right to talk about class war—the speaker had noted that he frequently did so—he would have to abolish class strangleholds. As to the size of holdings, just outside the Combroke estate were fifty-acre farms as well tended as the two hundred-acre ones within. Why not holdings of every size? He couldn't agree with his Lordship's theories at all, but they all found him a generous and genial landlord and they wished him well.

The Licensing Bill was a special case, for it was not altogether a party product. 'Brewster Sessions' of Justices were asking for greater powers; Temperance Associations and Friendly Societies approved the Bill's proposal to reduce the number of licences, with compensation for loss. Churches and newspapers gave support. But the official Conservative policy was opposition.

In Tysoe there was a meeting addressed by the Vicar, Tom Gardner and Joseph, with a view to a telegram to the Prime

Minister from a non-party meeting. The Vicar outlined the Bill, Tom gave figures for drink consumption. For Joseph's part he had, as usual, something to say upon Tysoe's own relation to the topic. Not so long since, Tysoe had had nine public-houses instead of its present one. There were men in the audience who knew where each had been and what their signs were. In times gone by it had been common for one house in six or seven to sell ale. Even now, villages no larger than Tysoe had as many as three public-houses. The way of drinking had changed as well as the number of inns. The older men knew stories of wretched vagrants, tramps, drinking heavily and committing crimes in drink; of drinking bouts in connection with the old rough games.

For something like five hundred years experiments had been tried, every one of them affecting this village. First, permission to sell ale given or withheld by justices; then expensive licences which drove gin-drinking underground. No good! Next, licences to be given only to respectable men and ratepayers. That was a success. Tysoe knew it; put a decent man in charge and the job is half done! There were yarns in Tysoe as to how the ancestors of more than one family had drunk their holdings away. Then, debts for drinks were made irrecoverable so that no publican could gain his neighbour's house and field through his tippling. And that was another success. There were still, now, far too many public-houses, but the new thing was the political power of the brewers. They subscribed to funds; their daughters married peers. (Here local examples were not mentioned but they came to mind.)

One need not have signed the pledge to support this Bill. It did not attack the harvest beer, or the neighbourly sup of metheglin, or the glass of wine with a meal. It was a question of temptation to drink away from your family, drinking down your family's welfare. There should be enough public-houses for social purposes, and yet no more than could be properly run.

Unanimous telegrams were sent from that and many such meetings, but the Upper House threw out the Bill!

That was in 1908, and in the same year the Old Age Pensions Bill was enacted, somewhat earlier in the year I think than the meeting on the Licensing Bill, for a quiet neighbourly celebration of this wonderful event seems in memory to have taken place in a keen spring air. Perhaps a tree had been felled or a high hedge lopped in Joseph's Little Field; at any rate a stack of twigs and branches was built there and all the Lower Town folk gathered in the dusk for the bonfire. Joseph said a couple of quiet sentences about the beginning of better times for old folk who had worked hard and lived rightly; someone lighted the oiled stick that Hannah held and she pushed it firmly in among the twigs.

Ten years before this Joseph had thought that Friendly Societies could provide opportunities for insurance and savings for old age. But wages stood even now at twelve and fourteen shillings. Saving was all but impossible.

After that there was less and less heart for bonfires. The resistance of the Lords to the 'hideous abnormality', as Lord Willoughby called it, of a strong Liberal Government produced a sense of frustration in all leftward politicians, and a sense of worse to come. In late April of 1909 came Lloyd George's Budget. Extra taxation had to be raised; fresh ways of finding money must be tried. Armies and Navies were growing. Land taxes would touch the pockets and ultimately the estates of landlords. Once levied they would be increased—to what point? Conservatives felt that the Budget was more than a money Bill; the Government claimed their right to have the Budget passed—a right acknowledged for two hundred years. But now in 1909 the Lords threatened to throw out the Liberal Budget.

So extreme a challenge raised the spirits of fighters. Arthur Ashby stuck a copy of Lloyd George's Limehouse speech in the frame of the rosewood and gilt mirror, laughing for the terseness of the attack on wealth and privilege and obstinacy. That feudal business must be finished now! But Mother asked where it would all end.

That was at the end of July. The depression in politics was paralleled in farming. The seasons in 1909 were late and wet throughout. Hay was spoiled, corn was threatened. There came a break in which Tysoe farmers, including Joseph, cut their wheat, and then the rain came back. Daisy Ashby, staying on a farm some ten miles away, wrote on 22 October that her hostess's wheat was still out. Joseph's wheat had been carried by then, but the last load of his barley did not come in till 8 November. Perhaps only defeat in war brings so much depression as such a harvest.

And then at the end of that month the Lords threw out the Budget. An election must take place in January. If the Conservatives won that election, that is, if the House of Lords won, the Liberal party would be finally defeated. And what then? Certainly not permanent rule for Lords and Tories, but the vast social gulfs in which revolution breeds. So Joseph thought.

Of the two local members of the House of Lords, one was a Liberal, a philanthropist, almost a Radical, and the other an extremist in resistance to the Commons, a 'Last Ditcher'. There had been a rule that peers of Parliament should not take part in electioneering, but Lord Willoughby at meetings in London and Lancashire turned himself about to display that strange animal a 'lord'. If land taxes took every one of his acres, a still more interesting career would be open to his Lordship it seemed—in the music halls! But Lancashire's appreciation of his turns suggested that some electors were no more serious than the peer himself.

Joseph at this time was ailing, as he was often to be from now on; in farming he could hardly keep his head above water; the children were going off on their own ploys and more work instead of less fell upon himself. And now political calamity threatened. Of minor ills one was the Liberal candidate for the Rugby Division, an Irish peer, who required to be fortified by whisky between meetings and so had to leave others to answer questions. He all but lost the seat; and nationally the Liberal party was only saved by Wales, Scotland and the Labour members.

Now the House of Lords had to be reformed or its powers reduced. Decisions on home matters were urgent; even Liberals believed that the Navy must be strengthened. Pictures of the Kaiser's sharp face, so fit to express extremes of feeling and sudden unreasoned decision, were appearing in all the newspapers.

Did the parents at The Orchards ever ask whether it was good for boys and girls to hear so much of politics? The doctrine to which they were exposed was not a narrow one and in any case the procession of 'Political' personalities who called at the house would have given them a notion that his politics were but a small part of a man's make-up. Candidates and agents visiting Tysoe called first on their father, always sharing a meal. Often visitors had much to ask about rural conditions and much to tell. The children liked the visits of a certain sober-sided academic historian of South Africa who nursed the constituency for a few months, but Arthur as a Liberal agent was glad to see him go. He was no fighter and South Africa was his King Charles's head. A candidate at one election was the handsome and solemn descendant of Sir Robert Peel. Neither of these, and certainly not the Irish peer, could hold a candle to Corrie Grant. But two candidates' wives struck new and remarkable notes. Such creatures might occur in the pages of Meredith but were an absorbing novelty in Tysoe. Lady Agnes Peel, an earl's daughter, sat beside the fire in the little sitting-room in exquisite clothes, palely striped, with lace cuffs and high whalebone collar, a sailorish hat with a garland of shining daisies, and lovely but rather frightened blue eyes. It was clearly a terrible new experience, taking tea in a farmhouse! But no one minded; she was so young, and might perhaps have some tiny exquisiteness of apprehension to match those delicate rare townish clothes.

But her shyness helped her husband to lose the election! The Countess was a society beauty whose portrait fashionable artists adored to paint, but she had been a local girl, the daughter of a gentleman farmer of ancient family on the Upton Estate. Having gone to London intending to be a famous actress she had become a chorus girl, the earl's mistress, and later his wife. Why? Had he charms, wit? They were invisible. But the Countess herself, with her high style and grace and kindness, made even a Victorian village and Puritan parents forget her story and eagerly help with her desperate enterprise of making a man and a politician of the whisky-scented Earl.

There were other callers, interested in rural affairs but not in party politics. Shy, inquiring young men were sent by Directors of Education and editors of journals, and came on their own account as writers or lecturers to be helped to an intimate understanding of rural conditions. Arriving to ask a few respectful questions, they would stay till dark, sharing meals, learning to milk and turning the separator, losing their hearts to the family life they saw. Little remains now of all the conversation the visitors stimulated, but a dramatic conclusion fixed an outline of one long talk in the children's minds.

Agriculture interested Joseph no more than many another subject, but in 1909 and 1910 there was a great deal of theorising on its future. This was the ferment that preceded the orderly approach to agricultural economics in which Arthur Ashby was to be a pioneer. One week at this time, no matter who dropped in the talk turned on farming. The 'Vet', the Chairman of the R.D.C., the corn chandler, the assistant Director of Education, all were drawn into discussion, on the rating of farms or farm schools or tariffs. On the Sunday after these visits the preacher at both morning and evening services was Richard Lean. Instead of driving his fine nag the few miles back to Kineton, Richard always stayed the day now for talk with Joseph. 'Father', the boys said, 'is up to something, Mr Lean. He talks of nothing but agriculture.' 'Well,' said Joseph, 'say I'm thinking about the Liberal party's programme.' Then they covered all the usual points—nationalisation of the land, provision of credit, increase of smallholdings, minimum wages. 'A party needing votes', said Joseph, 'will find that each of these loses as many votes as it gains.' In any case they were only expedients.

Richard was, that day, a pessimist. At what point could a reform movement begin? Landlords? They were devoted to their class interests. Bishops? (Arthur had lately read a paper on Bishop Grundtvig's Danish movement.) The English clergy's minds were full of social fantasies. The Labourer? Richard was only comfortable, so he said, with his labourers on a Friday evening when they could look at the money he was paying them and not at himself. In England it took an estate and a fortune to give a man the confidence and independence of a little Welsh hill farmer or of a peasant in a Swiss canton. That was what aristocratic dominance had done for us. The trouble was not agricultural but social. There was a little hope now in the farmers' and landowners' associations that were becoming active. True, all classes in farming pulled different ways ('A spider's web tug of war!' said a child). But in a meeting men's minds were more receptive than at home; fellows with ideas were listened to.

Joseph agreed that there seemed no hope of an inspired and practical movement, but, he said, he liked to imagine what the ideas of such a movement might be. It was plain that he had a plan.

Like all true revolutionaries, he said, he looked backward for his main motion. In the past land had been the basis of communities. No one, not even a corporation or a state, should have complete ownership of land. It should always be held in trust, not to provide incomes for younger sons and maiden aunts but for communities. A well-drawn trust could inspire generation after generation. Look at the Oxford colleges, at almshouses, even at the Tysoe Town Lands. But nowadays not only a village's or a town's interest should be recognised—the nation's also. Land had to do with the nation's safety—the children's education, with everything. And how to start? The new taxes would cause land to be sold, but not necessarily the breaking up of estates. Some would be run by companies for interest on money; why not by trusts for many-sided profit?

And the trust deeds? The size of estates and of communities? The units of cultivation? Conditions of tenure? Qualifications of trustees? To get the estates going, the first trustees must be of fortunate and liberal background—men of the widest, happiest education—Bolton Kings, Corrie Grants, Hon. George Peels, the Marquis. The estates would employ stewards of course.

An economic ladder? Oh yes! but also a ladder of responsibility—every man to have a share and a chance to bear more. The natural man liked responsibility. There would be estate committees from which a man could go forward, perhaps to a place on the movement's National Council. For of course there must be a movement—not national compulsion, not monopoly. No scheme should be universal. His village estates must prove themselves successful against every type of competitor. But they would be attractive! Away from the mere money-greed and the distinction-greed of the better-off, from the meanness of little men's co-operatives, towards villages worth living in, varieties of life and house and income, but scope for everyone and consideration given to all problems. He went on to practical details: the movement's statement of aim; the conditions of tenancy of land; the local estate councils. Suppose Tysoe were a communal estate; there were plenty of good men for a council! Their steward would be their leader as well as their servant—like the Directors of Education to Education Committees.

Stewardships would afford a career to active young men or to ambitious farmers. One must always think of the energetic, powerful personalities—give them something to do, keep them out of mischief, but control them.

The estates' trust deeds would show their part in education. Land must lie open for children to explore, so that they could really know their home. The estates must seem just in children's eyes; it was always important to notice how things appeared to children.

As to the techniques of agriculture, the movement would have its experimental farms and estates; its inventors would be told what to work at. Visits and tours would be arranged and shows, of course. It was minds you had to fertilise.

'And now, Father,' asked Arthur, 'what is the reason we've heard of nothing but agriculture for the last eight days?' 'Ah, I was coming to that!' The sound of teacups had been heard for a few minutes. Now Hannah came in. 'Joseph, we shall never be in time for Chapel! And Mr Lean must need a little time to think of the service.' But her husband was still deliberate. He took out from his watch-pocket two letters folded small, and soiled from being opened many times in the course of a week's work. He laid the first one where Hannah and Mr Lean could read it together, and then the other. Then the children seized both. The first letter was an invitation signed by the Marquis of Northampton and Mr King, asking Joseph in the name of a group of friends to be a candidate for the parliamentary division of Stratford, an entirely rural constituency, at the next election. He was to be independent of parties, his programme—mainly concerned with agriculture and rural conditions—was to be submitted only to the small group of friends. They would find the necessary money. The other, shorter letter, came from the owner of The Orchards. Joseph must shortly buy his home or receive notice to quit.

The little girls turned pale with ambition for their father. Arthur said, 'You'll stand, Dad? Won't we organise your campaign!' 'Don't be foolish, boy,' said Joseph, 'Haven't I been demonstrating that there's no possible programme for me? And can I leave you to do everything here? Who is going to buy The Orchards for us?' Hannah struck in with

'Arthur, you *must* get ready for milking.' And Father said his last word, 'I leave the parliamentary business for you.' 'I'm coming, Mother' said Arthur, and with a mocking, shining smile, 'I'll see to it, Father.'

Friends who liked to join the family at The Orchards often commented on the children's rich life, but Joseph realised that their education was a rustic one. He longed for them to have, also, such an education as many of his friends had received—one that afforded a well-oiled key to the chief mansions of learning and enabled them to go at their ease about the world. That was for the more intellectual; what of a boy ingenious and clever-handed? And girls who must find a way of earning a living? They all fared as they best could.

By that eventful year of 1910 Arthur had entered Ruskin College in Oxford, which offered courses in history, economics and social philosophy. The students were almost all urban Trade Unionists, himself the only countryman. From 'Ruskin' he brought home a long series of guests, mostly strangers to farms and villages. They varied greatly in outlook, of course, but some were ill at ease in the country, only happy in the evening when curtains were drawn and arguments began. Then they would prove that the dictatorship of the proletariat was inevitable, and take for granted that the struggle to hasten it was the only glorious mission. It was difficult for Joseph to maintain a host's courtesy through such politics of class and hate. He and Hannah began to be anxious about the effect of such companionship upon their son, but he was unscathed. The moment term was over he threw off his coat to help with the ploughing or to bring in the harvest; no gulf for him between thought and practical life. For him as for all the children, no friend was truly made till he had seen and appreciated his home. Soon he found first-class tutors in Oxford who valued what he brought to them and so could help him to rapid progress. Presently his energy of thinking, combined with that quality of his, of one born to be beloved, eased his way, bringing him in a year or two invitations to study in America and later to pursue research in England.

By 1910, also, Kathleen had started on a *via crucis* of scholarship-winning, first to a high school and then to a university. To her at school and Hall of Residence Arthur would send letters urging her to read this classic work and that. They were essential, he said, to her period or topic; he would somehow manage to buy her copies. But it was no good; Kathleen was so busy starting new subjects, passing examinations, spending whole days at lectures, that her mind was at a standstill. It was fortunate that a tough fabric had already been woven in her mind before her 'education' began.

Meanwhile William went off deliberately to learn farming by hiring himself to farmers in various parts of the country, studying methods and markets. The study of theology and philosophy were out of the question for him; but farm accounts, if so kept as to show with something like certainty what was gained in each operation, called upon a faculty for analysis; and it was pretty satisfying to conduct unaided experiments, as they had to be in those days, in feeding animals so as to improve yield. On most farms William soon 'had the idea' and took his leave, but once he stayed two years because he was given so much freedom to experiment, and because the farmer was drinking his farm to ruin and himself to death. An attempt to cure the dipsomaniac was one of Bill's experiments. Girls attended the County Council classes in cooking and dressmaking, and the demonstrations in the most charming of all itinerant vans—a small model dairy. A young woman coquettishly dressed in pink and white bonnet and overalls made butter and Devonshire cream. Then the County offered short residential courses at the Dairy Institute in one of George Eliot's early homes.

But in spite of forward movement, how troubling poverty could be. Arthur when he went to Ruskin could not manage without a dictionary, but the sight of the beloved old Ogilvy and Annandale on his table struck him with pain; it must be

daily, hourly, missed at home. Kathleen bought a sable brush
at five shillings for the school painting class when a nine-
penny camel-hair would have served, and could never forget
the fateful mistake. These trifles stick in the mind; there were
more lasting and pervasive effects of restriction. But there
was no sense of poverty in vacations and holidays, at their
Mother's table and in their Father's presence, its occasional
severity almost submerged now in a warmer and more
constant geniality.

The brothers and sisters had developed their relationship
to each other and to their parents till they fitted into a pattern,
like the sunward mosaic of leaves on a beech branch. Roles
had been accepted; one was to be the adventurer bringing
treasures from far off, another was critic and stimulant, two
gave grace and merry humour to the company. Such a moment
of unity in a large family's life is precious but can only be
transitory. Here it was broken once for all in a great storm
of May. Daisy, who in the family pattern was to contribute
a strength and constancy like her mother's and to be the
practical and devoted prop and stay of all, had gone from home
to stay with a friend a few miles away, and there on a great
friendly farmhouse hearth lightning had struck her. The
family pattern was broken and would never be re-knit. The
effects of this stroke of Nature on the minds of the children
were slow to develop and belong to another story. At first
the family noted chiefly the kindly human balm that was
offered. The girl's grave was smothered and heaped with
flowers, daisies from the lower orchard, bunches of flowers
from gardens of the village and greenhouse flowers from
more distant friends. And at the funeral service the Vicar stood
beside the Methodist Minister murmuring 'Amen' to the
prayers. He had asked permission to stand there in his own
churchyard. A strange young Vicar this, an Australian suffering from no old restricting social outlook. When he met a
carpenter he would doff his hat in honour of Christ. He
might be a fool who had to ask clever lads the meaning of the

word 'economics', but he had shown again and again that he well understood the meaning of service and humility.

It was in May, a few days before the Ashby family's loss, that King Edward VII had died. The new inexperienced monarch must be treated with great consideration and the Conservative and Liberal parties tried to reach agreement on the question of the House of Lords. They failed. What now could the Government do? They must ask His Majesty to create new peers who would respect the responsibilities of the elected chamber. The number of new peers would have to be large and King George declined to take the step till after yet another election. In December it was that the Hon. George Peel lost the Rugby Division; but Mr Asquith's majority in the Commons was almost as before. Now, surely —so the young folk thought at The Orchards—Liberal Bills would reach the statute book and a dead order in the countryside be removed. Lord Willoughby was now neglecting his foxhounds and almost ceasing to hunt: he was in constant attendance at the House of Lords. For him, the first of virtues was 'the defence of one's own order'. 'Class'—the girls at The Orchards had chidden their brother's Marxist visitors— 'is the meanest and most superficial of social concepts.' But at least the Ruskin men students had talked of ineluctable tendencies and not of lofty virtue.

Very soon after the election the Parliament Bill was read in the Commons. In May it reached the Lords, who amended the Bill so extensively that they might as well have thrown it out. And now King George was to be crowned. The Tysoe bonfire was not to be a homely affair on the green, but a pile was built on the hills above the site of the Red Horse where it would answer to fires on the Malverns and on the Dassett Hills, and be one in a milky way of lines and constellations of beacons all over England. After weeks of sun, 22 June was showery all day. By evening the fields were wet and the rain though soft was pretty constant. If some spirits were damped for those and less simple reasons it was not those of the young Ashbys, for they had with them watching the fire and talking with all and sundry a choice and interesting spirit, a Ruskin tutor, Charles Sidney Buxton. He had brought with him to The Orchards a plan for rural regeneration to which he meant to devote his life and fortune; a long, lanky fellow, a thought phlegmatic perhaps, not wonderfully practical, but with a nobility of character that showed itself in his every smile and word.

But much as 'Charles Sidney' was admired, the voice of the critic was not quite silent. 'And what', asked William, 'does he propose to do with this fifty thousand pounds that our Father has not done, without a five pound note to spare except the one that he absent-mindedly threw into the fire?'

Now, all classes having rejoiced in their new Sovereign and in the Constitution as they conceived it, Lords and Commons returned to their duties. A group of die-hard peers were all for the utmost resistance to a reduction of the powers of their House. Lord Willoughby became more and more fluent, more and more bold, the most prominent of all the Last Ditchers from the 'backwoods'. In the end, however, a majority of peers voted against their rash brethren. The struggle over, the great foxhunter was back on his estate, writing his charming essays on foxhunting and his auto-biography. The dead hand of the past had been loosened from English villages.

But aristocracy had still its influence. If Lord Willoughby was flanked on the Kineton Magistrates' bench by Ridley Brown and Joseph Ashby, he was still in the Chair. The Petty Session Court was 'no place for girls', and no lesser person than a university tutor could have persuaded Joseph to take a young daughter with him, but with this help Kathleen accompanied him once. It proved a sordid experience, not unrelieved. There was, for example, Lord Willoughby's royal progress, bowing right and left to the police, and the public and the trespassers and cyclists in trouble.

In times gone by Justices had been commissioned to 'inquire the truth more fully...of all manner of felonies, poisonings, enchantments, sorceries, arts, magics, trespasses, forestallings, regratings, engrossings and extortions whatever'—a highly coloured list. But that morning the magistrates dealt with a young man who had ridden his bicycle without a light, a woman whose dog had no collar, and some dreadful women from the slums of Birmingham who had defiled the neat streets of Kineton with foul language. More humour was provided by one of the magistrates. Mr Ridley Brown descended from the Bench into the dock, standing before his colleagues because he had allowed his cows to stray, not without excellent excuses. His short round person and round red face reminded one of Shakespearian comedy and so did his determination to set an example of respect to the magistrates. 'Your washups' he said, in his Northumbrian speech...'your washups', and again 'your washups'.

Misdemeanours dealt with that morning were typical. Kathleen, reading back numbers of the *Warwick Advertiser*, found that on other occasions men had stolen kale from a field, ridden bicycles on footpaths, or left a horse unattended. Poaching and trespassing occurred very occasionally. Tramps were now and then brought to court for sleeping out. But now they were nearly always men, and seldom young. Vagrancy was not what it had been even a few years earlier, though housewives left alone for the day were still a little alarmed by ragged dirty fellows asking for bread or for boiling water to make tea in their tin cans. Joseph thought the tramp problem had been cured as completely as possible, those who were left liked the life! Of course sometimes men were 'drunk and disorderly' but the number coming before the magistrates for this offence revealed little of the drink trouble; sensible policemen took care not to see everything, while cases of repeated drunkenness and disorder went to Quarter Sessions. Horrifying to a girl were the examples of cruelty to animals— driving a horse with a raw sore under a rough collar, or loading a poor old mare till she dropped. But the older generation said, 'Ah, but what stories we heard thirty years ago'.

Although he represented an economic class who had not previously had seats on the Bench, Joseph found himself very much at home, usually, with his fellows there. There were remnants of the feeling that poaching was a heinous crime and drunkenness a venial one, while in Joseph's mind the reverse was true; but faced with a delinquent in the dock, class-feeling was far less dominant than the Christian sense that there but for the grace of God, might the Justice himself be standing. The magistrates who made a practice of attending the Warwick Quarter Sessions—the most industrious and seriously interested—were sound even on the drink question: they had reduced the number of licensed premises as fast as the law permitted and wanted greater powers.

It was a good moment in rural society. Evangelical and humane movements had touched all classes, inciting the one side to tolerance of democracy and the other to forgiveness for past exploitation. At both extremes of the social scene, the ideal of the Christian gentleman attracted intelligent and sensitive minds. Tolerance, gentleness, high valuation of every individual, the grace of courtesy and love for books— all these were shared by members of every social grade.

About this time there died a greatly admired acquaintance of Joseph's—a fellow magistrate and member of the Brailes Rural District Council. A man of established family, a Tory, a landowner, though not of broad acres, he had been a most devoted public servant. Even in age he had continued to rise often at dawn and ride the long distance from his home to the county town. He was not, one gathered, brilliant in any way, but his justice and sound information and his scrupulous discharge of office had come to be recognised. As Joseph spoke of him one saw that he admired not only the man but his setting. His home had been a small ancient manor-house, manned by a very few but well-trained servants, so that his public duties did not cut him off from pleasure in his library and garden. In short he had been a Christian but also a 'country' gentleman—had lived just such a life as would best have suited Joseph, allowing him to develop his tastes and talents. Nor did Joseph think it a wrong style: it involved no dominance, and no privilege not balanced by service, while it allowed development of family accomplishments. Not everyone could have such a background, but then not everyone would care for it. For himself such a life would leave Heaven little to give.

CHAPTER XIX

LOOKING BACKWARD

FROM his drives with the old pony, Lady London, Joseph had
brought many a trophy—parcels of books from Stratford,
yellow archangels from Knoll End, orchids from Dishwater
Pool, odd bits of old cottage gear, but never booty like the
armful of shabby, dusty, old manuscript books that he brought
one early spring day in 1909. While he was driving through
Radway he had been hailed from the Vicarage gate. The old
Vicar had died recently at a great age. Some thirty-five years
before, when the spire of Radway Church was being rebuilt,
and Joseph was driving huge stones for it from Hornton
Quarry, Mr Sanderson Miller and he had had their first
conversation. There had been a number of talks, not so very
many. It was the son of the old Vicar who called to Joseph.
'I'm sorting my father's papers', he said. 'He left a lot of
old books relating to Tysoe. He said you'd know what to do
with them.'

Now, as Joseph laid the long, narrow, sheepskin-covered
books on the table, Hannah and the younger children crowded
round. One book, bound in dried and broken leather, bore on
its cover the date 1575 in elaborate figures: it was a register
of births, deaths, and marriages. Others were account books.
As Joseph turned the pages of one of these latter a pin fell out.
It had fastened a small piece of paper headed 'Corrigendum'.
'Handmade', said Father of the pin. 'Look at its head, like
a bulb—as bright as the day it was made.' Sybil, aged ten,
was holding it, and as Father added 'two hundred years old',
she shivered and let the pin drop: that was *too* much time.
Joseph glanced into the oldest book but the script was difficult
and much faded. He turned to the earliest of the account
books, and his eye and the children's eyes lit upon his own

name. It was contained in the List of Overseers for the few
years previous to 1727. Turning the pages he saw it again;
'Joseph Ashby, Overseer 1735'. Among the entries and the
headings were other familiar names—Jeffs, Walton, Durham,
Loveday, Lines. What elaborate, clerkly handwriting! Sometimes the ink was faded, but with care and a cheap magnifying
glass the account books were always legible. Here was first-
hand information upon three hundred and fifty years of Tysoe
life, with a thousand details of the two latter centuries.

By 1909 the children had begun to be scattered for much of
the year. Arthur had spent a winter at Ruskin College,
Kathleen had been two years at her High School, Richard and
William were making their sallies from home. In some ways
now their lives were being lived beyond their parents'
observation and influence. The stresses of new relationships
and new ambitions had begun: if their ways had not divided,
it could be seen that 'home' must soon lose its central place
for some of them at least.

But they had only to see the old books to know that here
was a large work for them to share with their father: in fact
it was to occupy them vacation after vacation for eighteen
months or more, the stay-at-homes getting ahead with the
farmwork to have leisure with the others. 'The job', as they
called the deciphering and study of the manuscripts was to be
a fine common adventure for their last. It was fit perhaps for
professors rather than babes and sucklings in history, but they
had their clues derived from their father's stories, and his
constant reference to the village's past, and he was there to
lead them in their first exploration of the manuscripts.

The registers and the overseers' accounts were only the
nucleus of the collection of documents that came to The
Orchards. When Joseph mentioned the books to his talk-
friends they fell to thinking about old documents in their own
cupboards and attics. Mr Tom Middleton arrived with a sack
full of ancient deeds, but these were in dog-Latin and faded, or
in infinitely repetitive lawyer's language. Old Mr Styles the

joiner produced a Vestry Minute-book; someone brought an old intermittent diary kept by a sexton and smallholder in a village in another county, but one with much in common, it proved, with Tysoe. The chest in the church yielded, among other things, a seventeenth-century recipe for a highly spiced and enormous cake; a blacksmith sent an envelope full of old farriers' prescriptions for the ills of horses and cows; and again there was a farmer's note-book kept during the middle of the eighteenth century. There was something for everybody!—human interest for girls, light on old agricultural ways for a budding farmer and on parish administration for a student beginning a training in economic history. For Joseph there was the opportunity to test the truth of that store of tradition and inference that he had built in his mind.

It is very easy for me to return in mind to the little study, the round rosewood table and Aunt Rouvray's old couch smothered with the old, long books, bound in stained white leather, and to reinstate mentally the quality of those days, but yet I am surprised by the childish, almost idiot script of the notes I turn over. There are transcripts made on Richard's rattling old typewriter: there is a book made up of Joseph's articles from the *Warwick Advertiser* on 'Two Hundred Years of Village History'. No one thought of making any record of Mother's contributions, but one or two of them were remembered. In one of the early pages of the first Register there was a word recurring among the baptismal entries, always cramped against the edge of the page and having, it seemed clear, nothing to do with babies. Something had happened, something novel and exciting, 'in our church of Tysoe'. Everyone else had studied each letter and copied the word a hundred times. Mother set her hot iron before the fire and left a sheet trailing from her ironing-board. 'R-e-c-h' said she, as she rejected the magnifying glass. 'When you cannot find a lost thing, never look for it. Sit down and think. Reched, wretched, reached, treached—in church. *Preached*, of course!' There were also her interjections into the talk, as on this occasion. William had made a rapid calculation. Preaching since 1580! At one sermon each Sunday in the church alone that is over seventeen thousand sermons, and Tysoe a wicked village still. 'Ah,' said his mother sadly, 'The fathers learn but the sons don't know', and the youthful cynic thought again.

Though the children usurped their father's study and his books and everything that was his, and he was obliged to wait till they had gone back to college or school to make his own study of the documents, he stood by as critic. He insisted, for example, on the students' pausing to find what was known of the pre-Elizabethan village. Several times he and Kathleen drove the sixteen miles, an all-day excursion, to the Shire Hall at Warwick. One could discover there from old books a great deal about the building of the church and something of the manorial organisation of the Three Towns. He made them use their books on social history and make clear to themselves where their findings were similar and where dissimilar to those of the authorities. The way he would laugh when some cherished hypothesis of his own was disproved by that passionately cautious student, his eldest son, was a lesson. But also for the most part, the children marvelled at the accuracy of his guesses, based, as he made clear, on the traditions of the village, and on knowledge of the fields, buildings, farms and families: the text-books were less to be trusted than the lifelong workings of this balanced mind.

There were two ways of approaching the old parish records —as a mere reader, or as a student. The first was Kathleen's way. She had been drawn to the registers by the beauty of the first page. The writing recalled the plainer parts of some illuminated manuscripts she had once seen in the Bodleian, though it had a vivacious elaboration of its own. She had experienced a shock in finding that the writer of 1575 had used a blacklead, as she did herself, to rule lines to write on. What a familiarity among so much strangeness! So she began, and read on as if the registers were an absorbing novel

—a thousand deaths, a thousand births, and marriages linking and relinking the families of the village, and the folk of Tysoe with the villages around. 'What is the good', asked her eldest brother, who thirsted for precise information, 'of reading as if the registers were one of your stories, meandering instead of making for some destination?' 'She does not meander', said brother William, 'so much as light a little fire of emotion under the entries and distil her own especial liquor, like old Mother Bowers' hedge-shoot wine, poor local stuff but her own.' The girl defended herself. 'If I ask questions, I half know already, out of the books, or from what you and Father say; but if I just read on something dawns on me, something I should never have thought of, something that perhaps even wiseacres from Oxford don't know. For example, did you know you could tell from these registers how many Tysoe families had never since surnames began lived more than ten miles away?' Many an inkling such as that came to her but she was particularly interested in her gleanings about children, how babies lived in the seventeenth century—and also how they died. Oh! such a lot were baptised in a hurry, before their hour-long lives could end. As to twins, there was no keeping them alive! They all died! And then, the children's names: after the stern high religious tradition and the occasional classical name of the sixteenth and seventeenth centuries (Mary, Grace, Joan, Matthew, Samuel, Hannibal) it was a keen shock to read the first diminutives in the eighteenth century (Nannie, Betty). Later in that century mothers had given to baby girls fanciful names of flowers and queens—Retta Maria or Violetta. But as a matter of fact mothers were only there by inference; they were never mentioned, their names never given, but only the fathers'—except the mothers of bastard babies! Poor bastards! Minister Edwards, the first of the ministers, was so ashamed of them that he entered their births in Latin.

Until the end of the eighteenth century, Tysoe, the registers showed, had been a village of yeomen, craftsmen, tradesmen, and a few labourers—not separate classes, but intermarrying, interapprenticed sections of the community, unified by farming in co-operation, and by as great mutual dependence in other ways. Only rarely was a 'gent' buried and still more rarely a 'servant'. A member of almost any family could trace a part of his heredity back to 1575. The Vicar was a 'minister' and a farmer till in the late eighteenth century the Seagrave family arrived and registered themselves as 'Reverend Misters', born, the phrase seemed to indicate, to direct and admonish, 'ministers' no longer.

But it seemed that there must have been many less successful communities. Vagrants rejected by or rejecting their home 'towns' travelled the roads and slept in the barns. 'A lad travelling on the high road' was found dead; a vagrant woman bore a child in the open, stony, church porch; a baby was found in a ditch. Kathleen, who had been used to shed tears over Dickens's stories, wept also over the boy who died alone on the road, but those were the last tears; there were simply not enough of them to keep pace with these hardships, though the terse register-expressions were so piercing. All that the reader could do was to identify herself with the poor outcasts. It was a small point but touching, that when the vagrants' babies lived and their mothers too survived their birth (it was not often both escaped the scythe), it was those babes who were given the far-fetched, fine names, such as Daniella or Velta.

It did look, as the girl read the registers and the diary of the yeoman and the smith's accounts, as though the sermons and the Bible in English might have had a good effect through a century and a half; life grew steadily gentler, as well as more comfortable and richer to the senses. Mothers smiled more often to their children, fewer girls died at the birth of their first baby, the variety of flowers planted at the foot of the house walls was greater; tea and tobacco ousted beer to some extent and doubtless soothed domestic life. But then came a change in the reverse direction. In the late eighteenth century, when plague came again, more people died. Somewhat later it seemed that the parish had to pay for the funerals of certain poor villagers, the Vicar writing 'Pauper' after their names, and presently as these burials became more numerous he would write only a large 'P'. If there had been parish assistance for funerals earlier they had passed without these signs of shame. Why this poverty, this retrogression? But she had arrived at the year 1812 and the end of the old informative registers. From that date a form had been used and nearly all the tell-tale variety of entry disappeared.

There was one thing all the students acquired—the sense of the complexity of 'simple' things. Even knocking on a door became an experience, when you had thoughts of its builders in the sixteenth century and of the girl who had disgraced with an illegitimate babe a stern upright family in the seventeenth, when such calamities were rare; and of perhaps exactly what had been sold from a tiny shop there in the seventeen-hundreds: or kicking against a stone accidentally, knowing it would have just as interesting a past, if you only knew of it, as the 'merestones' they had found in a ditch, flung there at 'The enclosure', or those lying about in Harbury Leys, that had been part of the base of the market-cross set up in the fourteenth century—though there had never really been a Tysoe market. Like all their varied farm and house jobs, this one gave them on some topics, useful examples and questions. Were you to tell them that the great houses had brought light, leading and beauty to rural parts, they would say, 'Well, not to Tysoe. You should look at the ugly farmhouses the Marquis's agents built in the Upper Town and then at the moulded doorways and mullions of the houses farmers built for themselves in the seventeenth century.'

But after all what are such vague gains to a scholar? There came the moment when Arthur became deliberately an imperious director of studies and the others obeyed, the first of his many admiring students and assistants. He took in charge the overseers' accounts for a thorough investigation, allotting tasks of note-making and decipherment and verification to his juniors. The book he finally wrote is a factual account of how the Poor Law was administered in Tysoe from 1727 to 1827, when the series of books came to an end. (But the Vestry Minutes enabled him to carry on the story in outline till 1834 when a new era began.) It must have been an achievement for so warm a temperament to limit itself so rigidly, for here in Tysoe during that century was enacted the Tragedy of the Village—a diffuse long drama, with only minor characters, and yet enthralling—the deepest of lessons in human affairs.

Try as Arthur might to make his assistants limit themselves in his way, they continued to visualise events and identify themselves with persons. One of the great amphitheatres formed by the curves of the Edge Hills contains the Church Town. Louis Napoleon Parker's Pageant of Warwick in 1906 had affected the children's minds, and now one or two of them, after a session with the Overseers, would run up Cow Lane and along to the top of Old Lodge and from there look down into the Town, seeing the figures moving there as if they were acting the scenes of the Tragedy.

Early scenes in the seventeen-thirties were not unhappy ones. Town meetings were held in the vestry of the church or in the still more central schoolroom. They were seldom very large, but in the course of two or three years many of the men attended and there are some signs that women were occasionally present. The members of the Town Meetings or Vestries were not 'electors' nor 'parishioners' but 'neighbours', and the method of the neighbours was to 'agree', and every man was Thomas, Jonas or Henry, as in a Quaker meeting: perhaps the Friends derived their customs from such meetings of neighbours. The Overseers of the Poor were the servants of the meeting, not elected but serving on a rough rota of persons of known capacity. That first year,

1727, only five persons came to the overseers asking for help —three widows, a child and an old man. They came at the appointed time to the schoolroom, not to make long pleas, for the officers knew their age and the blows that had fallen on them, but to tell precisely of their present need. The applicants were not 'down and out': the old man owned the cottage he lived in and had the right to turn a cow on to the Cow Pastures. One widow had only one dress, and it was worn; another who earned her bread by spinning had found her wheel past mending and must have a new one. The old man can no longer work; he must pay a neighbour to look after his cow. The orphan comes to say that he can go into Farmer C's house if the overseers will provide his clothes for the next year or two, till his work is worth a clothes allowance. The needs are modest and can all be met.

In many successive years there were similar processions, but growing a little longer, at first only because the number of the villagers was growing. Usually now the overseers were disbursing about fifteen shillings a week, growing to sixteen or seventeen. Besides helping to support the poor there were more occasional needs, giving to 'travellers', paying for the funeral of some breadwinner cut off in mid-course —no pauper's funeral, but a neighbour's, costly and decent as any other. Sometimes the overseers would receive rather out-of-the-way requests, and after attending to routine matters they adjourned to an inn to discuss the case. The ale they drank they charged to the ratepayers. The neighbours had little anxiety about the poor's rate and did not grudge the ale; deliberations were the better for being taken at ease. It would be nearly a century before anyone thought it improper to drink at the cost of the parish.

Long drinks were especially necessary when a letter was received from Quarter Sessions, giving directions and rules for the work of poor relief. Overseers would be bidden to keep their accounts carefully. (Ah! that was meant for other parishes, no need to bid Tysoe!) Once they were forbidden to give help from the rates in case of losses by fire or water: but when it was felt by the neighbours that everyone who could ought to help, was it not simplest to give aid from the rates? They very soon forgot that order. They must not, came one message, give to strolling beggars or soldiers and sailors without licence from magistrates. But when lame soldiers came hobbling through the village and there was no resident Justice, what could you do? A group of six poor men were relieved on the very next page after the message was recorded. But the magistrates appeared not to mind a modified and reflective obedience: the accounts were always signed without the disallowance of any item. The rules came from a still higher quarter and the magistrates themselves claimed a certain discretion.

That the spirit of relief was truly 'kind', recognising the kinship of neighbours, was clear. The Widow Claridge, very ailing in 1750, had a notion that the saline waters of a spring in a village seventeen miles away would do her good. So the overseers gave three shillings to Isaac Clark, who rode all the way to Leamington to fetch them for her. During long illnesses wine was supplied to patients. One of the greatest of mischances was to be 'drawn for a soldier'. In 1758 those upon whom the lots fell paid other, perhaps younger men, to go in their place, the overseers finding half these fees.

There were clouded moments during the first half of the eighteenth century. In 1741 the overseers spent nearly three times as much as in any of the ten previous years, for small-pox had come to the village. A 'travelling woman' arrived at the Lower Town carrying a 'pass'—a licence to beg. She fell ill; neighbours coming to bring her food and drink saw 'the pox'. In agitation they sent a lad to fetch the overseers. Then John Murray the roper came with his yellow face pitted all over and carried the woman on his back across the open fields, a mile and a half or two miles to a lone cottage in Westcote Manor. Daily, John took bread to the sick woman and salves for her sores. The overseers paid a weaver for

one warm new blanket for her. She grew better and returned
to the village to be lodged and boarded at a cost of four
shillings and sixpence—that is, as much as a man's wage.
The village could forgive a very ill turn; the effects of the
epidemic, which after all was not avoided, lasted a long time.
The overseers' expenditure remained high for two and a half
years and then dropped again to somewhat above the old
average.

In considering the condition of the village one had to
remember smallpox; it came again and again, at intervals of
two, four, and ten years. It seemed to become more severe,
probably with the rise in the price of bread and the increase
of unemployment. Cases were more numerous and death
from the disease more probable. There were signs of panic
about 1790: when there was a rumour of a case the neighbours
would gather together to insist that the overseers send post-
haste for the doctor, and then they waited to hear his verdict.
On the occasion it was thought that Mary Smith on the green
had the pox, the neighbours gathered in the open and waited or
discussed so long that the overseers felt that they must all be
refreshed, and spent fourteen shillings on beer for them. In
an epidemic, those earthly Fathers of the Village, the overseers, were very busy. In 1790 they organised the supply of
soups and milk, buying 'pease, pepper, beef and garden-stuff',
and paying a woman for 'trouble making soups'. They
supplied soap and firing and spent pounds on wine. Bread was
given for the asking. When cases were too severe for the
victims to be conveyed to Westcote, the schoolroom became
a supplementary pockhouse. Women were paid for nursing;
sometimes nurses were brought from Banbury. Throughout
the epidemics the overseers worked with evident devotion
and in a spirit of kinship.

As to general developments, it seems that from the seven-
teen-forties poverty was increasing all over England,
'Whitehall' was anxious; moral force must be used! Orders
arrived that relieved persons must wear a scarlet 'P' for

'poor' and thus be made to feel shame. Little harm, the overseers seem to have thought, could come of giving Tailor
William Gaydon (the name now spelt 'Geden') the job of
making six sets of scarlet letters, 'T.P.', standing for 'Tysoe
Poor'. When Kathleen first read of these letters she exclaimed in horror, but her father eased the shock. 'Let's not
be too sure the letters were ever worn. That's something that
would have been remembered. Can you imagine the Relief
Officer offering Mother Durham scarlet letters? It would
have been even less safe to offer one to her great-grandmother,
I imagine. Gaydon's bill was paid and that was the end of the
matter, I guess.'

The sickness coped with, there were the after-effects.
Young parents died and orphans came into the overseers'
care, to be apprenticed to 'mysteries' or set to farmers.
Sometimes much trouble was taken to put them to a desired
trade: a small boy would be escorted many miles, to some
craftsman relative of his own, or of some other Tysoe family.
Neighbours had need of beds, medicine, or a bleeding, or
Godfrey's opiate, or to go on a journey. Future welfare
might depend on help; they needed seed-corn, or a guarantee
to a landlord that rent for a cottage would be forthcoming.
In a single week of 1777 there were fifty-four entries in the
book. At mid-century, in 1750, eighty-seven pounds had been
spent; fifty years later the sum was nearly three thousand
pounds. Such an increase meant drastic, revolutionary change.

For a long time the overseers continued in the old way to
consider each need and to make a decision upon it. It was
difficult for neighbourly feelings and methods to be dropped,
for few of the ratepayers were securely elevated above the
poor. When their relatives were widowed or orphaned, these
would be in need of help. The names of paupers (the word
has come, and is even beginning to have the shameful meaning
the Government thought desirable) were the same as their
own or were also borne by men of broad acres, or rather of
many open-field strips.

What was causing such painful developments? Enclosures could not be blamed in Tysoe, for the rates had quadrupled while the open fields remained. War bore heavily on men seized for the Army or Navy, coming home lame or sick, but not before the Wars of the French Revolution did war have a visible general effect. The simplest, perhaps the superficial, explanation, lay in the price of bread and the fixity of wages. During the eighteenth century wages of men who had served no apprenticeship rose from four and sixpence or five shillings only to six or seven shillings. In the old intermittent diary kept from 1780 to 1830 which was among the miscellaneous documents at hand, the price of corn and bread was often given, interspersed among entries about the largest pumpkins, and the earliest floods. Entries relating to food were in the earlier years pleasant enough—'pease both blue and pounce-fir' for dinner in October, huge cucumbers in November, and bread at one shilling and twopence the peck loaf. But in 1801 the price of a loaf was six shillings and sixpence. From a labourer's budget for that year it seemed that a family of parents and six children required nine and a half peck loaves per week! Between 1801 and 1830 the price rose and fell in a most extraordinary way. On several occasions it reached six and sixpence again and once rose higher still. During those years, the entries in the journal about mid-winter primroses and stout cucumbers gave way to riots, machine-breaking, rick-burnings, deportations and hangings.

Of course, Tysoe folk had had to pay the same prices as others for their bread, but they had not taken to rick-burning or to murder. The overseers had long continued to administer relief in the old spirit, but they had had to try new methods. For example, when famine came in 1795, they built a bake-house, paid a baker, and arranged a rota of persons to buy flour and serve bread to the needy at a price below cost. In 1800 the bakehouse committee alone spent £600. This enterprise came easily enough to a village which had possessed a malthouse throughout the eighteenth century and perhaps earlier, besides sometimes having a brewhouse. With the increase in population the right to cut fuel from the waste had lost its value, for there was little wood to cut, and while gorse from the hills made a gorgeous blaze in the chimney, it burned away in no time. So the overseers bought coal and sold it to the poor, and at times to all comers. They acquired a barn which they used as a wharf or 'dock', near the 'Dock cottage' that Father and Mother had occupied for a short while. The toughest of problems was unemployment. It had made its first appearance in 1752 when one workless man was helped. In 1774 four or five men were without work for several winter months. It was the law that the able-bodied must be given work if they lacked it—not money or goods for nothing. The overseers endeavoured to obey, giving spinning wheels and hemp, money to furnish a pedlar's pack, or to pay the blacksmith for tools, or to go seeking work. When several men were out of work they were set to trenching for the common profit in the open fields or to the mending of the roads. Besoms were bought once for five boys to sweep the mud from the much-used village paths. It became difficult to find ways even of 'making out' that the overseers were finding work for several men but it was easy with women; there could be at least a fiction that they were tending some relative or neighbour. There was a tradition in the village that there had been 'parish carts' used by the unemployed men for drawing stone from the parish quarries on to the roads, but that must have been after 1827: there was no evidence for it in the books. The most usual method of relieving workless men was to pay them for 'going about by the yard land'. In 1763 Dan'l Wigson was paid 'one shilling per week that he was to have, going about by the yard land, four shillings'. It had been arranged that, having no work, he was to go in turn to several farmers and stay a certain time with each: the more yardlands each farmed, the longer Dan'l stayed with him. There are always jobs that need doing on a farm if only it would pay to do them! So the farmers paid a 'roundsman' three shillings a week and the overseers gave him another shilling, thus keeping his weekly receipts below the lowest wage—then four and sixpence—of the regularly employed workers.

Kathleen imagined the men 'going round by the yardland' or 'by the pound rent' (that was the term after the fields were enclosed). Of course, these men were the lame and halt, the clumsy workers, and the elderly. It was not always easy to tell from the accounts exactly how many there were of them or just how the work was organised, for the special book the overseers kept of men on the round had vanished; but in some years it was clear that over forty men and boys were receiving relief. Even for the employer, roundsman labour was a depressing affair, vexing and despised because irregular and cheap. For the men, even a full wage would not, in the seventeen-nineties, pay for adequate bread, let alone meat, which also had become dear. But in spite of all, the system developed. Possibly Tysoe left to itself might have found some better way, but it was subject to instruction and suggestion from outside. There were boys, younger and younger, on the round. Little girls of ten were sent from house to house, given twopence a day by the employer and twopence 'out of the book'. Old men, once good workers, went on the round for the same pay as boys. But the pay would not provide bread; hunger had still to be dealt with. Magistrates in Berkshire had ruled that the parish relief supplementing the roundsman's wage should be calculated on the number of persons in a family, and this became the general custom. So it might—it often did—pay a man better to be on the round. Farmers thus paid only part of their due wages bill; but all other ratepayers, tradesmen and small-holders, shared the supplementation of wages. Hard, was that, on small men who paid no wages on their own account. And what a muddle! The rates were subsidising the better off, but no one spoke of *their* being pauperised! The spirit of relief was changing and the problem was out of hand.

Meanwhile, in April 1796, an Act of Parliament was passed for the enclosure of the open fields of Tysoe. There was it appears no resistance to the project. Every parish but one that touched the border of Tysoe was now enclosed, and even in that one much land had been enclosed two centuries since. Enclosure was on the way for the whole country. It was undeniable that the land would yield more; the new crops could be grown. It might some day employ more labour. The paraphernalia of enclosure had a convincing appearance. Three impressive, patient gentlemen walked over the land. They viewed everything, heard every claim, every objection. When in doubt they sent to Banbury for a solicitor. Perfect lawyer's justice was done. For example the poor were well compensated for their right to cut non-existent wood; the Earl of Northampton and his heirs were put in charge of land whose rent would be spent on coal for them.

The Earl and his like, who ruled England, were satisfied with this lawyer's justice, being so happily wedded to their vision of 'the rich man in his castle, the poor man at his gate'! But the ordinary man's vision of a sound co-operative village of free men, free to get a living, free to say yea and nay in their own affairs, was less clear-cut, and he found no way to project it clearly for himself and others.

It was not till the hedges began to be planted that it became clear how deeply the village was going to be changed. The individualism of the nineteenth century sanctified the hedge and made it out to be beautiful, but the Ashby children began to realise its artificiality. The hawthorn growing free is one of the loveliest of smaller trees, but the cramped and cramping hedge-bushes carved up the hills and valleys absurdly. Before enclosure, every brook, every slight hill, every path, every group of trees had had its name and been called by it. Now, not one person in Tysoe, except those who had pored over the enclosure map, knew which was Shortmoor Shilch or the Ass Brook. Land had formerly been like the falling rain, free alike in some measure to the just and the

unjust. On foot or on your pony you could thread your way
by balk and headland over to any village in the neighbourhood, but some of these were set miles further away by the
new private fields. Now the very Red Horse itself had been
penned up within hedges, without even a footpath past it.
The old Whitsun Games were never held again. The enclosure of the open fields was a visible sign and symbol that
rampant family and individual power had gained a complete
victory over the civic community.

The labourers of Tysoe had hopes that at least enclosures
would bring incidental opportunities: they would be employed
to plant the hedges and drain the fields, but gangs of men
accustomed to the new jobs were brought in by the larger
owners. There was work for a few men on the roads for which
the Commissioners had provided, enough to prevent any rise
in the number of men on the round, but not enough to
reduce it.

No improvement followed enclosure, even after the lapse
of time. The number of relieved persons rose again, and their
name was now 'pauper'. The word gathered power to itself
and depressed men's spirit and their status. The text-books
said that degradation followed on pauperism. Did it here in
Tysoe? 'Relief in respect of each child led to early marriages'
said the books, and 'A single woman was better off with a
child'. True it was that in Tysoe the number of illegitimate
births grew somewhat, but it is easy to exaggerate. The great
majority of families kept free of bastardy.

It was in 1818 that the most intolerable entry was made.
The Easter Vestry Meeting 'unanimously agreed that all
men and boys who are out of employ shall walk from the Coal
Barn as far as the Red Lion Inn in Middle Tysoe, or stand in
the gateway near the Barn the full space of ten hours on each
day from the above date till Michaelmas next, and also it is
agreed that if any person enter any house during the ten
hours he or she shall receive no pay from the Parish'. The
roundsman system had broken down: there were at that time

forty-five men and boys in receipt of relief, besides girls and women. It might be that the churchwardens and overseers—few but these had been at the meeting—were desperate, and for the moment had lost their wits, which they recovered on reaching home. Possibly they never mentioned their strange decision again, even to each other; there was no reference to it in later minutes. But deduct all that a kindly reader might, the words were a knell tolled after community had died. It scarcely added to a young reader's sense of calamity that in the same year the overseers sent a number of small Tysoe children in a wagon to a cotton factory at Guyscliffe, twenty miles away, to be apprenticed to the machines there, in a small building beside the picturesque Avon, the most romantic spot in Warwickshire.

Starved, workless, indebted, browbeaten, and miscalled, how could the poor make their own lives tolerable? One could take for granted that some spent windfalls of money on getting drunk. But also Joseph pointed to a collection of Raphael's and Zadkill's astrological almanacs for the eighteen-twenties that a cottager had lent him: he had been told that many labourers' families bought them and studied the predictions, nativities and horoscopes. Talk of witches and wizards came back: in such ways hungering minds were windily filled. There was more of this mental bastardy, this foolishness of outlook, than of ill conduct. The decent clothes wore out; furniture was pawned and then sold. (Who in the village acted as pawnbroker?) The half-fed children whimpered, and exasperated parents repressed and be-laboured them, so that the second and third generations added a dull, inhibited appearance to all else—the same look the labourers' children still wore. Kathleen was amazed when she saw early eighteenth-century pictures of 'peasant' children—handsome, lively, adventurous! No artist could have seen such cottage children in a village from the seventeen-nineties to the moment at which she stood on Old Lodge pondering on the question (nor indeed till the nineteen-forties).

It was strange enough to have a 'system' of farming that starved the men who sowed, harrowed, and cut the corn; stranger that other workers in the industry, the farmers, should at the same time prosper. It was now, twelve years after they became possessed of an enclosed farm, that the Gardners built their fine brick house in the fields out towards Oxhill, now that large farmers joined the Hunt and bought their wives and daughters tickets for the Hunt Ball, each costing, as old copies of the *Warwick Advertiser* showed, more than a fortnight's allowance for a family 'on the Book'. Some Tysoe farmers made small fortunes from the high price of corn, and yet smaller farmers were losing hold: the Ashby holding was mortgaged soon after the enclosure to William Middleton, who later foreclosed.

In earlier years the division between classes in Tysoe had been no more than function or custom called for or worldly perspicacity earned; it could always be bridged by humour and good sense. After the years of wretchedness it was so deep a ditch that every foolish mind fell into it. The natural tendency to feel superior became a solemn claim when one's neighbour remained for generations half-starved and ill-dressed. The new foolishness was worse in women, living too much within their own doors; gentility invaded the farm-houses. Now was the time for a common religion to support a reasonable man's sense of common humanity. But instead, the labourers built the 'Primitive' chapel. They must get away even from more prosperous Methodists, into their own place where they could satisfy their hungers in a special relation to God—stressing spiritual salvation, how rightly for there was no other, praying with hot fervour for help and finding a brief comfort in loud singing of hymns that expressed their position. On the other hand, the Seagrave Vicars, friends and dependants for several generations of the Earls of Northampton, brought to the village the views and assumptions of the Castle Ashby dinner table, and grew high hedges and planted beeches between themselves and their 'parishioners', no longer 'neighbours'; the same hedges that still divided the Vicarage from the village. It seemed that it was the Vicars who led in that long effort to force the labourer to creep and cringe so obsequiously that he could never 'rise above his station' but would be a cheap servant for ever.

The young students were at times overwhelmed by what they learned. Had things not come, they asked, to a pass where 'crime' was better than patience? Were not the Tysoe men merely less spirited than other poor men of good character who stole sheep and hung for it? (The *Warwick Advertiser* for these years was full of cases of arson and machine-breaking.) Could one really believe, as Father did, that the Tysoe labourer kept to the straight way because the village had been once a true community? It was not that the labourer recalled those times, but that they remained implicit in his attitudes and customs and speech; they were in his cultural blood and bones. Why then did they not also linger in the minds of prosperous folk? This must be one of the needle-eyes the packed camel cannot pass through. And one must not exaggerate the labourer's hold on good, but recall certain old dark stories. There had been crimes, only the men stood together; no one was ever punished and the lapsed ones repented—and emigrated.

No one came to rescue the village labourer from his pit; but the students saw him finding footholds to climb out. First of all came emigration, which solved problems only for individuals. The French Revolution, the English poets, Methodism and the Evangelical Movement—all these afforded a little purchase, a little sustenance. But the Reform Act of 1832 was best. On Friday, 13 July, of that year the Banbury tradesmen celebrated their new power to vote. The 'drapers, grocers, printers, bookbinders, hatters, cork-cutters, wool-combers, dyers'—so wrote an onlooker—'carriers, saddlers, cordwainers, tailors, carpenters, sawyers, coopers', marched and sang. The last car in the triumphal procession carried a shepherd and shepherdess—a little fantastic, that; but behind the cars, a group of ploughmen with a plough had tacked themselves on, and some Tysoe labourers pushed through the crowd to follow the plough up the High Street and along the Horse Fair. They did right to feel that they belonged at the tail end of the procession. The Franchise would not come to them for half a century yet but it was something that men less distant from themselves could now influence legislation. The Reform Parliament promptly studied the question of the Poor Law. A Member of the Commission it set up came to Tysoe in 1833, but he only saw the village of the moment: could he have compared it with the Tysoe of 1753 he might have written a minority report!

The Poor Law of 1834 set up Poor Law Unions, combining several parishes into an area for relief, thus beginning the process of inventing new areas and authorities, taking from the village its ancient responsibilities, making its own business invisible to it, so that it could no longer be understood by simple folk. It set up the workhouses to curse the workers with dread of their last days.

Now the students had arrived at a time with which they already had acquaintance, the time of Grandmother Elizabeth's youth, not so long before their father's birth, before the Town Lands agitation, the land hunger, Joseph Arch, the Promised Land and all Tysoe's recent history. The job was at an end.

For two years Joseph had shared closely in his children's experience. He had kept them by his own strong interest and his encouragement from flagging till they had read all they could; he had led them perhaps unconsciously to see the village, the community, as the chief character in the long story they had pieced together. Looking back over the period he could see the children's gains—the beginnings of his eldest son's power to arm his passion for rural communities and their welfare with masterly knowledge; he noted another son's brief and insightful comments on changes in men, manners and farming; and hoped something might come of a daughter's interest in the children of the past.

The children had enjoyed their research in spite of gloomy findings and were proud of their father's long series of articles in the *Warwick Advertiser*, but that was not quite all. Perhaps Joseph gradually lost the sense that the documents contained strong meat for the young, or it did not occur to him that, for example, they would work out their own family's alliances and find some ancestors of their own sinking to the extremes of poverty and worse. It may be that he wanted them to feel, as they certainly did, that there was no one too poor or too far gone down the slopes of degradation to be their near relation, in some sense their own selves. Possibly an inkling of their father's own close connection with ancient rank and achievement might have balanced the self-suspicions engendered. But that would never occur to Joseph: it should suffice the young, he assumed, to be heirs of the ages and children of God. That children need smaller supports a later age knows.

CHAPTER XX

THE WAR: COLDSTONE FARM

BY 1912 my father's holdings had grown to about a hundred acres scattered through the three towns. The working of this farm, if you could call it so, was wasteful, no matter how well-planned the use of the sections might be. Some months before the beginning of the First World War in 1914, two friends, Mr and Mrs Sanderson Furniss, later Lord and Lady Sanderson, offered him the tenancy of two hundred acres in a Cotswold village twenty miles across the hills. They made their offer seductive: they would provide any extra capital that might be needed; they would put in order the ancient, spacious farmhouse. Coldstone Farm and its house were large enough to employ the older boys and to hold the turbulence of adolescence. A railway ran through the village of Ascott under Wychwood to Oxford, so that the youngest could go to school there.

'Joseph,' said Hannah, 'that farm is too big for you now. You have not the strength for more work.' But young William commented: 'Pity it isn't bigger still, then Father need only think about the work. It is thinking makes money.' Some such reflection ensured serious consideration of the offer.

Joseph, contrary to his custom, went alone on his first visit to Coldstone Farm. Driving Lady London at her modest elderly trot, he had hours of leisure for new impressions. The deep grass and heavy elms of the Red Horse Vale were left behind. The colour of the fields ceased to be bluish green and became lighter and thinner. The high veils of hedges gave way to stone walls, surrounding larger fields. Half-way through the village of Hook Norton the warm red and yellow stone and thick rustic roofs of thatch began to be replaced by higher, better houses of the pale grey and straw-coloured Cotswold stone, with their steep roofs. Looking from the top of the hills beyond Chipping Norton, Joseph saw the new country's essence. The curves of the hills were subtly flattened and long, quite unlike the rounded knolls he had left behind him; the distant colours in the valleys were light aerial blues. To go from South Warwickshire on a grey morning and spend a golden noon on the high wolds was like passing from stubborn facts to music. Arrived at the farm he found a roomy house, with high windows, a noble stone-roofed barn, and other spacious, oak-beamed buildings, set beside a quick-flowing stream with forget-me-not and figwort and purple loosestrife on its bank. Just beyond the house the stream passed briefly into a wider, shallower bed, full of water-cress in flower. Here, too, was moored a boat; and the river was full of trout, he learned. The presence of the lively stream after the great still plain of the Horse was a symbol for the greatness of the proposed change.

Sons and daughters were all in favour of going to Ascott, but Joseph and Hannah had more to weigh. Their loss in leaving Tysoe seemed likely to be in many ways balanced by profit. Joseph in crossing the county boundary would cease to be a magistrate; he would vacate all his small village offices. Declining health had already forced him to cease his work in the constituency. But if he had to be less active he might possibly do more writing. He would like to set down his thoughts on local government, and Arthur had more than once suggested that an account of his own experience would throw useful sidelights on rural movements. It was high time for change. Is there anyone in England now who bears such a burden as men like him bore then? The weight of farm and other manual work unlightened by machinery, the anxiety week by week as to whether by numerous activities enough money and produce had been drawn in to support the family—these, combined with an urgent sense of public duty, and a need for more personal thought and expression,

were some of the aspects of the 'simple' life they led. If the
farm were successful both Joseph's life and Hannah's would
be easier.

But the War came. The last week of July and the first days
of August, my mother and I harnessed a pony every evening,
and drove the five miles from the Lower Town to Kineton
Post Office to read in its windows the latest telegrams on the
news from Serbia, Austria, Germany, Russia and France.
Each evening all the wide valley was bathed in golden serene
sunset light, but on the third of August the weather changed.
The sunset was more gorgeous than ever; but the valley
was filled with mist of raucous purple. When my mother
recited the messages we had brought home there was a long
stillness that Joseph broke with the only possible words: 'Few
things will ever be the same again.'

It was but a few days later that a group of army sergeants
arrived in Tysoe, going from farm to farm selecting horses.
From the stables of The Orchards they took Captain, without
a by-your-leave. Captain, like Lady London and the small
pony Juggernaut, Beauty the Jersey cow, and Betty Alcock
the hen who lived to be nine, had achieved almost a membership of the Ashby family. He was a useful old horse still, if
you humoured him and knocked off promptly after his stint
of work, but under new men and at hard tasks he must break
down. Every farmhouse in Tysoe had some such shock and
grief that day. Emotion's proportions are odd; trouble's first
small swallow may seem the darkest, whatever follows.

In October the Ashbys' patriarchal trek to Ascott took
place. Sheep and cattle preceded the carts and wagon and gig.
Nothing unnecessary could be drawn by the reduced team of
horses. The farm's and kitchen's needs had to be considered
primary. Darling books of childhood were left behind, and
papers I now wish for were torn up.

The new farm was not a model of convenience: following
an ancient pattern the fields stretched in single file from hill
to hill across the valley of the Evenlode and the farm roads

were poor. But at first Joseph had a sufficient staff and was able to wander over the fields cogitating on their soil, the weeds they grew, and the shelter they had or lacked. Cows he had long understood, but now he must develop a shepherd's sympathy with the ewes, recalling what he had known as a lad on Bald Knob. His two sons on the farm were in the knowing, determined phase of youth, but he gave them spheres within which they could try out their notions.

Though the adjustment went well for a few months, it was not to be easy. Joseph needed new machinery for his increased acres, but engineering factories were all on direct war work and it could not be bought. Presently German submarines threatened our food supplies; farmers felt the public anxiety on this score but the Government gave them no priorities or privileges. The Army recruited agricultural workers as freely as any other labour.

Ascott was a different village from Tysoe. Till the railway had come it had been small and remote, left behind in an older day with its inhabitants almost exclusively farmers and their labourers, and no love lost between the two. The men in 1914 were good, old-fashioned workers, but the young ones were going to the War. The women preferred field-work to domestic chores and Joseph employed a group of them for a while. But if their humour was salty, they also swore and pilfered: to appreciate their jokes you had to accept their low standards for themselves and that was more than Joseph could do. It was not easy, but presently he had to accept his seventeen-year-old daughter as one of his workers. He had hoped to see his slight, merry girl grow into a 'lady' and the old view that outdoor work coarsened a woman's mind had its local corroboration. The Victorian father was forced to give way and Sybil rode the haymaking machines as blithely as any boy. But could a girl plough with a three-horse team? Again prejudice lost the day, and this time his old power to look at a problem freshly came to the fore. He considered every operation Sybil undertook, teaching her at every point to save herself exertion and shorten her journeys. The girl and the big ailing man went from field to field, from one job to the next, in partnership.

Presently, young William was forced to 'join up'; then the work became hard indeed. There was one new source of labour: 'conscientious objectors' were being excused military service if they would work on the land. A series of young men slept in William's bed and failed to do his work. They were all talkative, all urban, some strange; at last came one good, cheerful worker, though unskilled.

Indoors the situation was similar. The family was enlarged by a refugee child and tired relatives from towns, besides resident labourers. Old-established farmers fared better, no doubt, but everywhere the basic story was the same.

It was never possible now for the Ashby family to meet as a whole. Till late in 1915 Arthur was in the States and after that William was away at the War. But from their journeys the children were sending news of foreign ways in agriculture and country life. William in Belgium had seen old dames spinning wool at cottage doors and had marvelled at the intensive labour on French holdings. Arthur, returned from the University of Wisconsin, then pioneering at Madison in Agricultural Economics, had at once joined the Ministry of Agriculture in its Wartime Enquiries Branch. Fresh from American stimulus and also from the anxieties and difficulties of Coldstone Farm, he was able to suggest types of inquiry and methods of work. Later, when a Food Production Department and an Agricultural Wages Board were set up at the Ministry he worked upon both. The scheme for the survey of conditions of agricultural labour made in every county was Arthur's, based on his father's work of more than twenty years earlier. Kathleen, inheriting a taste for the peripatetic life, found work involving a wide acquaintance with village schools.

'Ah, Mother,' Joseph would say to Hannah, 'we can leave everything to the young ones now.' But it remained for him to prove that to live in and for one village is not to be narrowed and cramped. Joseph's knowledge of local government had become known to the organisers of adult education in Oxford, and now for a brief time he became a lecturer. He had not intended to be a lay preacher in his new Methodist circuit, but with so great a shortage of young men he could not refuse. It was the same work, but done now in a different way. The War and the brevity of his own prospects led him to drop from his sermons the old careful arguments and references, to deal with everyday and ultimate matters in a simple-seeming way. He could foretell the composition of the congregations in the chapels of tiny high villages in the Cotswolds; to an audience of young farmers and their wives he gave a charming homily on child life (his first two grandchildren brought him serener pleasures than had his own children). To an ageing congregation he gave a stern realistic talk—as one may who speaks for himself—on the risks and duties of old age. The long, deepening trouble of failing power, the temptation to refuse the trivial duties that might still be carried out, the possibility of falling off from such height of character as might have been attained—all these were simply dealt with. But he turned from the theme of his text, 'The soul that sinneth it shall die', to another, 'Create in me a new spirit'. In age there is time for thought, time to review life and events, and to cleanse the spirit. The old were said to be habit-bound and merely conservative; it was often not so. Free from the pressure of passion and great needs, with no prospects at stake, they could try at least to penetrate to the heart of ideas and of movements.

There was one direction in which Joseph's work was finished when he rode over the county border into Oxfordshire. Except in his direct relationship as employer to a handful of them he could do nothing more for the agricultural labourer. Within a few months the Government's recruitment policy, taking men equally from luxury trades and from the plough, raised the remaining labourers' wages. After a time the German submarines made each labourer so important that he positively gained social consideration, not to say prestige. In 1918 the Corn Production Act (passed in 1917) in effect linked wages to the price of corn and thus bound together, at long last, the interests of labourer, farmer and landlord. The machinery for determining wages brought labourers to the council table in equal numbers, on equal terms, with farmers. Labourers could now afford to subscribe to their unions and the unions had a legal duty of representation. 'So now', Joseph commented, 'it is not so much a question of the labourer's living as of his quality.' He had seen signs that the labourers were ceasing to get inspiration from Chapels and Friendly Societies and solace from the work itself; to what new source were they turning?

Now the ebb of Joseph's strength left for him a last small gift of leisure. The War brought Londoners to the village for rest from raids and excessive work. A young writer and publisher settled his family in the next farmhouse. Politicians came to stay with his nearby friends and landlords; his children's friends included scholars and artists. Conversation was not lacking but he would decline long talks on politics and the future of farming. 'I leave all that to Arthur', he said. (Arthur was now a member of the Royal Commission on Agriculture.) But he would listen to Michael Sadleir who chid him for too narrow a view of literature and made him sample the books he was bringing out. Resting from his supervision of the farm, Joseph would sit on a high knoll and take delight in the delicate colours of the wolds. Now that the Government was encouraging the growth of corn the scene became more and more brilliant. The hills turned into slopes of straw-gold and pearl, with short lines of bright green and splashes of modulated strawberry. Beside him would sometimes sit an artist friend of his children, telling him of a painter's problems in recording colour and demonstrating to him the total inadequacy of words for such a work. 'I'm at school again,' he said to Hannah, 'all the young folk teach me.' But sometimes he plainly wished to be alone on the hillock, free to contemplate, looking beyond the gold light of sunset, above the silver-rimmed clouds, into the clear green serene of air.

He died in 1919. When the end was at hand he knew it well and took thought to leave all his concerns in order. His last words were no homily but of what must be grown next season on the Holly Ground, and how Beech Hangings must be tilled; his last action a pressure of the hand for his Hannah.

If Miltons are never mute, it is also true of some of the finest minds and characters that their development is away from the direction of fame. Quick to respond to all the duties and beauties of local situations, they must reject the concentration and specialism by which genius builds its own monument. It is so with great women in their homes and so with Joseph Ashby and his like in their villages.

'And his like.' Was he not an exception? He would have thought it an infirmity to suppose so. How came he to be what he was? Born into poverty, to a family which had sunk almost to disgrace, of illegitimate paternity, he not only came to have a well-furnished mind and to discharge many offices with faithfulness and influence, but also, a greater achievement, to confront life happily. When I had almost finished the first draft of this book the identity of his father was by chance put beyond doubt. The latter was a member of an ancient family of high rank and of some, though not great, achievement in science and letters. From this half of his physical inheritance he must have derived much, yet there is reason to suppose his maternal family was not ill-endowed. No doubt the aristocratic succession had been admirably nourished and exercised through its many centuries. Perhaps it passed to him some richness of physique that contributed to a generous presence and to his humour and balance. But his mental content and his development he owed to his village—to its folk, its history, its churches, but possibly above all to its civic tradition.

As I wrote this study I came to feel that he and his mother Elizabeth were the product of a very different community from their contemporary Tysoe, the ill-balanced and wretched village of the early nineteenth century or the anaemic one of Queen Victoria's later years. They seemed to have come out of a more vigorous community—one still possessed of that first of the things of the spirit—responsibility. It seemed to me that during their time their village was struggling back to an accustomed balance, imperfect but basic. A well-shaped, well-populated village came, as I wrote, to seem the finest school of life. Such a community is seen as a whole by its members; the workings of human nature and of institutions can there be followed in all their deviations and amusing ways. Minds are formed having the scepticism and humour which are health, immune from the extremes of doctrine. Variety of trade and talent ensure leadership and comment for many occasions and give minorities courage and comfort. Such a village can sometimes rise, even in bad periods, above divisions and interests into fun and charity, as Tysoe did.

Yet to treat Joseph merely as a representative of any community or class is of course wrong. A man should also be unique and universal and plainly he was so. The ease with which he moved from sphere to sphere—from manual work to thought or from leadership to silence in a retired seat was one of his characteristics. He loved to talk but could suspend all he had to say while an old illiterate man or a child fumbled for a word or a thought. He believed in the power of the simplest to achieve wisdom, but let them exhibit the contrary, and they were to know it. 'When you have finished your foolishness, Robert,' he said quietly in a meeting to a loquacious speaker, 'I have a word to say.' His angular, illegible writing bore no mark at all of the copy-book. The power of his body and mind to walk apart was the source of many stories. He strode, it is said, deep into a house which had been his home ten years before and sat down in a chair, before coming to

himself with the exclamation, 'God bless my heart and soul!'
Or he had been met at the top of Tysoe Hill with a horse
and cart, totally unable to think how or why he had arrived
there.

Doubtless his influence as a villager was exceptionally
wide through his varied acquaintance and very directly
through his family. His eldest son's eventual influence on
agriculture, reaching out as far as India and China, and his
devotion to rural welfare shown in his serving rural Wales
'as a priest his parish', were the fruit of a tree planted by
Joseph. His daughter's study of rural education, found useful
occasionally in Africa and the colonies, had its roots in his
reflections on that subject.

But I cannot escape my sense that he was, after all, representative; that is indeed the whole point of this study. It has
been the special destiny of Englishmen to be at once good
citizens and highly individualised—to be very serious pil-
grims, like Bunyan's, but telling fine tales on the way, like
Chaucer's. The scale of our lives is different now; for us all
the world is our parish; all the more need to practise our wits
and skills in Joseph Ashby's way, on the home acres.

INDEX

Agricultural Holdings Bill, 248–9
Agricultural Labourers' Union, 62, 63, 77, 81, 86, 88, 155–6
Agriculture, Ministry of, 58; Royal Commission on, 294; *see also* farming
allotments, 50, 72, 117, 120, 123–9, 133, 134, 145, 148, 162–3, 175, 183, 187, 188–9, 198, 249; use of, 163–4, 168–9, 176
Allotments Acts, 122, 183
almanacs, astrological, 283
Arch, Joseph, 30, 58–9, 60–2, 73, 79, 145, 179, 286
Ascott under Wychwood, 288, 290, 291
Ashby, Arthur Wilfred, 134, 152, 183, 196, 203, 205–7, 209, 211, 218, 225, 241, 248, 251, 253–4
Ashby, Elizabeth, 1, 4–13, 24, 26, 28, 40, 46–52, 63, 77, 85, 88–9, 172, 286, 296
Ashby, Hannah, 70, 88, 90–1, 93, 98, 100–4, 107, 108, 111, 129, 135, 151–2, 157, 194, 197, 211, 214–15, 220, 221, 226, 251, 257–8, 266, 268–9, 289, 292–3, 295
Ashby, William (son), 242, 246, 259, 262, 267, 270, 292
Ashby, William (uncle,) 3–5, 58, 78, 85, 87–8, 90

Back Lane, 8, 10, 42, 105, 109, 110, 127, 151, 193
Bald Knob Farm, 24, 28, 38, 45, 291
Banbury, 1, 7, 17, 26, 27, 37, 56, 61, 94, 112, 146, 150, 218, 276, 281, 285
Banbury Guardian, ix, 30, 34, 51, 57, 58, 94, 106, 130
Barford, 59
Bellamy, *Looking Backward*, 241
Bench, *see* Justices of the Peace
Bibby's Annual, Bibby's Calendar, 244
Bible, 5, 14, 22, 30, 34, 52, 114, 166, 202, 222–3, 233, 271
Birmingham, 56, 120, 150

Boer War, 117, 125, 194–7, 228
Boy's Own Paper, 242
Brailes, 39, 59, 218
bread prices, *see* corn prices
Brown, Capability, 179
Brown, Ridley, 176, 221, 262, 263
Budget, Lloyd George's (1909), 251, 252
bull-baiting, *see* sports and games
Buxton, Charles Sidney, 262

Castle Ashby, 128
cattle-maiming, 2
Chairmakers' Guild, 41
Chamberlain, Joseph, 117, 118, 184
Charity Commissioners, 48, 49, 50–1, 117, 133, 187
Charity Estate, *see* Town Lands
Chipping Campden Grammar School, 206
Chipping Norton, 289
Church of England, 2, 6, 23, 36, 42, 118, 126, 193; disestablishment of, 182
Church Lads' Brigade, 194, 196
Church Reformer, 151, 153, 154
Church Town, Tysoe, 7, 8, 10, 14, 15, 65, 70, 87, 126–7, 131, 133, 142–3, 196, 273, 282
Civil War, 55, 56
clothes, 107, 130, 136
Club day, 8, 68, 69, 70, 231
Cobb, Mr and Mrs, 113, 122, 181–3
cock-fighting, *see* sports and games
Coldstone Farm, 288, 289
Collings, Jesse, 114
Commons, House of, 182, 183, 185, 248
Compton, Earl and Lord William, 127, 133, 165
Compton, William George Spencer Scott, fifth Marquess of North-ampton, *see* Northampton, fifth Marquess of
Compton, William Bingham, sixth Marquess of Northampton, x

299

Index

Compton Wynyates, x, 29, 55, 62, 64–6, 106–7, 120, 124, 202

Comptons of Compton Wynyates, x

Conservatives and Conservative party, 122, 178, 182–3, 193, 239, 240, 247–9, 251, 261

Corn Laws, 56

corn prices, 85, 86, 90, 114, 146, 185, 239, 240, 276, 278

Corn Production Act (1917), 294

cottages, labourers', 105, 159–60

County Councils, 140, 180, 186, 188, 227, 229, 234, 236, 259

Court Greenwood Tree, 69, 71, 73, 74, 193

Court Leet, 9

Daily News, ix, 58, 196, 240, 241

Dickens, Charles, 48, 178; effect of his work on country life, 94

diseases, infectious: cholera, 11; diphtheria, 39; smallpox, 37, 275–6; various, 87; whooping cough, 79

Disraeli, Benjamin, 113, 125

'Dock', the, 105, 109, 279

Dodge, Mr, 16, 18, 19, 230–3

domestic work, 90–1, 98–9, 105–6, 161, 215–18

drink and drunkenness, 102, 164, 250, 263–4

Economic Journal, ix, x, 145, 157

Eden, *State of the Poor*, 241

Edge Hills, 7, 55, 150, 155, 244, 273

Education Bill (1902), 228, 233, 238, 248

Edward VII, King, 230, 261

Election, General (1906), 238

Eliot, George, 108, 243, 259

Emigration, 11, 63, 85, 88–9, 161, 285

Employers' Liability Bill, 183

Enclosure(s), 7, 38, 115, 281–2

English Labourers' Chronicle, 145

Estate Agents' Record, x

fairs, 7

farmhouses, 225, 272

farming, 254–7, 284, 289, 291; co-operative farming, 7, 97–8; dairying, 213; drainage, 15, 87; harvesting, 24, 252; haymaking, 24;

leasing (gleaning), 25; plough oxen, 37; *see also* agriculture

Fenny Compton, 59

Feoffees, 114, 117, 120, 127, 129–31, 187–8

Feoffees' Estate, *see* Town Lands

Fessey, Daniel, 124, 130–1

Fire Brigade, Tysoe, 189, 193

Flower Show, 202

food, cottagers', 110, 145, 172

footpaths, 7

Foresters' Friendly Society, 30, 69, 71, 73, 161

franchise, 112, 113, 117, 126, 178, 195, 286

Free Trade, 86, 238

Friendly Societies, 81, 97, 161–2, 187, 191–2, 249, 251, 294

Fuel Lands, 131

Furniss, *see* Sanderson, Lord

furniture, 106, 172–4, 175, 202

gambling, *see* sports and games

Gardner, Tom, 118, 196, 228–9, 235, 249, 284

Gaydon (village), 181

Gaydon, John, 84

Gaydon, William, 83, 277

Gee, Muster, 15

George V, King, 261

George, Henry, *Progress and Poverty*, 95, 115, 151, 153

Gillett, Joseph Ashby, 1

Gipsies, 149, 150, 201–2

Girl's Own Paper, ix, 104, 108, 172

Gladstone, W. E., 113, 117, 122, 125, 139, 181–3

Good Words, 172

Grant, Corrie, 183–5, 207–8, 216, 238–9, 241, 253

green, the village, 8, 9

Guardians, Board of, 190–2

Hardwick, 45, 54, 198

Hardy, Thomas, 243

Harte, Bret, 129, 208

Hartshill Stone, 62, 111

Hasbach, *History of the Agricultural Labourer*, 158, 242

Herbert, George, *A Shoemaker's Window*, x

Highway Board, 142–3, 186

Index

Home Readers Union, ix
Home Rule, *see* Ireland
Hook Norton, 38, 288
Hornton, 53
Hornton quarries and stone, 45, 111, 234, 239, 266
Housman, A. E., 243
hunts and hunting, 180, 185–6, 262, 284

Idlicote House, 1
insurance companies, 162
Ireland (Home Rule), 117–20, 122, 181–2, 184
Isle of Wight, 98

Jasper, Carter, 29–35, 38, 46–53, 58
Jeffs, Fred, 95, 115, 267
Jubilee of Queen Victoria, 125, 133
Justices of the Peace, 179, 247–8, 262–3

Kineton, 50, 54, 146, 175, 181–2, 207, 218, 238–9, 254, 290
King, Bolton, 96–7, 107, 130, 145–8, 157, 207, 229, 241

Labourers' Friend Magazine, 72
Land Agents' Record, 135, 214
landlordism and squirearchy, 9, 179, 180–1
Land Magazine, ix, 55, 57, 59, 74, 135, 145, 191, 198
Land Restoration League, 148, 151, 155
Land tax, 155
'Last Ditchers', 272
Leamington, 110, 238, 275
Leamington Chronicle, ix, x, 151
Leamington Gazette, v, ix
Lean, Richard, 221, 254, 257, 261
Liberals and Liberal party, 122, 128, 165, 175, 178, 181–4, 189, 193, 238, 247–8, 252–5, 261
Licensing Bill, 249–51
Lighthorne, 96
Local Government Bill, 183
Lords, House of, 120–2, 145, 181–3, 240, 248, 251–3, 258
Lower Town, 45, 54, 127, 131, 133, 143, 211, 212, 251, 275, 290

Makepeace, John, 28, 29–33, 35, 37
Marx, Marxism, 95, 261
Masefield, John, 101–2
Methodism, village, ix, 2, 11, 36, 83, 105, 142, 285, 293
Methodists, 32–3, 49, 77, 80, 83, 148, 181, 193, 195, 228–9, 235, 242, 244–7, 260, 284
Methodist Times, ix, 196
Middleton, Tom, 4, 48, 51, 52, 53, 62, 196, 231, 267, 284
Mill, *On Liberty*, 95, 153
Miller, Sanderson, 57, 266
Missionary meetings, 42–3
Mormons, 85
Morris, *News from Nowhere*, 241
Murdoch, John, 151–6

names (Christian), 270
Northampton, fifth Marquess of, (W. G. S. S. Compton), x, 10, 18, 62, 65–7, 71, 228, 257, 281, 284
Northamptonshire, 152

Oddfellows, 161–2
Old Age Pensions, 192–3, 251
Old Lodge, 37, 44, 114, 245, 283
Orchards, The, 211–14, 224, 240–1, 253, 257–8, 261–2, 290
Ordnance Survey, 93, 95
overseers, ix, 105, 143, 192, 266, 273–9, 282–3
Oxhill, 14, 47, 55, 59, 70, 84, 239, 284

Paine, *Rights of Man*, 95
parish constables, 9
parish councils, 140, 183, 185, 187, 188, 189
parish registers, ix, 125, 268, 269, 270
Parliament Bill (1911), 261
Passing Years, The, x, 178, 180, 273
paupers, pauperism, 272, 276, 277, 282; *see also* Poor Law
Peacock Inn, 2, 9, 10, 48, 116, 118, 119, 125, 138, 188, 190, 232
pedlars, 201
Petty sessions, 190
pig clubs and pig keeping, 97, 115, 116–17, 119, 163–4
Pillerton, 239

Index

Plymouth Brethren, 193–4
poaching, 4, 33, 214
Poor Law, x, 12, 286; see also Guardians, Board of; overseers
Price, John, 224
Primitive Methodists, 8, 62, 77, 80, 82, 118, 137, 152, 202, 221, 224, 284
Primrose League, see Conservative party
Priors Marston, 86
Pro-Boer, see Boer War
Promised Land, see allotments
pupil teachers, 228, 230

Quakers, 6, 10, 32–3, 46, 55, 78
Quarter sessions, 54, 231, 264, 274

Radway, 57, 176, 266
Ratley, 150–1, 201
Realities of Irish Life, 119, 120
Reason, Charles, 48
Reason, Charlie, 16, 49–52, 58
Red Horse, 261, 282, 288
Red Vanes, 147, 151–2, 156, 169
Reform Act, 285–6
religious teaching, 169–70
rents, farm, 86
road-making, 111
roundsman system, 279–82
Rouvray, 3, 41, 65, 173–5, 208, 217, 244, 268
Rugby division, 113, 122, 181–5, 207, 252, 261
Rural district councils, 186–90, 219, 242, 254; Brailes, ix, 186, 264
'Rural Vignettes' (J. A. Benson), x
Ruskin College, 241, 258–9, 262, 267
Russell, Lord John, 56
Ryde, 98–9

Saddlers' Lane, 77, 142–4
Salisbury, Lord, 183
Samuelson's factory, 57
Sanderson, Lord, 288
Sanitary authority, 124, 186
school, 8, 10, 16, 17, 20, 50, 87, 204, 228, 233–6; inspection, 18, 204; board, 228; feoffees', 20, 49; managers, 187, 229; secondary, 229
Scott, Gilbert, 8, 99
Scott, Sir Walter, 108

Shakespeare, 21, 34
Shenington, 6, 38, 59, 116
Shipston on Stour, 190, 242
Shutford, 54
Sibford, 2, 6
Sick and dividend clubs, 72, 97
Sick and provident clubs, 69, 193
Single tax, 95, 148; see also Land tax
Smallholders' Association, see allotments
smallpox, see diseases, infectious
Southam, 112, 123, 124, 149, 151
Speenhamland, 192
sports and games, 180, 282, 136; bull-baiting, 9, 36; cock-fighting, 36; gambling, 36; wrestling, 36, 42, 124
Stratford on Avon, 1, 2, 7, 56, 59, 95, 107, 219, 220, 257, 266
Sturt, George, xi
Styles, Mr, 10, 67, 68, 222
Sunday schools, 43, 59, 136, 170, 226, 241
Sunrising Hill, 37, 45, 54–6, 127, 129, 209, 219
Surrey, 92
surveying, 106, 203

Tariff reform, 240
Temple Tysoe, see Lower Town
tithes, 31
Tories, see Conservatives
Town Lands, 46–53, 71, 117–20, 127–33, 187, 228, 255, 286
tradesmen, itinerant, 201
transport, 182, 209
Tribune, The, 247
Tysoe Temperance Society, 69, 249

Ullyett, Mr, 234–6
unemployment, 86, 89, 161, 276, 279
Unionists, see Conservatives
Upper Town, 7, 10, 39, 53, 64–7, 70, 88, 126, 231
Upton House, 56, 198–201, 254
Utility Estate, see Town Lands

Vagrancy, 263, 271
Verney family, 179, 180, 181
Verney, Richard Greville, x, 178, 179, 182, 183, 184, 185; see also Willoughby de Broke, Lord

Index

Vestry meeting, 49, 51, 123, 132, 140, 142, 144, 187, 282
Vestry minute-book, ix, 268, 273, 276
Vicars of Tysoe: Australian, 260; Dodgson, Rev. F. V., 189, 193, 195, 197, 205–6, 228, 232, 234, 236, 249, 250; Francis, Rev. C. D., 6–8, 9, 22, 29, 35, 43, 44, 46, 48–9, 50, 53, 60–1, 63, 69, 70–2, 83, 85, 94, 113, 119, 122, 125–6, 129, 131–4, 137, 141, 142, 144, 187–8; Seagrave, 271, 284
Victoria, Queen, 125, 172, 197, 296
votes, *see* franchise

wages, agricultural, 86, 100, 146–7, 158–9
Warwick, 7, 58, 91, 94, 98, 231, 269
Warwick Advertiser, ix, x, 122, 130, 165, 198, 214, 240, 263, 268, 284–7
Warwick Pageant, 213, 277
Warwickshire, 92–3, 107, 148, 178, 181, 289

Warwickshire County Council, 111
Waywarden, 54, 131, 141–4
Wellesbourne, 57
Wells, Mrs, 40, 55
Wells, W. B., 206–8
Wesley, Charles, 82
Wesley, John, 28, 80, 82–4, 242
Wesleyans, 8, 59, 77–8, 82, 137, 151, 182, 196, 220–3
Westcote, 37, 275–6
Westminster Gazette, 209
Whatcote, 29, 59, 70, 150, 151
White Cross, Brotherhood of, 193
'whisky money' classes, 194, 227
Wight, Isle of, 98
William and Mary elm, 185
Willoughby de Broke, Lord, 94, 180, 221, 239, 249, 251–2, 261, 262; *see also* Verney
witchcraft, 10, 16
World War I, 117, 158, 288, 290
wrestling, *see* sports and games